Media Policy

Media Policy

An Introduction

DAVID HUTCHISON

BLACKWELL
Publishers

First published 1999

2 4 6 8 10 9 7 5 3 1

Blackwell Publishers Ltd
108 Cowley Road
Oxford OX4 1JF
UK

Blackwell Publishers Inc.
350 Main Street
Malden, Massachusetts 02148
USA

British Library Cataloguing in Publication Data

A CIP catalogue record for this book is available from the British Library.

Library of Congress Cataloging in Publication Data

Hutchison, David, 1944–
    Media policy: an introduction / David Hutchison.
        p. cm.
    Includes bibliographical references (p.) and index.
    ISBN 0-631-20433-4 (alk. paper). – ISBN 0-631-20434-2 (alk. paper)
        1. Mass media policy. I. Title
    P95.8.H88   1999
    302.23 – dc21   98-8093
                                                                         CIP

Typeset in 10$\frac{1}{2}$ on 12$\frac{1}{2}$ pt Palatino
by Best-set Typesetter Ltd., Hong Kong
Printed in Great Britain by MPG Books Ltd, Bodmin, Cornwall.

This book is printed on acid-free paper

Contents

Acknowledgements

This book arose out of a conjunction of circumstances. I have taught a policy course on a media studies degree for a number of years, and while I have always found that there is an abundance of excellent material available for students to read, it has never been easy to settle on one volume which covers all of the territory I have wished to consider. Despite that fact, I doubt if I would ever have written the book, had it not been for the persuasive powers of Jill Landeryou of Blackwell, who cajoled me into producing an outline proposal, then secured some extremely useful critiques from her readers, and thereafter let me get on with the job as I saw fit.

I owe debts of gratitude to a number of people, first to my students at Glasgow Caledonian University with whom I have explored the issues dealt with here, and secondly to several friends and colleagues with whom I have discussed and argued about media policy over rather more years than I care to put a figure on. I am fortunate to have spent some time on the edge of the policy-making process as a member of the BBC General Advisory Council and the Scottish Film Council, and that experience is reflected in what follows. I would wish to acknowledge in particular the various debts I owe then to – Fiona Ballantyne, James Boyle, John Brown, David Bruce, Pat Chalmers, Richard Collins, Norman Drummond, Graham Hills, Stuart Hood, Bill Hull, John McCormick, Watson Peat, Nigel Smith, Brian Wilson, Kath Worrall and Willie Young.

My colleagues, Neil Blain and Bill Scott, made many useful comments on a draft of the manuscript while Ian Mowatt did the same for chapter 7. I offer my thanks to all three of them. Responsibility for errors and omissions remains of course with me.

Earlier versions of parts of chapters 10 and 13 appeared in the *Canadian Journal of Communication* and the *Canadian Review of American Studies*, to both of which I happily make due acknowledgement.

My wife, Pauleen, remained remarkably tolerant when this project, like others before it, reached the obsessive stage, and, as ever, I am very grateful for her forbearance.

David Hutchison
Glasgow, March 1998

Introduction | 1

Media policy is constantly discussed, but the forms which that discussion takes vary considerably.

Towards the end of 1997 a senior BBC executive was giving a talk to an audience, composed of members of the public, who had applied for tickets to the university which was sponsoring the event, in order to hear him address the challenges facing the Corporation as the twenty-first century loomed. The speech ranged comprehensively through the issues of digital broadcasting, joint ventures with commercial companies, licence fee funding and the impact of political devolution – among others. When the time came for questions, the first member of the audience to speak made the point that despite the fact that the colour licence fee cost over ninety pounds a year, black and white films were frequently broadcast, and asked the executive what he proposed to do about it. The next two individuals urged greater coverage of events in the sporting and musical fields with which they were associated. Throughout the twenty minutes or so of questions there appeared to be little engagement with the issues which had been raised in the lecture.

A few months before this talk was given Diana, Princess of Wales, was killed in Paris in a car crash which occurred as she was being pursued by freelance photographers. In the aftermath of that event people in all walks of life made it clear in ordinary conversation and in more public forums that they thought press intrusion into the lives of prominent individuals had gone too far and ought to be restrained in some way. The British Press Complaints Commission felt obliged to propose very quickly that its Code of Practice be amended in order to respond to the clear change of mood.

In both cases – the lecture in Glasgow, and the aftermath of the car crash in Paris – media policy was a central concern, but in the one case the public seemed to have difficulty in reacting directly to the issues before them, while in the other they reacted clearly and unambiguously. There are several reasons for this, not least the rather startling intensity of emotion released by the Princess of Wales's death, which served to fuel the desire for curbs on the media's behaviour, but one crucial factor is the difficulty which arises when those who inhabit a world, where the formation and implementation of policy is the *raison d'être* of their professional existence, seek to engage with the rest of the population whose experience of policy is highly specific – the cost of housing, the incidence of burglary, the length of hospital waiting lists. Establishing the link between the general and the specific in public discourse is a constant challenge in modern democracies.

This book will attempt to explore that link in the media field. The basic issues of principle will be discussed, as will the processes of implementation and the actual consequences in practice. Media policy is an area of continuing controversy, in which argument rarely stops for any length of time. That makes it an exciting field, if at times an exasperating one for those who teach or write about it. Since practice too is continually being modified, it is therefore very important to clarify what the underlying basis is – or indeed ought to be – so that specific policy decisions can be evaluated in that light, rather than in an unsystematic *ad hoc* fashion. We all react spontaneously to life as it happens, but when we move on to take a more considered approach we must of necessity ask questions about what we believe and how we justify our positions. That is as true of media policy-making and debate as it is of other areas of experience.

A number of assumptions are being made throughout this book, and it is as well that these should be explicit at the outset. The media are central to modern life in several senses. First, and most obviously, they are very difficult to avoid. How do we insulate ourselves from television, radio, cinema and the press, even if we make a determined effort to do so? Opinions vary as to how we actually 'read' or understand media messages and as to what exactly their impact upon us is, but it is assumed here that the media fulfil a number of crucial functions: they act as a two-way channel of communication between governors and governed and as an arena of public debate and contention; they operate too as a major force for social cohesion. It is a mistake however to overemphasize their political aspect, for much of what the media offer us in the way of entertainment, diversion and cultural enrichment cannot accurately be represented as merely the terrain on which power struggles between conflicting interest groups or classes are played out. The media can and do enlarge the possibilities of life, and extend horizons of understanding and experience in ways that no other systems of communication can.

The book seeks to consider the media as a whole, but for reasons of space there are areas which are not as thoroughly treated as they might have been. The basic aim has been to ensure comprehensive coverage across broadcasting, press and cinema, but as a con sequence of that, on occasion, depth has had to be sacrificed for the sake of breadth. The book falls into three sections. The first seeks to illuminate the contexts – intellectual, economic and technological – in which media policy is formulated and realized. The second considers the basis of policy as it has developed over the last two-hundred years or so, and examines and critiques the fundamental principles which have driven it. In the third and final section the actual implementation and revision of policy are explored through a series of case studies, which cover a wide range of topics, and in which I seek to relate what has been said in the earlier part of the book to contemporary practice.

Although the book was written in the United Kingdom, and the British experience is central, reference is made frequently to both Europe and North America – Canada and the USA. This is done not only to set the issues under discussion in a broader context than would otherwise be the case, but also to provide useful contrasts and comparisons.

It is common nowadays for authors to forswear any pretence of objectivity and declare where they are situated ideologically. I do not imagine that I am totally objective, but I hope that I am tolerably fair to ideas to which I am not personally sympathetic. The reader ought however to know from the outset that I am uneasy about the growth of relativism in both aesthetics and ethics. Relativism seems to me to be an apparent solution to the problem of grounding a world view on any kind of secure base, which can in its turn lead on to a dangerous nihilism which is not only morally and intellectually disabling, but is also remote from the everyday perceptions and judgements of most of our fellow citizens. I am however well aware that not only is total certainty in these spheres unobtainable, but also that the illusion of certainty in the arena where ethics and politics interact has brought several appalling disasters on humanity. The position I am adopting is really a kind of sceptical liberalism which, I suspect, owes as much to Scottish Presbyterianism as it does to political conviction. I hope that the spectacles I am wearing do not cloud my vision overmuch, or become blinkers.

Throughout, the objective is to encourage questioning and argument. What I want to do is to involve the reader with the issues and complexities of media policy and to provoke engagement with the actual decisions made, remade and then revised again, for, as noted earlier, media policy-making is an on-going process, and it is one which responds to changes in the social structures within which it is embedded. It was Heraclitus, the ancient philosopher, who is reputed to have observed that 'upon those who step into the same rivers different and ever different waters flow down'. In so doing he was drawing attention to the coexistence of change and stability in the world. In the study of media policy one is reminded constantly of Heraclitus's remark: there may well be underlying stability of principle and approach, but there is also constant change, whether cultural, economic or technological. Policy has to mediate between change and principle, and in democratic societies the process whereby it does so is one in which we are all, directly and indirectly, involved. The members of the audience in Glasgow were not simply complaining about particular aspects of broadcast output, but were raising questions about programming balance, the difficulty of catering for sub-audiences within a mass audience, the role of broadcasting as cultural patron and the economics of television. These are all important policy issues, and it is the aspiration of this book to illuminate at least some of them, and a few others as well.

Part I
Contexts

Age of Darkness, Age of Enlightenment? The Intellectual Background | 2

Here is the distinguished literary critic, F.R. Leavis, writing in 1930 about films emanating from a 'Hollywood engaged in purely commercial exploitation':

> They provide now the main form of recreation in the civilised world; and they involve surrender, under conditions of hypnotic receptivity, to the cheapest emotional appeals, appeals the more insidious because they are associated with a compellingly vivid illusion of actual life.[1]

Sixty-six years later, here is the musicologist, Wilfrid Mellers, on Broadway music:

> Urban songs may have been produced by industrial technology for a mass audience, with the goal of material gain, but that doesn't alter the fact that the songs, dealing verbally and musically with adolescence, sex, love and loss (though not often with death), are about the things that make the world go round. Moreover, there is evidence that commercial success may often be proportionate to the degree to which words and music grapple, consciously and unconsciously, with the springs of feeling.[2]

Such a contrast in approach to commercially produced culture is startling. How can it be explained, what relevance do such divergent attitudes have to the processes of media policy-making and what light do they cast upon these processes?

Revolution and upheaval

The age of the media dawned with great rapidity: newspapers had existed in Europe since the seventeenth century, but the first mass circulation journal of the modern age is generally taken to be the *Daily Mail*, founded by Alfred Harmsworth in London in 1896 – in fact he established the *Daily Record* in Glasgow the year before – and by 1902 that paper had attained a national UK circulation of one million, then the highest in the world. The Lumière brothers presented their famous film show in Paris in 1895, and within twenty years cinemas were to be found throughout Europe and in the USA, catering for an apparently insatiable demand from both urban and non-urban audiences. The arrival of sound in the late twenties strengthened cinema's position, but already it was facing competition from radio, which had emerged after the First World War, as a new public use of a technology, which until that point had been monopolised for military and other non-public purposes. Station KDKA in Pittsburgh, which went on the air in November 1920, was the first regular broadcasting station in the world, but it was soon followed by others, with, for example the British Broadcasting Company, as it was then known, beginning operations in 1922. Although television had still to come, and would not be a mass medium proper for another quarter of a century, any observer in the mid twenties could look back at thirty years of a genuine revolution in communications.

If that observer had cast an eye a little further back, (s)he would have been aware that the media revolution was only one of a number of related upheavals which characterize the modern age. The biggest of these, and the one which had the most profound effects, was the Industrial Revolution, which in Britain, where it began, lasted roughly from 1760 until 1840. Its consequences included the massive movement of populations from the land into towns, where they worked not in agriculture but in factories, and the sharpening of the conflict between the elites, who had real political and economic power, and the vast majority, who had very little. As part of an attempt to redress the balance between worker and employer trade unions emerged, as did radical social movements, which were hostile both to the system of capitalism which was developing with such rapidity, and also to the civic impotence of most of the population.

There had been two major political revolutions in the late eighteenth century, and although neither could be characterised as a revolt of the workers against capitalism, they did involve the overthrow of established hierarchical orders in favour of less undemocratic ones. The American Revolution, which began with armed clashes in Massachussetts in 1775, was primarily a rebellion of colonists against the imperial power, but it was also fueled by the ideas that rational men – not, as yet, women – of means and position were entitled to a say in the conduct of the state, and that sovereignty rested not with the governing class, but the governed. The French Revolution, which broke out in 1789, was more thoroughgoing in its determination to eliminate hierarchy and privilege, and although it degenerated into the bloodletting associated with *la guillotine*, and paved the way for Napoleon Bonaparte's dictatorship, its significance was all too apparent to onlookers, not least across the Channel in Britain.

Over half a century later in 1848 yet more revolutions erupted in Europe, propelled to a large degree by nationalism, but also by political radicalism. Earlier that year Marx and Engels had declared prophetically in their *Communist Manifesto* 'A spectre is haunting Europe – the spectre of Communism'.[3] The 1848 insurrections were suppressed, as was the working-class revolt known as the Paris Commune in 1871, but only the most blinkered observer could have failed to conclude that, if more conflagrations were to be avoided, then at the very least political adjustment and compromise were called for: the *ancien régime* might be restored temporarily, but it could not be expected to last; the alternative to evolution was revolution, as events in Russia in 1917 were to conclusively demonstrate to even the most obtuse reactionaries.

As a consequence attention focused urgently on such matters as power and authority, the nature and justification of social and economic structures, the relationship of the individual to society and the survival and development of culture – largely, though not exclusively, defined as the arts – which until that time had been very much the territory of an elite. And all of these issues had to be discussed in relation to 'the masses'. Not everyone is comfortable with that term: Raymond Williams famously remarked that 'Masses are other people. There are in fact no masses; there are only ways of seeing people as masses', and his very important point is that the term is often used to imply a homogenous group of unthinking people, rather too close in behaviour to a mob for comfort.[4] The problem is that while the term may in itself be objectionable – if a group of men and women is asked 'how many of you consider yourselves to be members of the masses?', few hands go up – there is no doubt about the sheer physical fact of the congregation of large numbers in urban centres in the last two-hundred years, and the continuation of that process to the present day, whether in towns and cities themselves or in their adjoining suburbs.

Cultural pessimists and cultural optimists

Intellectual responses to the situation which was emerging in the nineteenth and early twentieth century took a number of distinct forms. First, there were elitist approaches, the main thrust of which was that it was vital in the interests of order and civilization that hierarchical social structures should be preserved. Elitist thinkers who discussed culture often took a very gloomy view of its prospects in the new age, and for that reason they are sometimes described as cultural pessimists. Secondly, there were those who looked more positively at social and political developments in general and at the outlook for culture in particular, and they are often called cultural optimists. There are several variants on these two basic positions – and some cross-dressing – but they do provide useful points of reference. In what follows attention will be given to members of both camps; some of them were more interested in society in general and some in the specific situation of culture. 'Culture' is of course an extremely difficult term, the several overlapping meanings of which can provide hours of debate. For the present purpose, it is less culture as way of life but more culture as expressive artifacts with which we are concerned, and these expressive artifacts can encompass not only the traditional arts such as literature, classical music and painting, but also cinema, the press, broadcasting and popular music. The two groupings have sometimes been loosely characterised as 'high culture' and 'mass culture', although that distinction is less frequently made than once it was, since in the last twenty-five years the impact of post-modernism has meant that the boundaries between 'high' and 'mass' have become much less rigid, and tend to shift constantly. But in the earlier period, with which we are concerned here, that was not the case.

Mass culture can be seen as itself very much a product of the Industrial Revolution for, not only is much of it created and disseminated in ways which are similar to factory production and distribution, but also the appetite for entertainment and diversion was encouraged by the gradual expansion of leisure time among the working class; other social classes of course already enjoyed recreational pursuits, included among which was high culture. In the late twentieth century, as an ever wider range of possibilities offers itself, it has become common to talk of the leisure industries, a concept which would have been meaningless two hundred years ago, and which is now taken to encompass everything from theme parks and pubs, to concerts and television.

The problems of democracy

Alexis de Tocqueville (1805–59) was one of the first Europeans to address himself to the problems of the new age. A Norman aristocrat, some of whose family had perished under the Revolutionary Terror, he visited America with a friend in 1831–2, when he was still in his twenties. The ostensible purpose of the journey was to examine American penal practice, and Tocqueville and his colleague dutifully reported on that, but what really came out of the trip was *Democracy in America*, an extensive study of the American political system. Tocqueville went as an aristocrat, but an open-minded one who was convinced that America represented the future. For Tocqueville, if the aim of society is:

> to raise mankind to an elevated and generous view of the things of this world . . . to hope to engender deep convictions and prepare the way for acts of profound devotion . . . refining mores, elevating manners, and causing the arts to blossom[5]

then it is not wise to choose the democratic path. However:

> if your object is not to create heroic virtues, but rather tranquil habits . . . if in place of a brilliant society you are content to live in one that is prosperous, and finally if in your view the main object of government is not to achieve the greatest strength or glory for the nation as a whole but to provide for every individual therein the utmost well being[6]

then democracy is the model to aim for. It is clear where Tocqueville's own sympathies lie, but his objective is not so much to attack as to understand the system which he knows will triumph. In this respect his approach contrasts with two later thinkers who are often cited in discussions of responses to democracy, the German, Friedrich Nietzsche (1844–1900), and the Spaniard, Jose Ortega y Gasset (1883–1955).

Nietzsche has had a profound influence on Western philosophy, and his supposed impact on Nazi thinking raises disturbing questions about the connection between ideas and their ultimate political incarnation; it also has considerable ironic resonance, for the philosopher fell out with his friend, Richard Wagner, on account of the composer's anti-semitism. Nietzsche was driven by a hostility to what he perceived as Christianity's destruction of human potential through its emphasis on meekness and humility; society should, he believed, be organized not for the benefit of those enslaved by the Christian obsession with humility, but in the interest of the few natural aristocrats – the 'higher' or 'super' men. The happiness of other people is immaterial, for what matters is opportunity for the higher men, who are motivated by a desire for power and a determination to achieve noble deeds, deeds of which they alone are capable. Women exist for recreational purposes, and the common rabble should be ignored, as the higher men pursue their objectives. Nietzsche is unashamedly anti-egalitarian; he declares of the 'labour question' – 'if one wants an end, one must also want the means: if one wants slaves, then one is a fool if one educates them to be masters'.[7]

The tone in Ortega is less strident, but he too sees society as being split between a mass, seeking comfort and security for little effort, and an elite which has a sense of history, makes demands on itself, and has an awareness of the fragility of what has been attained. For Ortega the new 'mass man' is extraordinarily self-satisfied:

> This contentment with himself leads him to shut himself off from any external court of appeal; not to listen, not to submit his opinions to judgment, not to consider others' existence. His intimate feeling of power urges him always to exercise predominance. He will act then as if he and his like were the only beings existing in the world; and consequently, will intervene in all matters, imposing his own vulgar views without respect or regard for others, without limit or reserve, that is to say, in accordance with a system of 'direct action'.[8]

Democracy in America is much more generous in tone, and remains to this day a wonderfully suggestive book – Tocqueville is both perceptive and witty about the ability of the majority in a democratic society to be every bit as tyrannical as a despot towards those who hold unpopular views, a theme to which the English philosopher, John Stuart Mill (1806–73), was to return later in the century. As far as culture is concerned, Tocqueville was writing before the dawning of the age of the media proper, but he does have some interesting things to say about the place of the arts in a democratic society. In an evocative image he recounts sailing up the East River to New York, and noticing what appeared to be several little marble palaces along the shore. However closer inspection on land revealed that the 'palaces' were constructed of whitewashed brick, and their classical columns were made of painted wood! Thus, suggests

Tocqueville, in a democratic society, where there is increased pressure from the newly prosperous for works of art, inevitably the premium will be on the appearance of quality rather than on the quality itself; the aristocrat demands – and can afford – the very best, the democrat the passable. The theme which is articulated here is one which recurs in writing about the media: in a mass society commercial pressure to meet and profit from the demands of the many leads inexorably to a glut of inferior goods. The literary critic, F.R. Leavis, who was quoted at the beginning of this chapter, referred to a 'Gresham's Law' of culture, whereby bad coinage – the original 'Law' referred to the currency – drives out good coinage, and so the whole is debased. Cultural pessimists are fond of such analogies, and behind these analogies there lie assumptions about the essentially exclusive nature of high cultural activity, which is seen as being the preserve of the few, and simply not universally accessible.

Not all writers on the subject take that view however. The English poet and critic, Matthew Arnold (1822–88), is a case in point. Arnold, like Tocqueville, was aware that the future would be a democratic one, and he shared Tocqueville's reservations about the operation of majority rule in America. However, mindful of what had happened across the Channel within living memory, he was very concerned that social change should move forward in evolutionary fashion, in order that revolution could be averted. By the time Arnold came to write *Culture and Anarchy* in 1869, Britain had already embarked on the slow process of extending the franchise, and many working men in towns had just been given the vote. The very title of his essay sets out a stark – and some might think rather odd – choice: either we shall have anarchy in the new democratic era, or through culture we can avoid chaos. Arnold, despised the 'mechanical' character of his age with its emphasis on economic activity as the criterion of a society's success, and was more than a little neurotic about the possibility of a breakdown in law and order: he found even modest street demonstrations in favour of reform difficult to stomach. However he accepted that it would be necessary to educate society's new masters, and this is where culture comes in. As was remarked earlier, culture is a difficult term to define, and it is not always clear in what sense(s) Arnold is using it. But the basic force of his argument is that since culture embodies the finest human insights, knowledge of which leads people to behave in a reasonable fashion, then the dissemination of culture throughout society will ensure that there is no breakdown, and that

what he terms 'sweetness and light' will prevail. Crucially therefore, Arnold is a diffusionist.

> Plenty of people will try to indoctrinate the masses with the set of
> ideas and judgments constituting the creed of their own profession
> or party. Our religious and political organisations give an example of
> this way of working on the masses. I condemn neither way; but
> culture works differently. It does not try to teach down to the level
> of inferior classes; it does not try to win them for this or that sect of
> its own, with ready-made judgments and watchwords. It seeks to do
> away with classes; to make the best that has been thought and known
> in the world current everywhere; to make all men live in an atmos-
> phere of sweetness and light[9]

As to how this objective is to be achieved, Arnold does come up
with the rather improbable notion that 'aliens' drawn from existing
social classes would carry out the work. Despite the implausibility
of that idea, Arnold's own efforts as a schools' inspector, and those
of the Victorians who were the driving force behind the movement
which produced art galleries, museums and libraries, all free to the
user, regardless of income, were exactly what would have been
expected from such 'aliens'. A Marxist might well regard the whole
Arnoldian enterprise in theory and in practice as essentially an exercise in incorporation, whereby a significant section of the working
class was deradicalized by being persuaded that its interest lay in
the continuation of the social traditions which had produced high
culture; in so doing it was being sucked into support, or at least
acceptance, of a fundamentally unjust economic system. Arnold
would have been baffled by such a characterization, for he saw
himself as being engaged in an urgent, but perhaps impossible, task.
In many ways he can be regarded as a Victorian who was acting on
the twentieth-century Italian Marxist, Antonio Gramsci's, injunction – 'pessimism of the intelligence, optimism of the will!' [10]

High culture under siege

F.R. Leavis (1895–1978) took some of his cues from Arnold, and like
Arnold he regarded education as having a vital role to play in the
preservation of culture, but he is much more of an exclusivist than
Arnold was. Leavis, and many of his associates were imbued with
a bleak hostility to the modern world. In this they echoed Arnold's
disdain for the materialism of the Victorians, but Leavis goes

further, and harks back to a golden age when labour and leisure were intertwined in organic fashion, a relationship which, he maintains, has been destroyed by industrialization. Allied to this rather mundane romanticism is a passionate belief in the value of literature, for, Leavis argues, since we essentially live through language, and literature represents the most elevated use of language, then literature is clearly of supreme importance. But literature is under threat, and indeed has always had to depend on the safe keeping of a relatively tiny elite:

> In any period it is upon a very small minority that the discerning appreciation of art and literature depends: it is (apart from cases of the simple and familiar) only a few who are capable of unprompted, first hand judgment. They are still a small minority, though a larger one, who are capable of endorsing such first-hand judgment by genuine personal response.[11]

The media represent a potentially catastrophic threat to literature in particular and high culture in general. Leavis attacks advertising, newspapers, cinema and broadcasting, and some of what he says about the easier targets he selects, such as the popular press, hits home. What is extraordinary however is his refusal to discriminate: he simply cannot bring himself to make the kind of distinctions that as a critic he made so effectively between the good, the bad and the mediocre in literature. And in the end he undermines the salient points he makes. It has to be added nonetheless that the Leavisite approach to the media has had a major impact on educational practice in Britain, where until relatively recently many teachers – particularly teachers of English – felt it incumbent upon them to seek to innoculate their charges against the dangers of which Leavis warns.

The issue of discrimination also arises with the American critic, Dwight Macdonald (1906–82). Macdonald too looks back to a golden age when high culture and folk culture coexisted. Folk culture, which Macdonald regards as a genuine, if uncomplicated, expression of ordinary people's feelings, posed no threat to its more sophisticated cousin, with which it might on occasion interact. All this has changed, for alongside high culture, which continues to emphasise the individual response to the complexities of experience, we now have Masscult:

> Masscult is indifferent to standards. Nor is there any communication between individuals. Those who consume Masscult might as well be

eating ice-cream sodas, while those who fabricate it are no more expressing themselves than are the 'stylists' who design the latest atrocity from Detroit[12]

There is a new more sinister danger, argues Macdonald, the growth of a kind of imitation high culture, which offers the appearance, but not the substance, of the real thing. His examples of Midcult, as he calls it, include the Revised Standard Version of the Bible, Hemingway's novel, *The Old Man and the Sea* and Thornton Wilder's play, *Our Town*. Midcult is also:

> the transition from Rodgers and Hart to Rodgers and Hammerstein, from the gay tough lyrics of *Pal Joey*, a spontaneous expression of a real place called Broadway, to the folk-fakery of *Oklahoma!* and the orotund sentimentalities of *South Pacific*[13]

This is a most interesting passage, for what Macdonald is doing here is what the critic must always do, discriminating between texts, and giving his reasons for making the judgements that he offers. What is not explained by Macdonald however is how the Rodgers and Hart collaboration, which drew its sustenance from the commercial theatre and the commercial music industry, is superior to Richard Rodgers's later partnership with Oscar Hammerstein, which operated in exactly the same milieu as the earlier association with Lorenz Hart. Somehow or other it is the fault of Midcult, rather than Rodgers and Hammerstein, or the changing nature of the times. And of course Macdonald has chosen easy targets. If his essay had been written some years later he could have swooped with relish on *The Sound of Music*, but would his argument have seemed so persuasive if instead of the two shows mentioned he had cited *Carousel*, another Rogers and Hammerstein musical? Too many attacks on mass culture, or indeed mid culture, abandon the rigour and discrimination which are required of critics in other spheres. It is one thing to prefer Richard Rogers's collaborations with Lorenz Hart – I might happen to think that *On Your Toes* is a wonderfully inventive and exhilarating show, and not hold *Oklahoma!* in such high regard, despite its many attractive qualities. Likewise, while acknowledging Andrew Lloyd Webber's undoubted theatrical talent, I might wish to argue for the superior musicality of Stephen Sondheim's work. But I am surely obliged in any discussion to explain my reasons; two word dismissals are not good enough.

Macdonald was a former Trotskyite, who latterly described himself as a 'conservative anarchist', and he is at pains to insist that he is in favour of cultural diffusion, if only it could be made to happen. An interesting comparison can be drawn between his work and that of the Frankfurt School. This is the title given to a group of social analysts based during the interwar period in the German city from which they took their name. The rise of Hitler led to their departure for the USA, though some of them returned to Germany after the war. Prominent among their number were Theodor Adorno (1903–69), Max Horkheimer (1895–1973) and Herbert Marcuse (1898–1979). They were all of a radical Marxist orientation, and sought to understand the emergence of Fascism and the failure of revolutionary movements in the West. The explanation which they offered suggests that in a capitalist society the people are beguiled by the manufacture and satisfaction of consumerist false needs. Thus they are deflected from an analysis of the underlying power relations, an analysis which would radicalize thought and action, as they realized that they were in fact living under a form of tyranny. The 'culture industry' has a crucial role in this anti-revolutionary process, for mass culture has a narcotic and deadening effect, unlike the best of high art, which encourages reflection and criticism. Here are Horkheimer and Adorno taking a similar approach to cinema as does Macdonald:

> That the difference between the Chrysler range and General Motors products is basically illusory strikes every child with a keen interest in varieties. What connoisseurs discuss as good or bad points serve only to perpetuate the semblance of competition and range of choice. The same applies to the Warner Brothers and Metro Goldwyn Mayer productions.[14]

It is very tempting to reply that 'every child' who had actually seen films from these two studios would be well aware of the sharp contrast between, for example, the lavish Technicolor optimism of the musicals which emerged from Arthur Freed's MGM unit in the forties and fifties, and the much harsher social realism of Warner Brothers Pictures Inc. productions in the interwar and immediate postwar eras. Again, there is a tendency to generalize, and here it appears to be linked to plain ignorance of the material being referred to. But even when the Frankfurt critics do seem to have some, albeit limited, knowledge of mass culture, they lack discrimination in their judgements.

The escape from pessimism

This is a point to which the English critic, Raymond Williams (1921–88), turns in his much more open-minded discussion of the media. Despite his reservations about the use of the term 'masses', Williams is all too conscious of the dangers of cultural snobbery, and is mindful of how the novel, when it first appeared in the eighteenth century, was regarded by many elitists of that time as a rather vulgar and inadequate literary form. Williams cannot see the objection to multiple transmission, and takes a generally optimistic view of the outlook for both high and mass culture:

> If the readers of bad newspapers have increased in number, so have the readers of better newspapers and periodicals, so have the users of public libraries, so have students in all kinds of formal and informal adult education. The audiences for serious music, opera and ballet have increased, in some cases to a remarkable degree. Attendances at museums and exhibitions have in general steadily risen. A significant proportion of what is seen in the cinemas, and of what is heard on the wireless, is work of merit. In every case, certainly, the proportions are less than we could desire, but they are not negligible.[15]

As the use of the term 'wireless' makes clear, this passage was written some time ago – 1958 to be precise – and even then Williams had some catching up with contemporary developments to do, but the points he makes are representative of the way thinking about the media has developed in the second half of the twentieth century. For Williams, given his own background as a railwayman's son, it would never have been easy to engage in blanket condemnation of the leisure habits of the vast majority of the population, and he is also acutely aware that our society squanders many talents and offers most of its citizens limited access to education and culture.

Williams can be located in a radical English tradition which goes back to William Cobbett (1762–1835) and William Morris (1834–96). Cobbett, writing in the pre-democratic era, agitated in favour of social and political reform, and against rural and industrial exploitation. For his pains he found himself jailed by the authorities, but he lived to become MP for Oldham in 1832 in the first parliament which was elected after the process of electoral reform began. Where Cobbett focused on the political and the economic, Morris operated on a broader canvas, literally as a painter and interior decorator, and metaphorically in his writing on social and cultural questions. For Morris, capitalist society is essentially in a state of war and will remain so until four basic rights are made available to all. Each citizen, he argues, is entitled to health, education (including leisure), a fair share of pleasant – and not so pleasant – work and beautiful material surroundings. Morris has little to say about mass culture, which was in its early stages towards the end of his life, but, although he is politically much more radical than Matthew Arnold, he too is a diffusionist:

> What I claim is liberal education; opportunity, that is, to have my share of whatever knowledge there is in the world according to my capacity or bent of mind, historical or scientific; and also to have my share of skill of hand which is about in the world, either in the industrial handicrafts or in the fine arts; picture-painting, sculpture, music, acting, or the like: I claim to be taught, if I can be taught, more than one craft to exercise for the benefit of the community.[16]

Richard Hoggart (1918–) can be regarded as being in the same political tradition. Like Morris and Williams he was a firm believer in, and practitioner of, adult education. Like Williams, but unlike Cobbet and Morris, he came from a solid proletarian background, in his case the Yorkshire industrial town of Leeds. Hoggart's description of working-class life in *The Uses of Literacy*, although lacking the rigour of academic sociology, vividly creates the feel of the kind of community in which he grew up. However Hoggart is much less sympathetic to mass culture than Williams. Like Macdonald, he has a tendency to choose rather easy targets, such as 'Sex-and-Violence' paperbacks, in order to argue that the working class is being culturally robbed:

> Most mass-entertainments are in the end what D.H. Lawrence described as anti-life. They are full of a corrupt brightness, of improper appeals and moral evasions. To recall instances: they tend towards a view of the world in which progress is conceived as a seeking of material possessions, equality as a moral levelling, and freedom as the ground for endless irresponsible pleasure. These productions belong to a vicarious, spectators' world; they offer nothing which can really grip the brain or heart.[17]

Although the main object of Hoggart's attack is the press, he has doubts too about some forms of broadcasting, and for all his political radicalism, he does come across as a cultural pessimist, at least in what he wrote. But that is not the whole picture, for Hoggart was much involved in media policy-making, in which role he too has seemed to act on Gramsci's precept and sought to improve the quality of broadcasting and the opportunities for access to the arts.

The decline of certainty

The reader will have been struck by the tone of most of the views quoted so far: they have about them an air of certainty; the observers who articulate these opinions seem absolutely confident in the validity of what they are saying. That kind of assurance is much less common as we approach the end of the twentieth century, for across a range of spheres – politics, ethics, culture – there is a reluctance to profess certainty, and an eagerness to stress the tentative and localized nature of judgements. There are a number of reasons for this. For one thing, many in the West are acutely conscious that much of the behaviour of colonial powers was arrogantly insensitive to indigenous beliefs and customs, and there is now a desire to make intellectual amends. Secondly, the whole Enlightenment project, the movement in thought, which reached its climax in the eighteenth century, and which cast off superstition and prejudice in favour of the exercise of reason and science as guides to human conduct, has come to seem deeply flawed in its promise of universal happiness. Not only that, the belief deriving from the Enlightenment that the resources of the planet are there for *homo sapiens* to do with as his reason tells him can be regarded as potentially destructive of the very basis of life itself.

By way of reaction to Enlightenment certainty, some commentators have gone so far as to suggest that not only do we have Western ways of looking at social organization, as opposed to say Islamic or Oriental ways, but also that there are Western science and other non-Western sciences. This position is difficult to come to terms with, for although it is clear that the native peoples of, say British Columbia, are likely to have a different view of humankind's relationship to the forests from the one held by logging companies, it is not at all obvious how, for example, the DNA in the plants and animals of the forest will behave any differently when viewed from the perspective of these allegedly varying 'sciences', even if allowance is made for the possibility that the very act of observing may make some minute difference to the behaviour of the phenomena observed. But although we may well take the view that relativism – or pluralism – has little place in the physical sciences, we may be reluctant to insist on absolute or semi-absolute ethical and aesthetic standards, and this is part of the overall process of retreat from Enlightenment certainty. We are now much more aware of the conditional and contingent nature of value judgements than once we were. That may well be a good thing; however there is also a serious danger that a reluctance to be certain can lead to an inability to believe anything at all. Be that as it may, moral relativism and aesthetic relativism are part of the zeitgeist now.

Ideas in action

Media policy-makers at the beginning of the century did not have to deal with such a complex situation. But they were only too well aware that for many critics the media meant inevitable cultural debasement, and commercial exploitation of gullible and ill-educated publics. They were also conscious however that there was a respectable tradition in Europe – and in America too – of cultural diffusion, which was deemed to be a desirable aspect of public policy.

Broadcasting was the arena in which these contrasting ideas were most clearly foregrounded and engaged with, particularly in the UK. Before the British Broadcasting Company (BBC) was established as a government sponsored monopolist, officials carefully studied what was happening in the USA. Despite various brave attempts to insist on the educational and cultural potentialities of radio – David Sarnoff, for example, later to head America's first network broadcaster, the National Broadcasting Company, commented in 1922 'broadcasting represents a job of entertaining, informing and educating the nation, and should therefore be distinctly regarded as a public service'[18] – very quickly the new medium became a branch of selling. It offered the advertiser the opportunity of direct access to the home, and in a society which in the twentieth century has been by far the most capitalistic, it was not easy to resist that use of the airwaves. As one commentator has put it, before very long 'The industry had developed what was already known as the American system of broadcasting, which made the salesman the trustee of the public interest, with minimal supervision'.[19] British observers of the American scene did not like what they saw, and their distaste informed the approach to the establishment of the BBC. Under its first Managing Director, later Director General, John Reith, the policy was firmly Arnoldian:

As we conceive it, our responsibility is to carry into the greatest possible number of homes everything that is best in every department of human knowledge, endeavour and achievement, and to avoid the things which are, or may be, hurtful. It is occasionally indicated to us that we are apparently setting out to give the public what we think they need – and not what they want, but few know what they want, and very few what they need. . . . In any case it is better to over-estimate the mentality of the public, than to under-estimate it.[20]

It is difficult to imagine any Director General (DG) of the BBC speaking in these terms today, but the Corporation's mission remains the provision of 'sound and television programmes of information, education and entertainment'. Reith was in practice rather less of an elitist than the pronouncement quoted suggests, and he very shrewdly saw to it than on most days of the week there was a judicious provision of lighter fare alongside more demanding material – although frivolity on Sundays remained firmly off limits for a stern Presbyterian like the DG.

It can be argued that the establishment of the BBC was the most overtly Arnoldian response to the coming of the media that there has ever been, although the efforts by communist regimes to disseminate through radio and televsion high cultural forms such as classical music, opera and ballet also have an Arnoldian flavour to them. Arnold's ideas have continued to inform the development of broadcasting policy in Britain to this day. Although few politicians, officials or broadcasters in the 1920s who subscribed to his diffusionist ideals, shared Arnold's fear of anarchy, many of them were keenly aware that broadcasting would be a major force for social cohesion. The climate of the times in the twenties was conducive to what was being embarked on, for the idea of government provision of certain vital services had become acceptable during and after the First World War, and there was also a feeling that the excesses of the press during that conflict, such as propaganda claims about the behaviour of German troops which were shown to be absurd, rendered a thorough going commercial approach to broadcasting untenable.

Unhappiness about the American experience was an additional factor at work, as has been noted, and that was also the case in America's northern neighbour. Canada, faced with a developing commercial sector, set up its own state-regulated broadcasting system in 1932. The Canadian Radio Broadcasting Commission was clearly expected to behave like the BBC, with one crucial difference:

it was to have an explicit role in nation building. The Conservative Prime Minister, R.B. Bennett, put it this way:

> this country must be assured of complete Canadian control of broadcasting from Canadian sources, free from foreign interference or influence. Without such control radio broadcasting can never become a great agency for the communication of matters of national concern and for the diffusion of national thought and ideals, and without such control it can never be the agency by which national consciousness may be fostered and sustained and national unity still further strengthened.[21]

Canada's unease was very much a response to the danger of its airwaves – and its sense of its own identity – being swamped by American programmes, either transmitted directly across the border, or relayed by Canadian stations, but it was also a reaction against commercialization of broadcasting on the US model. Tocqueville's foreboding about the impact of America on culture was to produce many such echoes among policy makers. Although the concern with broadcasting's role in the creation and sustenance of a sense of national identity is central to the Canadian approach, it is also to be found, if less explicitly, elsewhere too. Indeed, as Scannell and Cardiff have demonstrated in their history of the BBC, by relaying a range of sporting, cultural and social events the Corporation did much to develop and disseminate a particular sense of what Britishness meant in the first half of the twentieth century.[22]

The cinema was well into its stride when broadcasting emerged, and it was never to be run as a state industry in democratic societies, but the state did become involved, and continues to be so, particularly in Europe. In Canada policy makers agonized about what to do about the flood of American feature films which in effect eliminated the possibility of an indigenous cinema until more recent times. While civil servants worried ineffectually in Canada, they took a more robust line on the other side of the Atlantic. The history of European cinema is one characterized by a whole raft of measures – quotas, tax allowances, production grants – designed to encourage home-grown work. The clear objective of policy makers was to prevent the destruction of their own cinemas by the economically powerful American industry. The concern was commercial, for cinema offered employment and export potential, but it was also cultural, motivated by the desire to see the nation telling its own stories on its own screens. Many of these policy makers, although they probably went to the pictures rather more often than F.R. Leavis, shared, at least in part, his view of Hollywood. Some of them also had reservations about 'mass man' similar to those expressed by anti-democratic thinkers like Ortega. So considerable efforts were made to ensure that 'dangerous' or 'subversive' material did not appear on-screen, lest social disorder result, from the 'wrong' ideas being let loose. These were to be found in both the political and moral spheres, and the history of censorship in the cinema is a narrative of struggle between the official guardians of public behaviour and those who believed in a more libertarian and democratic approach. Today in the West there are few political controversies over films. The emphasis in debate is now on sex and violence, but that should not blind us to the fact that there were many such disputes in the past in our own societies, and still are in countries such as China, where the elite distrust the masses as much as an Ortega or a Nietzsche did, and cinema censorship is seen as crucial to the maintenance of order.

If we can detect the influence of the thinkers whose work we have considered on broadcasting and film policy in the twentieth century, that is not quite so easy with the press. There are a number of reasons for this, not least the fact that newspapers had existed for rather a long time, and were firmly established in private hands. Indeed, it was the firm belief of the proponents of a free press in the eighteenth century that newspapers must be owned privately, in order to ensure that they were not subject to government intimidation. So, it would have been extremely difficult for democratic governments to act in response to the disdain of some intellectuals for the popular press, even although they might well have shared that disdain. The issue of enforcement of standards of good journalism is still bedevilled by this history, as we shall see when we come to look at the work of bodies such as the British Press Complaints Commission.

The cultural situation now

It has to be said one hundred years after the Lumières' first show and Northcliffe's invention of the modern tabloid paper, that critics hostile to the media are more subdued than they were in the first part of the century. When they do comment, they tend to be much more selective than some of their predecessors. The tabloid press in Britain still attracts a great deal of criticism for its alleged triviality and offensiveness, as do particular broadcasting channels and much Hollywood output. But dismissals of the media and all they produce are rarely offered. There are a number of reasons for this. One is the growth of relativism alluded to earlier. Also it is much more comfortable to say 'this does not appeal to my taste' than 'this is offensive, anti-life kitsch'. Then there is the simple fact that high culture, the potential loss of which alarmed so many commentators, is still in reasonable health, and 'the Masscult depths [and] . . . the agreeable ooze of the Midcult swamp'[23] have failed miserably to choke the life out of classical music, serious literature or theatre: critics may deplore the current state of, for example, the English novel, or American poetry, but they cannot argue that novels and poetry with serious artistic pretensions fail to get published on either side of the Atlantic. Matters are far from perfect, particularly given the constraints on public funding, but there is no likelihood whatsoever of extinction. Indeed, since the first jeremiads were issued, in Europe, and to a lesser extent in North America, the state has become the principal funder of high culture. It can even be argued that the establishment of bodies such as the Arts Council of Great Britain was in itself a response to the dangers seen to be posed by the existence of a commercially driven mass culture, to whose appeals it was all too easy for people to succumb. Be that as it may, the individual who draws his or her pleasures from high culture has no difficulty in finding much of interest. Furthermore, in Britain and many European countries at least one medium, broadcasting, still gives a fair amount of attention to the arts, as do broadsheet newspapers, even although some of them seem less inclined to the view that there are cultural hierarchies than once they were; there may well be many vacuous films and television programmes, the tabloid press may appear disgusting and offensive, but it all exists in a rather different realm, from which one can avert one's eyes and ears.

This is perhaps to caricature an attitude, but it is one which undoubtedly exists, and does raise uncomfortable questions about the nature of common culture and experience in the kind of society in which we live. Indeed it could be argued that one major disadvantage of the 'go as you please' possibilities offered on the cultural front today is that there is not enough serious engagement with many aspects of media output by critics and analysts. It is also true however that many observers, whose inclinations would make them gravitate to the 'elite' arts, accept what earlier commentators were reluctant to concede, namely that it is necessary to discriminate between the good and the bad in mass culture just as it is in high culture. This is not necessarily aesthetic relativism, but a simple acknowledgement that Manichean oppositions are of little help in understanding the complexities of the situation with which we are now confronted.

Summary

The media age dawned at the end of a period of economic, social and political upheaval, when there had been much discussion about power and authority in society. As far as culture was concerned, there was widespread anxiety, expressed by several commentators, that mass society and the mass media represented a serious threat to the traditional high arts. Other commentators took the view that a process of cultural diffusion would spread appreciation of the arts across social classes, and that art forms deriving from the new media were capable of producing work of value. All of these ideas fed into early policy discussions about the development of both broadcasting and the cinema.

Questions for discussion

1. What evidence would a cultural pessimist cite to justify his or her position in the contemporary situation?
2. What evidence would a cultural optimist cite to justify his or her position in the contemporary situation?
3. How difficult is it to establish agreed standards for the evaluation of cultural artifacts such as films, novels and popular music?
4. How relevant are the principles laid down by John Reith, which are quoted on page 22, for media policy today?

Markets, Media and Moguls | 3

The media are businesses, first and foremost, that is to say they are organizations which produce goods and services for purchase by consumers. When matters are put so bluntly, many of us recoil, for we do not always think of the media like that, and indeed there are some media organizations, most obviously public service broadcasters, like the BBC in the UK or NOS in the Netherlands, which do not seem to be at all the same kind of bodies as, for example, Sky Broadcasting, or even terrestrial broadcasters such as Carlton Television. And in the newspaper world there are examples of titles which are not operated in a completely commercial fashion, such as the *Guardian* in the UK or *Le Monde* in France, before financial pressure forced change upon it in 1994. In cinema too there have been state-run enterprises, most obviously during the Communist period in Eastern Europe. Nonetheless the initial statement stands, despite the existence of what might be called modified commercial organizations, for, as we shall see, even they have to compete in the market place and behave to a degree as if they were fully-fledged businesses.

Media businesses

It is sometimes said that it is the function of business to make a profit. This is a half-truth: it is the function of business to provide society with a range of goods and services; profit is one indication of how successfully a particular company is doing that. Businesses which fail to make a profit usually do so because people are unwilling to buy what is offered at the stated price. The logic of the capitalist system is ruthless in this regard, and those most committed to that system will argue forcibly that it is the customer who benefits from the competitive process, although the employees of companies which cease trading as a consequence are bound to suffer, at least in the short term. Few however would claim that all of our needs can be met by capitalism, and there is a general acceptance that there are some things that can only be done fairly, and even perhaps efficiently, by society as a whole. The most obvious examples of community-based services are the armed forces and the police, but in many Western countries it was received wisdom – at least until the 1980s – that such commodities as water, gas and telephone systems should not be provided by private businesses. That logic has been challenged, and as we approach the twenty-first century, it is clear that the growth of the state sector has not only been halted but reversed in many parts of the world, as privatization programmes have been pursued enthusiastically by governments of varying political hue. It would therefore be surprising if public sector media organizations did not feel that it is now more difficult to justify their *modus operandi* and dependence on state funding than was the case thirty years ago. It is not only in the countries of Eastern Europe that life has become more difficult for those in charge of such bodies.

The word 'industry' in the phrase 'media industries' needs a little explanation. Strictly speaking, manufacturing industries produce tangible items – soap, electrical pumps and refrigerators, for example – and services provide less tangible things such as banking facilities, medical assistance or entertainment. Although this distinction remains a valid one, in common parlance it has been blurred, as, for example, insurance companies, and even educational institutions talk about offering customers and students ('clients'), 'products'. It is usually foolish to inveigh against changes in the use of language, but this one is potentially very misleading, for its effect is to elide an important difference.

If it is possible then to make a distinction between manufactures and services, into which category do the media fall? This is a tricky question: newspapers and magazines are clearly tangible goods, and so are video cassettes and CDs, but what about broadcast programmes, as we experience them in our homes? Clearly the machines we buy, on which to receive these transmissions, are 'goods' but do the programmes come into the same category? There is not much help available from official sources. The British Standard Industrial Classification of Economic Activities, for example, puts newspapers under the category, 'Manufacture of pulp, paper and paper products; publishing and printing', but this category also includes the reproduction of video recordings, although the production and distribution of these comes under 'Other Community, Social and Personal Service Activities'.[24] The most sensible way to answer the question posed at the beginning of the paragraph would be to acknowledge that the media produce tradeable services and tradeable goods. For practical purposes we shall continue to talk about the media industries, but with reservations about the term.

Imperial Chemical Industries (ICI), if it is to survive and prosper, has to satisfy a number of 'constituencies'. Most obviously, if it fails to produce chemicals and paints that customers wish to buy at the prices charged, then it will soon be out of business. Additionally, it has to please its shareholders, the people who actually own the company. Nowadays ownership of a large corporation is in the hands not only of the thousands of individuals who have purchased shares on the Stock Exchange, but also in those of insurance companies who manage the cash which has been placed with them by the millions of people who buy life assurance, investment policies and the like. Those who own companies expect that not only will their shares increase in value, but also that there will a regular dividend paid. The pressure is therefore on the managers of such companies to maximise profits and growth; doing both at once can be difficult, since short-term profits can sometimes only be generated at the expense of long-term investment. Thirdly, a company like ICI has to answer to government and government-sponsored regulatory agencies. It is obliged to abide by legislation on such matters as safety at work, pollution control and dismissal procedures, and to pay taxes on its profits. In the countries of the European Union companies have to take account of pan-European regulations as well as national ones, while in federal states like the USA and Canada they have to deal with both national and state/ provincial legislatures. Furthermore, there are now strong public expectations beyond legal requirements that corporations should behave responsibly and should not, for example, exploit their workers, either at home or in foreign countries, or pollute the environment.

A media corporation is no different. Time Warner Inc., which is the largest media company in the world, if it is to stay in business, must sell its magazines, for example *Time*, and *Sports Illustrated*, its recordings, on the Warner label, its films, and the television programmes offered on its Home Box Office cable channel.[25] It keeps its shareholders happy by doing so, and through a vigorous programme of acquisition-led growth. Like ICI, it must abide by government regulations, and pay its taxes. The fact that much of what it produces is more intangible than what ICI manufactures does differentiate it to some extent from that company, and there is one additional distinction to be made: all companies operate in a climate of uncertainty, for it is never possible to be sure about how consumer demand might shift in the future, but the media customer is rather more fickle than the purchaser of industrial chemicals. It has been calculated, for example, that of 212 films released by the major US studios in 1995, only 67 broke even or made a profit.[26] So, the media company has to find ways of balancing the inevitable risks in parts of its business against more dependable investments, such as well-established television stations in lucrative US markets.

Media companies compete with each other for custom, but they also have to compete with a myriad of other companies which offer consumers ways of passing their leisure hours and spending their disposable income. A few examples demonstrate the point. Sales of evening newspapers in the UK have declined substantially as early evening radio and television news coverage has grown. When television began its expansion in the 1950s, cinema attendances dropped and have never recovered to their previous levels, and although the introduction of multiplexes has had some impact in reversing the decline, it is the video cassette which has proved to be the real saviour of the film industry. All of the media industries face stiff competition from home computers, shopping trips, foreign holidays and a range of alternative uses of non-working time.

The world's top ten media companies by turnover are listed in table 3.1.

As can be seen, there are four US corporations, one Japanese, one Australian, one German, one French, one British and one Canadian. In *Fortune* magazine's listing of the top five-hundred global corporations, Walt Disney is put ahead of Time Warner, but even then it only comes in at number 192. Media companies are actually rather small: Walt Disney's worldwide turnover in 1996 was 18.7 billion dollars, while, by contrast, General Motors's was 168.4 billion and Mitsubishi's was 140.2 billion.[27]

Media companies take different forms. Although, as has just been noted, the largest of them cannot compete in size with industrial giants, a number of these giants have substantial interests in the media: General Electric, for example, which is ranked by *Fortune* as

Table 3.1   The world's major media companies

Company	Headquarters	1996–7 Revenue ($M)
Time Warner	USA	20,925
Walt Disney	USA	18,730
Bertelsmann	Germany	12,300
Viacom	USA	12,080
News Corp	Australia	11,216
Sony (Entertainment)	Japan	8,400
Havas	France	8,200
Tele-Communications	USA	8,022
Universal	Canada	6,514
Granada	UK	6,450

Source: *Variety Magazine*[28]

the fifth largest American corporation, and the twelfth largest in the world, owns NBC, the oldest US broadcast network; Sony, which makes most of its money from video and audio equipment, moved into the media business in the late 1980s with the purchase of American CBS records and Columbia Pictures, so its media company is merely a subsidiary of a much bigger organization; Matsushita is another Japanese company which draws most of its revenue from the manufacture of electrical goods, but it too decided to expand its holdings into the media with the acquisition of MCA, which owns Universal Pictures and several record labels, but after a relatively short period of ownership it sold most of MCA to the Canadian drinks company, Seagram.

All of these companies are large multi-product, multinational concerns. A more common pattern is the media company which expands within the field, from, for example, newspapers into broadcasting and publishing. This is the route News Corp has followed, as has the German company, Bertelsmann, which began in publishing and has moved into broadcasting. A striking feature of the behaviour of many of these businesses as the twentieth century ends is the linkups they are forging with much larger telecommunications and computer companies. The thinking here is that with the deregulation of telecommunications and the opportunities for delivery of programming material via telephone systems, rather than through the air or cable, and other moves towards communications convergence then there may be substantial growth of video on demand systems. Because computers interface with each other via telecom-munications, and because of the rapid expansion of the Internet, media companies feel obliged to make alliances which will enable them to exploit whatever opportunities arise in the future. None of these firms is the least bit certain how new services will develop, since the evidence about unsatisfied demand is very mixed, and returns on investment may be derisory for years to come, but it is vital to have a stake in the territory as the media field enlarges.

By way of contrast to the kind of companies which have just been discussed, there are still a number of relatively small organizations, specialising in, for example, regional and local newspapers: al-though larger multinational operators, such as Pearson Longman, which owns Penguin Books and the *Financial Times*, until recently had substantial holdings in the regional field, it is also the case that at the other end of the scale companies like the Scottish-based, Johnston Press, for example, have made a great success of concen-trating on the local newspaper market in Britain, and have deliber-ately restricted their holdings beyond the core business.

The News Corp story

As ICI operates internationally, with 75 per cent of its sales taking place outside its home base in the UK, so do many large media com-panies.[29] News Corporation, the fifth largest media business in the world, which is headed by Rupert Murdoch, conforms to that pattern. Murdoch is probably the best known 'media mogul' since William Randolph Hearst, the American newspaper owner whose life Orson Welles used as the basis for his *tour de force*, *Citizen Kane* (1941), still one of the best movies about the power of the press. Murdoch, like Hearst, is an American, but only by adoption, when it became clear that an Australian would not be allowed to acquire television stations in the US. The basis of Murdoch's company is a chain of newspapers in Australia, which he inherited from his father. News Corp is still substantially controlled by Murdoch and his family, which is one reason why he has been so identified with the company in a way that few other media chief executives are. From Australia he moved on to Britain in 1968 where, first of all, he acquired the successful *News of the World*, and the then ailing *Sun* newspaper. He turned that title from a left-of-centre tabloid, aimed at skilled upwardly mobile working-class citizens, into the most commercially successful down-market right-of-centre newspaper in the world. Thereafter he went on to acquire three other titles, and by the mid 1990s controlled over thirty per cent of the British daily and Sunday market by circulation. From Britain Murdoch expanded into America where he began in newspapers, and then, in 1985, with the acquisition of Twentieth Century Fox Films and of a number of television stations, created a fourth network, Fox Television, which challenged the existing three networks, and reduced their market shares. The film studio has been an invaluable source of material for the Fox network, and for Sky Television. That satellite service, which had been in existence on a pan-European basis via cable since 1983, was relaunched in ABS form early in 1989 as a pre-emptive strike against British Satellite Broadcasting before it came on air, and in effect Sky put that organization out of business in 1990, when a merger of the two companies took place. BSkyB dominates satellite broadcasting in Britain: in the mid 1990s it had a 5 per cent share of viewing – roughly half the total figure for satellite – and was available in over one quarter of all homes, mainly via receiver dishes, but also through cable services.[30] Sky was a risky venture, and it took some years for it to move into profit, but Murdoch was able to use revenue from elsewhere in News Corp to sustain it through lean years. Similar cross-subsidization enabled him to cut the prices of both the *Sun* and *The Times* in 1993 in a bid to crush rival British newspapers in both tabloid and broadsheet markets. That strategy led to a remarkable increase in the circulation of *The Times*, and more modest gains for the *Sun*, and although the only title that went out of business was News Corp's own mid-market *Today*, pressure on other titles has been intense and could ultimately lead to another closure.

From one perspective this story is a justification for the capitalist system itself. Rupert Murdoch has taken risks in fickle markets, and he has triumphed against less fleet-footed rivals. Millions of consumers clearly wish to buy the papers his company produces and watch the films and television programmes he beams to Britain and the USA, not to mention Asia, where he also has satellite broadcasting interests. It is not however quite as simple as that. News Corp most certainly does meet some of the needs of many consumers throughout the world, and no doubt it keeps its shareholders happy most of the time, although they were subjected to a rather bumpy ride in the early days of Sky. However, as far as fullfilling wider obligations to society is concerned, News Corp has had a remarkably easy run: it appears to have minimised its tax liabilities to a startling degree, and it has enjoyed extensive generosity from broadcast regulators.[31] In Britain it has not had the wide ranging programme obligations, which are laid on terrestrial competitors, imposed upon it, and it has made little effort to meet European Union programming quota requirements, so it has been free to transmit mainly American movies, old – and new – American television material, and sporting events. Its programming costs have been far lower than those of the BBC or Independent Television (ITV), which are both expected to provide not merely movies and American programming but also indigenous drama (by far the most expensive kind of television production), documentaries and entertainment. Sky, unencumbered by such obligations, has used its subscriber revenue and the resources of News Corp to buy up sporting events which were once available free of additional charge on the terrestrial channels. So much outrage was provoked by this development in the UK that in 1996 the House of Lords forced the British government to place limits on such transactions. Murdoch has also managed to persuade the American Federal Communications Commission that his violation of the twenty-five per cent limit on the foreign ownership of television stations, through the vesting of control of his US stations in his Australian holding company, was more apparent than real![32]

News Corp has happily used its British newspapers in order both to promote Sky Broadcasting, and also to run anti-BBC and anti-ITV stories as regular features. Furthermore, although Sky News is required to offer an impartial service – that obligation *was* laid on it by the regulators – News Corp's titles took a clear political stance in favour of the election of Conservative governments for many years; the company's dominance of the British newspaper market reinforced the Conservative bias in that market and made it increasingly difficult for non-Conservative parties to secure fair treatment in the press. The abandonment of the Conservatives during the 1997 general election appeared to tip the balance towards the Labour Party, but it remains to be seen how deep and long-lasting the conversion actually is, and whether it is ideologically or commercially motivated. In the Far East, when China complained in 1994 that the BBC World television service, which could be picked up in that country, was 'slandering' the Communist government, News Corp promptly ejected the BBC from the Star satellite, which had come into its ownership. The desire to ensure a sympathetic environment in China, as his business interests expand there, appears to have been the motive in 1998 for Murdoch ordering his publishing company, Harper Collins, to abandon plans to publish the memoirs of the last governor of Hong Kong, Chris Patten. Patten is not noted for his pro-Peking sympathies.

Media businesses are special

So the rise of News Corp is not simply the tale of a buccaneering entrepreneur from the Antipodes demonstrating to envious rivals how to seize investment opportunities, and to satisfy millions of consumers world wide. Its success certainly demonstrates what can be done by a company which is prepared to take risks in its pursuit of growth, but it also shows that, to adapt an old phrase, what's good for News Corp is not necessarily good for the USA, or the rest of the world either for that matter. The media industries divert and entertain us, and it is a mistake to forget just how much of what comes to us not only in broadcasting and cinema, but also in the press, has little or no overt political significance. However, because the media also provide us with information vital to our active citizenship, and contribute to our general awareness and knowledge of the world, then they have to be treated rather differently from other industries. All democratic countries acknowledge that fact, and have sought to develop rules specific to the field.

The Berlusconi experience in Italy reinforces the need for such an approach. Silvio Berlusconi has built up a chain of companies under the Fininvest umbrella, which cover construction and property as well as media. With considerable acumen, and a clever exploitation of loopholes in Italian law, Berlusconi gained control of the three commercial television networks, which compete with the the the three state-controlled RAI channels. In 1993 he launched a new political party, Forza Italia, and used his own stations to promote that party, with no pretence at balance, other than during the immediate pre-election period. Forza Italia won the election and formed a coalition government with Berlusconi as Prime Minister. The new government then began to exert pressure on RAI to operate in a more 'sympathetic' fashion. It was not long however before Berlusconi found himself being investigated for corruption, which allegedly took place under a previous administration, and out of government after electoral defeat. His behaviour in office however was a vivid demonstration of what unfettered power in the media industries could be like.

In the USA too there has been growing unease about the ability of huge media organizations to affect the news agenda. In 1997, for example, a spokesman for the Progressive Caucus, a grouping of over fifty congressmen within the Democratic Party, noted the ignorance of many Americans about the existence of publicly funded healthcare systems and the more even division of wealth in other countries, and commented:

> The reason is pretty simple. Most Americans get their news from the four big TV networks. ABC is owned by Disney. NBC is owned by General Electric. CBS is owned by Westinghouse, and Fox is owned by Rupert Murdoch. You just don't see those corporations reporting on trade unions, on the wealth gap, on the fact that over 90 per cent of the budget cuts the last Congress passed were taken from the poor.[33]

The point was made in the previous chapter that when broadcasting began it was the clear view in the UK that commercial organization of the new medium was not desirable, and so the BBC came into existence. But how different is the BBC – the archetypal public service media organization – from a company like News Corp? Of the three constituencies which ICI and News Corporation have to satisfy, the BBC also has to take account of the wishes of governmental and pan-governmental regulatory authorities on a range of matters, some of which, like the safety of its employees, are not peculiar to the media, but some of which, such as the requirement of balance and fairness in news broadcasting, are. It also has to satisfy its customers, though the relationship is not a clear-cut one like that of Sky, which is selling a service directly to subscribers. Nor is it the same as that between commercial broadcasting companies and their listeners and viewers. In the end the customers whom the commercial companies have to satisfy are the advertisers, for they provide the funding to keep these organizations alive; they will continue to do so only if the broadcasters deliver enough of the right kinds of audiences at prices which the advertisers are prepared to pay. That is the basic relationship between ITV companies, or the American networks, and their principal clients, the advertisers, to whom they sell their audiences. It is a relationship which is mediated by the public service obligations laid on them by government appointed regulators, but it is the fundamental fact of their existence from which there is no escape. Channel Four in Britain is now in the same situation, except that special provisions are in place to ensure that if it cannot raise enough commercial funding, the ITV companies, which collectively constitute Britain's principal commercial television service, are required to bail it out (in practice in the mid 1990s the reverse was taking place with Channel Four subsidising ITV, much to its annoyance), and there is a direct government subvention to support its operations in Wales.

The BBC's activities are financed in three ways, primarily by the licence fee, which funds domestic broadcasting, secondly a government grant which pays only for the World Service radio operations, and thirdly profits from programme, book and recording sales, a small but growing source of top-up revenue. The licence fee is basically a compulsory tax on all television-owning households, the level of which is set by the government of the day, and non-payment of which leads to criminal sanctions. So viewers pay for the Corporation's channels, whether they use them or not – and subsidize non-television-owning households which listen to BBC radio. The customer does not have the right to stop paying for the service as he or she can with cable or satellite. It might therefore be argued that the Corporation is immune from the market forces which affect other broadcasters. In practice this is not the case. In the mid 1990s the BBC's two television channels had over forty per cent of total viewing, but if its share were to drop below thirty per cent, it would not be long before Members of Parliament were calling for a review of the compulsory tax system of funding, So the pressure is on the BBC to behave at least to some extent as if it was directly dependent on its customers to stay in business. What it does not have, unlike a private broadcaster, is shareholders who are looking for a return on investment; it is not required to make a profit to hand over to the British government, unlike, for example, the Royal Mail. However, it is still expected to balance its books and to behave in many ways as if it were a private company. The BBC is ultimately owned by the citizens of Britain, but that ownership is exercised through parliament, which in practice means that MPs in general, and the government in particular, act as both regulators and shareholders, an arrangement which would be regarded as rather improper in ordinary business.

The BBC is almost unique in the world in being a publicly financed broadcaster whose revenue is not topped up by advertising; the Australian Broadcasting Corporation, whose income comes in the form of a government grant, is in a similar position, as are the public broadcasters in Norway and Sweden, which are licence fee supported. However advertising, whether as the sole source of finance, or, more commonly, as a supplement to licence fee funding, is crucial to the survival of most of the world's radio and television systems, and to the media as a whole. The dependence is most historically rooted with newspapers, which have carried commercial messages since their inception. In North America today the press as a whole draws over seventy per cent of its income from this source, while in the UK tabloids take over half their revenue from sales, but broadsheets are nearer the North American pattern.[34] What this means is that newspapers – and this is equally true of magazines – not only sell themselves to their readers, but they also sell those readers, as commercial broadcasters sell their viewers and listeners, to advertisers. If sufficient advertising cannot be generated, publications with perfectly respectable circulations may struggle for survival. It is also a distinct possibility that newspapers which depend heavily on advertising from a particular sector may skew their contents towards that segment of their market to a greater extent than the actual percentage of readers in the relevant category would justify; so they may, for example, produce extensive business-oriented sections and supplements, and they may even modify their editorial line in deference to the business interest.[35] Advertising finance then is not just a convenient source of revenue, but a significant influence on the behaviour of the press.

A curious feature of American life which puzzles visitors from Europe is that in a country where the landscape and the airwaves are dominated by advertising, one commercial-free zone is the cinema. But it does not therefore follow that the only source of revenue for the film industry is the paying customer, whether in the form of the movie attender, the video tape renter or the television viewer. Film companies derive much of their income from their percentage of exhibitors' returns, but the exhibitors themselves rely also on considerable revenue from the sale of edibles and refreshments, as the pervading odour of popcorn in cinemas eloquently attests. In Europe, by contrast, cinema advertising is long established, and is a source of income to exhibitors, albeit not a very large one. It should be added however that, although the American cinema industry does not derive revenue directly from advertisers, product placement, whereby, in return for payment from the manufacturer, a commodity is conspicuously situated within range of the camera in certain scenes, has been growing in recent years. It is a practice which does raise serious questions about where exactly artistic control resides in a movie.

The media industries are regarded by many governments as important components of the economic life of their countries, for although, as was noted earlier, individual companies can be rather small, taken together they can be much more economically significant. Audiovisual goods are now America's second largest export, after aerospace manufactures, so even allowing for the fact that exports represent only 11 per cent of US Gross National Product, Hollywood is a very significant industry. In 1996 foreign generated revenue from films alone amounted to 8.5 billion dollars.[36] Britain's gross receipts in 1996 from film and television sales were just over one billion pounds, but after deduction of payments to other countries, mainly the US, the net deficit was £113 million, compared to a net surplus of £50 million in 1994, since when the position has been deteriorating.[37] It is not therefore surprising that the British government, in common with other European governments and the European Union, regards the audiovisual industry as an important one, which in theory at least it is committed to encouraging, if only to bring the trade balance into surplus again. Furthermore, a very useful characteristic of this industry at a time of intractable unemployment levels is that it is labour intensive. In addition, the media as a whole are 'knowledge-based', and many Western governments have come to believe that the future of their economies lies in such industries rather than in other areas where less-skilled labour is needed, and is plentifully available at rock-bottom wage rates elsewhere in the world.

What then are the policy challenges which arise from the circumstances which have been outlined in this chapter?

The impact of economic policy

The first point that must be made is that because the media are industries, general economic policy will have an impact on their operations. For example, if a clampdown on a perceived inflationary threat leads to a recession, then newspaper sales and advertising revenues will decline; conversely, a fiscally generated housing or employment boom will generate an increase in classified advertising. A similar point can be made about commercial radio and television: a buoyant economy will usually boost advertising spending, and hence revenue and profits. Likewise, if a government decides to legislate in the industrial relations area, then that will have an effect on all of industry including the media.

However some policy changes might well have a disproportionate impact on the media, as indeed happened in Britain in the early years of the Thatcher governments. Under new industrial relations legislation the power of trade unions to pursue disputes with employers was substantially curtailed. As a direct result several newspaper proprietors felt able to confront the print unions' dogged opposition to the introduction in national newspapers of computer based technology – technology which had long been the norm in North America and in some British regional papers. In 1986 outside News Corp's plant in Wapping in London, where new equipment had been installed, and new staff recruited, police clashed repeatedly with dismissed Murdoch employees and demonstrators, but the plant continued operating. The legislative changes were an integral part of the Thatcher programme, and were not specifically geared to the needs of newspaper companies, but after the Wapping confrontation computerized technology rapidly spread throughout British newsrooms, and many traditional printing jobs disappeared. A number of new titles, such as *The Independent* and *Scotland on Sunday* emerged, though rather fewer than some of the supporters of the Murdoch approach to modernization had prophesied.

Legislating for the media industries

As was noted earlier, although the media operate as industries, they are also important – perhaps the most important – sources of information for citizens about what is happening in the democracies in which they are voters. Therefore media businesses cannot expect to be treated in quite the same way as say a company manufacturing soap. It would not greatly matter if there were only a few major producers of that commodity, provided consumers had reasonable choice, there was competition among producers, and it was possible for new entrants to find a space in the market. Anti-monopoly and anti-cartel legislation is designed to ensure these conditions are met. However, when it comes to the press, it is generally accepted that the greater the number, and the wider the range, of sources of information and comment available, the better, even although there may be a loss of efficiency, and newspapers are as a consequence dearer than they might otherwise be. What this means in practice is that anti-monopoly and anti-cartel rules are tightened in order to take account of considerations which do not arise with soap. The existence of such special provisions has had some effect in arresting the trend towards increased concentration of ownership in a number of countries, though rather less impact than many observers would consider desirable.

As some industrial statutes have been adjusted to take cognisance of the perceived roles of the media in society, so inevitably governments have been obliged to legislate continually for the one media industry which in many countries still has a substantial public sector, namely broadcasting. Even where that industry is almost entirely private, as in the USA – which is the exception rather than the rule in this respect – there is a significant body of law concerned both with frequency allocations, and also with ownership and content. In Europe not only do national and regional parliaments structure and restructure broadcasting systems, often specifying detailed programming requirements, but the European Union has also become involved. What is very striking about much recent legislative activity, for example in the area of digital broadcasting, is that it tries to find a balance between the cultural obligations of broadcasters and their obligations as businesses seeking to maximise opportunities for revenue growth.

The continuing trend towards multi-media linkups has also become a concern of policy makers. The British government, for example, in 1996 introduced new legislation on cross-media ownership, and in the White Paper which preceded that legislation it argued that the new regime which it was proposing would 'allow the media industry to evolve in a way that exploits the opportunities created by technological change', but would also 'continue to safeguard the public interest in a free and diverse media'. The White Paper was at pains to stress the distinction between the media industries and other businesses:

> General competition legislation is mainly concerned with securing economic objectives, although it can also encompass other non-economic objectives. However, wider objectives are important as far as the media are concerned. A free and diverse media are an indispensable part of the democratic process. They provide the multiplicity of voices and opinions that informs the public, influences opinion, and engenders public debate. They promote the culture of dissent which any democracy must have. In so doing, they contribute to the cultural fabric of the nation and help define our sense of identity and purpose. If one voice becomes too powerful, this process is placed in jeopardy and democracy is damaged. Special media ownership rules, which exist in all major media markets, are needed therefore to provide the safeguards necessary to maintain diversity and plurality.[38]

This is an exemplary defence of pluralism. It is quite extraordinary that during the subsequent parliamentary debates the British Labour Party argued – unsuccessfully – for fewer restrictions on cross-media holdings than the Conservative Major government, for its part mindful perhaps of the poor record on limiting concentration to date, wished to introduce.

Broadcasting and the press also attract legislative attention in some countries in respect of non-domestic ownership, since it is felt that again the normal rules of commercial operation need to be modified to take account of the particular functions which the media serve. On the one hand, foreign companies may own British mainstream broadcasters, provided they are based elsewhere in the European Union – there are no longer such limitations on the ownership of cable television operators – and newspapers may be purchased by companies from anywhere in the world. On the other hand, it is not quite so easy for British businesses to buy up European broadcasters, and while Conrad Black's Toronto-based Hollinger can own the *Daily Telegraph* and its stablemate, the *Sunday Telegraph* – not to mention the *Jerusalem Post* – because of Canadian tax laws it is extraordinarily difficult for foreign companies to purchase Canadian papers.[39] The central policy issue here is the extent to which non-domestic ownership poses a threat not to the commercial viability of the press or broadcasting – it might well strengthen that – but to the national cultural role of the media. It is therefore a paradox that in the USA, while there are some limitations on foreign involvement in television stations, there are no corresponding restrictions on the ownership of the film studios which are the production centres of the national narratives and myths through which Americans to some degree know themselves, and by which they are known to the world outside; as was noted earlier in the chapter, two of the Hollywood 'dream factories' have recently been in Japanese hands; a third, MGM, has been passed from one foreign owner to the next.[40]

Governments, particularly outside of the USA, do intervene in the cinema industry for both cultural and economic reasons. As far as the latter are concerned, the objective usually is to boost employment and exports, and the methods chosen include tax and investment incentives. The Irish government, for example, has developed very generous fiscal provisions to encourage the making of films in the country, regardless of whether these films have Irish themes or not. The policy is an employment-driven one, but the hope has been that in time not only will Hollywood companies use Ireland for location work, but the indigenous industry will be helped on its way to a more significant international presence, and so there will then be a cultural as well as an economic benefit. The apparent success of Ireland led many British film makers to castigate the British Conservative government, which since 1980 had dismantled many of the support mechanisms which had previously been in place, in the belief that market forces should operate without modification. Here the UK administration was taking what appeared to be an American attitude: a film company is much more like Procter and Gamble than the BBC, and therefore should be treated like the former, without special privilege. However that is very much a minority view in Europe, where policy makers have generally allowed cultural considerations to come into play, as they have also done in Australia and Canada, where state-funded support mechanisms have been in place for several decades. It should also be noted furthermore that, so far from being left to its own devices, the American film industry has historically enjoyed generous fiscal encouragement, and continues to be actively assisted by the US government in its efforts to expand overseas sales.[41]

The role of globalization

The term 'globalization' is much used in discussion of the nature of contemporary social reality; it has been succinctly defined by Anthony Giddens as 'the intensification of worldwide social relations which link distant localities in such a way that local happenings are shaped by events occurring many miles away and vice versa'.[42] For the present purpose we are interested in the economic aspect of this process.

It was remarked earlier that News Corp has taken great pains to minimize its tax liabilities. It has been able to do so to some extent, because, like many modern corporations, it operates on a global scale, and is able to shift much of its revenue across frontiers to subsidiaries located in countries with lenient fiscal regimes. Globalization is a phenomenon which poses serious difficulties for any government seeking to regulate economic activity. It is misleading however to suggest that this is a completely new development, since the history of, for example the British Empire, offers us many examples of companies, such as the Paisley-based textiles business, J. & P. Coats, whose activities spanned the globe long before the term was used. The shipyards of the Clyde, for their part, built one-fifth of all the ships in the world in the early part of the twentieth century. Both Coats and the Scottish shipbuilding industry are indicative of the dominance of Britain at its imperial zenith. The Empire was both a source of raw materials and a semi-captive market for finished goods; the institutions of the City of London provided the financial services which kept this system functioning smoothly. Britain was even prepared to go to war in order to force other countries to acknowledge its trading dominance: in the mid nineteenth century, for example, China was compelled, after defeat in the so-called Opium Wars, to accept the right of British India to sell that drug to the Chinese; the profits were used to finance British purchases of goods such as silk and tea. So globalization of economic activity is not a recent occurrence. However there are a number of significant differences between current international patterns and those which obtained during the heyday of the British Empire.

Most obviously, that Empire no longer exists, and indeed it can be argued that the United Kingdom's relatively weak economic performance in the twentieth century owes much to its over dependence on Empire, and the assumption that its world dominance would therefore continue.[43] The United States is now the largest exporter in the world, and, as neon signs proclaim from the rooftops of cities in every continent, its major corporations, like its films and television programmes, are everywhere. But, as was noted earlier, a relatively small part of the United States's Gross National Product (GNP) derives from trade, with Britain, for example, exporting over twice the US percentage of GNP; America's dominance arises from the fact that it is the richest country in the world, and eleven per cent of its GNP is colossal by the standards of many smaller nations. However the USA is far from being the only major economic power, as an examination of the same neon signs demonstrates, for Germany and Japan, after their defeat in the Second World War, have established themselves as significant players, albeit helped on their way by substantial American investment. To many in the West, German success was only to be expected, since it enjoys long established industrial strength, based on a commitment to technical excellence. It is Japan which has surprised by its rapid evolution into a kind of honorary Western nation by virtue of its economic progress, progress which is based on a strategy of selective concentration in a relatively small number of industrial sectors.

The United States, Germany and Japan, three major economic powers in three continents, symbolize the modern phase of globalization. And Japan is no longer alone in Asia, for it has been joined by the so-called 'tiger economies', such as Taiwan, and South Korea, which have rapidly industrialized, again with much American help. So back in the United Kingdom it is not only Japanese and American electronic businesses which are wooed by governments desperate to increase employment opportunities, but also television tube manufacturers from South Korea.

The significance of the multinational companies based in the dominant economies has increased substantially. As one observer has commented:

> Foreign Direct Investment has been growing four times faster than trade since 1982 . . . Central to this growth has been the role of multinational corporations in reshaping the world economy . . . At some point during the 1970s, the output from assets located in one country but owned and controlled by another exceeded the volume of world trade for the first time. That output is highly concentrated. Just 420 of the largest of the roughly 35,000 multinationals account for over half of the total output.[44]

It is hardly surprising then that financial reports on radio and television in the West refer not only to the FT and Dow Jones indexes, but also to the (Japanese) Nikkei and the (Hong Kong) Hang Seng ones. Stock exchanges remain crucial components of the global economic system, and ease of electronic communication means that they now interact very rapidly with each other. Furthermore, the lessening of restrictions by governments worldwide on external financial transactions, a development which owes much to the Reaganite commitment to free markets, means that it is now much easier to move stocks, shares and money around the planet, and that is a crucial aspect of the contemporary phase of globalization. For the individual company this can bring many benefits, as it seeks to maximise profits and minimise liabilities, but it can also leave a business vulnerable to sudden movements in share prices which it cannot control, and which may not be directly related to the real value of its current activities. Governments likewise find that their powers can be rather less than they would wish. The financial turmoil which began in the Far East in late 1997 demonstrated to many observers not only that the opportunities for large-scale dishonesty had increased dramatically, but also that some kind of reregulation was urgently required in order to prevent regional crises becoming global ones. It also exposed the hollowness of some of the claims which had been made for the 'tigers', and the overdependence of some Western countries upon them for new investment capital.

What all of this means is that media policy-makers look out on a much more complicated economic landscape and culture than their predecessors did fifty years ago. The pace of change, particularly in multi-media mergers can be bewildering, and adjusting policy to keep abreast is a daunting task. It would not be surprising if, confronted with such complexity, civil servants and politicians concluded that there are processes at work which have a life of their own, and are outwith the control of individual governments or even pan-governmental organizations. This is an understandable reaction, but it is a dangerous one, for it concedes to the corporations at the centre of the globalization process far more power than they are entitled to, however agreeable they might find its exercise. Media policy and general economic policy in a liberal democracy are fundamentally about asserting the instrumental role of business: it exists to serve society, society does not exist to serve it. In the post-1989 world few would challenge the effectiveness of the market system in creating wealth, but few would wish to live in a society where there were nothing but markets. Indeed it is striking that the triumph of capitalism has not led to universal rejoicing, but rather to a profound unease about the tendencies of that system left to itself to take little or no account of people's needs for security, community and fulfillment, needs which are basic to happiness and contentment.

Businesses, yes, but something else too . . .

This chapter has been about the economics of the media, and too much discussion of the business aspect could make us forget that, although many cultural goods are produced by organizations which seek to maximise profit, it does not therefore follow that these cultural goods will be imbued through and through with the ideology of wealth creation and accumulation. Robin Wood in a stimulating essay has argued just that point about Rouben Mamoulian's film *Silk Stockings* (1957). The film contains some wonderful dance sequences performed by Fred Astaire and Cyd Charisse, which move the viewer into a realm of pleasure remote from the movies as a business, and remote also from the explicit pro-capitalist ideology of the film. As Wood says:

I would suggest . . . that . . . one might talk of certain aspects partially escaping ideological determination. I would suggest, in other words, that there are indeed certain fundamental drives and needs that are not ideological but universal – drives which certain ideologies can suppress but which no ideology creates – and that such things as freedom of expression, delight in bodily movement, instinctual spontaneity, are among them.[45]

A similar point can be made about the exhilarating banter between Humphrey Bogart and Lauren Bacall in *The Big Sleep* (1946): the film was produced by Warner Brothers Pictures Inc. to make a profit, but, to use Marxist terminology, the superstructure is substantially independent of the base, and the skilful exploration of sexual relationships which develops under Howard Hawks's direction takes on a life of its own unrelated to economic considerations.[46]

Hollywood has always had a predilection for happy endings, and it could be argued that such endings are good for business, in that they encourage customers to return to the cinema. Even if that proposition is accepted however, it does not inevitably follow that all American films will come to cheerful conclusions: the patriotic feel-good *Forrest Gump* (1995) certainly does, but the same could not be said of *Leaving Las Vegas* or *Casino*, which appeared in the same year. Both of these films are set in the desert gambling city, and while one offers an uncompromising picture of a movie scriptwriter drinking himself to death, the other paints a very unflattering portrait of the relationship between organized crime and legitimate business. All three pictures were offered to the public by large capitalist corporations. The economic circumstances of the production of texts are certainly important, but, as these examples suggest, they are far from all determining.

Summary

The media are businesses, and act on the imperatives which govern the operations of the capitalist system, but they are very special kinds of businesses: they do not simply provide us with goods and services, but supply us with information which we need as citizens of democracies; they also offer us representations of life in our societies. Because of these distinguishing characteristics special laws have been introduced to deal with the problems that could result if there is not a sufficient number of independent sources of news and information to guarantee pluralism of ideas. Policy makers have also sought to ensure that film and television companies have the resources to 'tell national stories', and, where possible, to sell them abroad. The phenomenon of globalization poses challenges in the media field, as it does in other areas.

Questions for discussion

1. If media businesses are 'special', how many 'special' rules do we need to deal with them?
2. Why are governments reluctant to restrict the growth of media conglomerates?
3. Are there ways in which globalization of the media can be matched by globalized regulation?

Technology –
Chance, Fate and Choice 4

It is often said that we live in a technological age. There is a sense in which this is a vacuous statement, for human beings have depended for thousands of years on technology for survival, whether the technology of weapons used to hunt animals, the technology of fire employed to cook the carcasses of these animals or the technology applied to create clothing out of their hides. However the phrase 'technological age' is designed to draw attention to the complex nature of the systems on which we now depend and their all pervasiveness. We may still use the same technologies as our ancestors of 75,000 years ago, or updated versions of them, but we draw on a much greater range of technologies than they did. If one of the characteristics of the modern age is the appearance of the masses, another is the wholesale application of science to every aspect of living, whether it be in the provision of lighting and heating systems, transport systems, medical procedures or communications.

Technology often seems to be partially invisible: when we switch on a table lamp we may well be aware that the electricity which flows into it is turning into light rather than into the heat that emanates from an electric fire, or the motive power which drives a vacuum cleaner, but few of us consciously think of the process by which in a power station water is heated by coal, natural gas or nuclear fission and the steam thereby produced driven through turbines in which electrical impulses are generated in copper conductors, and the resulting energy is distributed throughout the country. Likewise, the astounding advances in computer technology, linked via telecommunications, which have made electronic mail and the Internet possible, have very quickly been taken for granted by many of us, and the processes which lie behind them naturalized and forgotten. What we do not forget however is how much we depend upon technology, and how different life can be when one of its major components ceases to function, as happens, for example, when there is a power cut, and we find ourselves shivering in darkness, devoid of diversion from our home entertainment centres.

The mid-nineteenth-century Victorians who worried about the cultural consequences of mass society were well aware of the power of technology to change their way of life, for they had witnessed at first hand the Industrial Revolution, in which the combination of coal, iron and steam had turned a largely agrarian society into a factory based one. But the industrialization of communications had still to come. The technology of printing was well established, for it was in the late fifteenth century that the print/paper conjunction utilising moveable type had been developed in the West by Johannes Gutenberg in Mainz – several centuries after the Chinese had first invented it – but the mass circulation newspaper had yet to appear, and film and broadcasting, although occasionally prophesied, were mere fantasies. Yet in a relatively short space of time between 1895 and 1925 all of the technical components of the modern media were in place. That the media are based on sophisticated technologies is incontestable. What is open to question is the extent to which their development is driven by technology, and the extent to which it is propelled by other factors, such as the relations of production in economic systems.

Technology and social change

The interaction of technological change and social change is a complex one, and to understand it we need to look at the total context within which technology operates, which means that we have to consider economic forces, political attitudes and choices, and general social attitudes. The process whereby a technology is developed and applied is easy to chart retrospectively, but not quite so easy to predict at the onset of the innovation in question.

By way of example, let us look at the motor car. The basic question which needs to be addressed is whether the astounding growth in the number of automobiles and their impact on our way of life are due entirely to the invention in the late nineteenth century, by Nikolaus Otto and others, of the internal combustion engine, which thereafter dictated the growth of private transportation and all that

stemmed from it. If that is the case, then the fundamental determining factor is the technology itself. Leaving aside for the moment
the issue of why particular technologies are developed, rather than
others which were also practical possibilities at the time, what is
being argued is that once a particular technology does appear, then
other things inexorably follow on. This line of reasoning is sometimes referred to as technological determinism, determinism being
the idea that our ability to choose particular courses of action is very
heavily circumscribed, perhaps even completely constrained, by
factors outside of our control. In philosophy one of the perennial
debates is over the extent to which human beings choose to behave
in certain ways through the exercise of free will, and the extent to
which biological, social and other factors combine to compel us to
act as we do, even although we may have the illusion of choice. The
discussion about the role of technology in the process of change has
many similarities.

To return to the motor car, might it be the case that the invention
of the internal combustion engine could not of itself have brought
about the upheavals which followed? Might there not have been
other factors at work, such as Henry Ford's development in Detroit
of a particular kind of production line which made the manufacture
of affordable family cars possible? Indeed, if the general level of
wealth had not been rising at the beginning of the twentieth century,
would there have been any point in building Ford's Model Ts at all?
When it comes to the interaction between private and public transport, do we need to consider the role of, for example, the oil companies, which had a vested interest in the expansion of the 'great
car economy' – the phrase is Margaret Thatcher's – and at one point
bought up the suburban tramways in Los Angeles and closed them
down, thus paving the way for the development of the most
automobile-dependent urban settlement in the world? And would
any of this have happened if human beings did not have a deep
attraction to the sense of freedom and control which privatised
transport seems to offer? If we look at subsequent developments, it
is clear that the car has brought far higher levels of personal mobil-
ity than were known in the nineteenth century; it is also the case
that millions of people have lost their lives or been very seriously
injured as a consequence of its omnipresence, there has been a
massive increase in health threatening pollutants, and cities – and
to some extent the countryside too – have become unbearably con-
gested. With or without the machinations of oil companies, public
transport has suffered a substantial decline, particularly in North

America, Britain and rural parts of Western Europe. Possibly as a consequence of that decline, urban streets have become emptier in the evenings, and to individuals on their own, often places to be fearfully avoided.

All of this, it might be argued, arises inevitably from the operation of the technology of the internal combustion engine. But what then is to be made of a more recent set of developments, including pedestrianization of city streets, restrictions on motor vehicle access to towns and parts of the countryside, such as national parks, and reinvestment in public transport? Even Los Angeles has been rebuilding suburban railways, and British towns, which abandoned tram cars in the 1950s, are keen to establish modern light rail systems. Governments are now openly anxious to find ways of balancing the 'freedom to drive' against other freedoms such as the right to breathe relatively unpolluted air, to enjoy a pleasant urban environment and not to have one's life prematurely ended by a motor vehicle.

What this brief history suggests is that, while technology may have an enormous impact on how we live, the nature of that impact depends on the ways in which technology interacts with wider social and economic processes. We chose the motor car as our preferred mode of surface transport for much of the twentieth century, but it looks as if that choice may be a little less popular in the twenty first, as its negative consequences are now very clear. In the twentieth century we also chose to develop very sophisticated weaponry, and the effort put into that was rather greater than was put into, for example, producing labour-saving devices for the home, or effective contraception, which have freed women from backbreaking toil and given them control over their own reproductive processes. The fact that it took longer to make these things possible than it took to manufacture machine guns and tanks is not only because some of the scientific work involved, particularly that related to the contraceptive pill, was long and arduous, but also because liberating women from what was perceived as their traditional domestic role was not considered a priority. Here social attitudes – patriarchical attitudes some might say – were just as important as scientific and technological advance. Developments which are technically feasible can be held up because of such attitudes; conversely, they can also be embarked on when they do not appear to make much economic or social sense.

An excellent case in point is the Concorde supersonic aircraft, which wings its lonely way back and forth across the Atlantic, a symbol of the British and French governments' desire to steal a march on American aerospace companies and enhance national prestige. Concorde has not led to the establishment of a European supersonic aircraft industry, and its development costs will never be recovered; it is an example of the way in which politics and technology can interact and seduce governments into squandering resources. The British civil nuclear power programme, by contrast, arose out of a conscious decision to spend money on a commercially non-viable method of generating electricity for clear military reasons, the production of weapons-grade plutonium. That was needed for the manufacture of nuclear bombs, although it can be argued that this decision too was driven by a desire for political prestige – the prestige conferred by the possession of weapons of mass destruction – which got the better of economic judgements.

What all of these examples suggest is that when we consider the role of technology in the development of the media, and in particular the approach of media policy-makers to new possibilities, we are as well to be sceptical about the reasons given for the choices which are apparently being made, not because these same policy makers are necessarily engaging in duplicitous behaviour, but because technology, or rather the supposed inevitability of particular kinds of technologically driven changes, can be used consciously or unconsciously to mask the real economic or political forces which are at work.

Technology and the media

The modern newspaper utilises a number of technologies: there is the print technology itself, which has a long lineage, but there is also the technology of paper making, which in the nineteenth century took a huge step forward when it became possible to manufacture that substance from wood pulp rather than rags, as previously had been the case. Paper now became cheaper and more plentiful. Then there was the technology of the steam-driven rotary press, the operation of which meant that far more copies could be produced within a given timespan than was the case with older flatbed presses. But it is difficult to see how these advances would have had much of an impact if a new reading public was not also coming into being as a consequence of improved schooling – basic education became compulsory after 1870 in Britain, rather later than in some continental countries – and a greater political awareness, and if a growing number of people had not had the money to buy papers, initially on a Sunday, then on a daily basis. So the modern press arose from a conjunction of technological, political, economic and social developments.[47]

The role of a technology outside of the newspaper industry altogether was a crucial factor in Britain – and to a more limited extent on continental Europe – in the creation of a national press. In the middle of the nineteenth century 10,000 miles of railways were constructed in the United Kingdom, and similar programmes were underway elsewhere in the world. Because the UK system was centred on London it became progressively easier, as the speed of rail transport increased, for that city's newspapers to print in the evening and to be circulated by train to most of mainland Britain by the next morning. As a consequence, many well-established titles in the regions, faced with direct competition from the metropolitan press, were unable to make the transition to the modern age, and simply disappeared. Today there are only a few strong morning newspapers outside of London, although there are many localized evening titles. The exception to this general rule is Scotland, for trains in the nineteenth and early twentieth centuries were simply not fast enough to reach the north in the time available, so the Scottish press grew in strength and still dominates its market, despite intense competition from London titles which now use electronic communication and local printing plants in order to be available at the same time as the indigenous papers.

North America offers an interesting parallel. For obvious geographic reasons it was not possible to print daily newspapers in New York or Toronto and circulate copies to the rest of the country in the space of a few hours, so the press in the US and Canada developed on a regional basis with papers like the *New York Times*, the *Los Angeles Times* and the *Toronto Globe* dominating both their home cities and their hinterlands. When it became possible in the latter part of the twentieth century to use electronic transmission via satellite to printing plants across the country, attempts were made to establish national newspapers in both the United States and Canada, so that it is now possible to buy the *New York Times* and the specially created *USA Today* throughout America, and the *Globe and Mail* throughout Canada, but none of these titles has been able to dominate its national marketplace as a whole, since reader loyalty to regional titles remains strong, for historical as well as for cultural reasons.

One of the striking features of cinema is that while it could not exist without the chemistry and the engineering required to record moving images, and then put them on a strip of celluloid to be projected onto a screen, that basic technology has not changed radically. The illusion of reality may be much greater because of improvements in colour cinematography and the utilization of stereo sound reproduction, but to create the effect on the screen a strip of celluloid is still pulled past a source of very bright light in a projector.

The illusion of movement in cinema stems from a phenomenon known as persistence of vision, whereby the brain retains an image for a fraction of a second longer than it actually exists, thus leading to an overlapping of still photographs, and hence the sense of movement. Broadcasting for its part depends on the existence of the electromagnetic spectrum, and the fact that it is possible to create radio waves on which messages can be superimposed, and then to transmit them at the speed of light, to be picked up and decoded by receiving apparatuses. What is striking about the development of radio is that the technology was being employed as an alternative to wire-based telephony for almost twenty years before it was utilised for public communication, and the question to be asked therefore is why broadcasting appeared when it did, just after the First World War.

Again we see a complex of factors at work. First of all, there had been important technological advances, which made feasible the manufacture of radio receivers which did not require of the listener that (s)he use earphones. Secondly, a number of commercial concerns saw the possibility of exciting new markets opening up. Linked to that was the perception, particularly in the United States, that public communication via the airwaves would be a wonderful method of advertising. Governments for their part, although under pressure from the military to restrict the use of radio, sensed that a new mode of instantaneous communication, which could do much to promote the flow of information, and to encourage national cohesion, was coming into being. Because of the limited space in the electromagnetic spectrum, and the need for some kind of orderly allocation of frequencies, governments realised too that they would have to play a pivotal role in the organization of the medium. Broadcasting was the first of the media to be centrally regulated from its inception for overtly technological reasons. Governments had always sought to exercise some control over the production of newspapers and books, whether through licensing or criminal sanctions, and the cinema too had been subject to similar constraints, but the reasons were political, not technological. The authorities may well have taken advantage of the situation in which they found themselves in order to ensure that they had greater control in broadcasting than they had in the other two media, but there is no denying that there were pressing technical reasons for their involvement.[48]

As was noted above, manufacturers realised that radio technology offered them markets for new products, and the history of broadcasting is to a significant degree the history of large electrical companies, such as the British concern, EMI, and the American one, RCA, investing large sums of money in the attempt to exploit radio and television. In that sense, as Raymond Williams has argued, broadcasting was no accident, but something which was being consciously sought for commercial as well as for other reasons.[49] The drive for new markets in the capitalist system encourages continuous product development, but it would be wrong to invest that process with an aura of inevitability, since consumers have to be persuaded that they need or want goods and services, which until that point they have survived contentedly without. The Sony Walkman is a case in point. Miniaturised technology made it possible, but unless young people had come to believe that their lives were going to be enhanced by having portable music systems, then the company's investment would have been futile. The marketing strategy Sony adopted achieved that objective, but the one employed when the same company developed the Betamax video tape did not prove at all effective: the Betamax standard is regarded as technically superior to the VHS standard, but Sony refused to license Betamax manufacture, whereas the company's rival, Matsushita, was perfectly happy to license production of the format it had developed jointly with JVC. Matsushita's marketing strategy defeated Sony.

The very existence of home video technology illustrates another aspect of the interaction of the technical and the economic. The video recorder was developed by the Ampex Corporation of California as a solution to a problem the broadcasting industry had: how could it eliminate live television programmes, with all the hazards they involved, and make better use of its large production complexes by recording material at times of the day when no transmissions were taking place. Having successfully resolved the broadcasters' difficulty, Ampex considered the possibility of building a domestic version of its new machine, but baulked at the development costs involved. In Japan the closely linked business and civil service elites saw an opportunity, and government and industry committed themselves to an investment programme, the success of which is clear for all to see. It is not an accidental success, but one which stems from conscious political and economic choices and the further development of existing technology. However, unless consumers had been persuaded of the value of the video recorder in the home, it would not have been a success at all.

With any one of the media then technological change interacts with other factors and processes constantly. Furthermore, the actual form of media ouput is continually modified. In the early 1960s, for example, artificial satellites orbiting the earth made possible not only improved telecommunications between different parts of the world but also live television coverage. We now take for granted that a news programme can go in real time to any location on the planet where there is a reporter who has even the most basic of equipment through which (s)he can uplink to a satellite. So we can see and hear correspondents in Baghdad or Washington speaking as we watch, something which would have been impossible in the 1950s. ('Liveness' can, however, very quickly become a substitute for analysis, and this technologically induced problem manifests itself all too clearly on twenty-four hour-a-day news channels.) Sports television has also benefited enormously from the availability of live coverage, and indeed satellite and cable channels which specialise in this area depend on the technology concerned for their very existence.

To take another example, the improvements in voice quality and the introduction of subscriber trunk dialling on telephone systems have led to the proliferation of phone-in radio programmes, which were technically possible before these developments, but subject to constant breakdown and regular lapses into unintelligibility.

The technological fix

The point was made in the previous chapter that Western governments have become very concerned that in the globalized economy they must emphasize knowledge-based industries. Information technology is seen as a crucial component of that sector of the economy. Here, for example, is the European Commission talking about the need for action to ensure that Europe's 'strong position in mobile communications and in the race towards personal communications services' is maintained:

> Current barriers impeding the development of a Union-wide market for mobile communications must be overcome. Union-wide solutions need to be found to issues of standardisation and frequency and numbering coordination and a common regulatory framework needs to be formulated to promote the emergence of pan-European services, operators and service providers.[50]

What strikes the reader is not so much the specific objectives being put forward, but the tone, which is one of urgency. It is an understandable urgency, given the anxieties which have developed about Europe's ability to compete in a changing world marketplace, and the persistently high levels of unemployment which are to be found in many of the countries of the Union. However a kind of technological/commercial determinism tends to creep in to such pronouncements. The imperatives of business and technology must be prioritized and barriers at national state level must be removed in order to allow the entrepreneurial spirit to flourish. That may well be appropriate in the sphere of mobile communications, but when it comes to the media there are real dangers in the assumption that what is technologically – and commercially – feasible is necessarily desirable.

The experience of Canada in this regard is a cautionary one. As was explained earlier, that country has had to contend with the problem of media encroachment by its powerful southern neighbour. It also has had to face very serious internal communication obstacles, for its relatively small population is unevenly distributed across a huge land mass; so, it has been obliged to devote an enormous amount of time and energy to ensuring that there are effective communications throughout the country. The great nineteenth-century achievement in this respect was the transcontinental railway, which was built from the east coast across the prairies and through the Rockies in a remarkable feat of engineering. As the railroad became a symbol of national unity in the nineteenth century, so broadcasting has been seen as exercising a similar function in the twentieth. The principal national broadcaster, the Canadian Broadcasting Corporation (CBC), has always been compelled to spend a high proportion of its budget on transmission costs because of the nature if its terrain and its obligation to talk to all Canadians. So the effectiveness of technology has been crucial to its cultural effectiveness. Not surprisingly then, policy making in Canada has often been characterized by a willingness to embrace new technology, such as cable delivery, as if an ongoing commitment to the latest technical possibilities would ensure that the cultural role of broadcasting would be enhanced. Service after service has been licensed by the regulatory body, the Canadian Radio-television and Telecommunications Commission (CRTC), and innumerable promises have been made by the licensees about their willingness to provide quality Canadian content. In practice what has happened, particularly in English Canada, is that the market has simply fragmented, and there has never been enough money to produce the range of indigenous programming which is taken for granted in a country like Britain. Part of the problem is clearly endemic, because of the size and population base of the country, but part of it stems from a regulatory enthusiasm for technological advance, an enthusiasm which has been taken advantage of by commercial operators who have seized opportunities to generate revenue by scheduling American programming and cheap home imitations, and then pleaded shortage of resources when taxed with non-fulfilment of pledges made to the licensing authority.[51]

Britain – cable then, digital now

In Britain a similar approach was apparent in the government's response in the early eighties to the possibility of a cable revolution. There were perfectly good reasons for hoping that cable communications would expand, since Britain enjoyed a lead in fibre optics, a technology by means of which a much greater number of signals can be carried than through conventional copper wire, and that technology had already established itself in telecommunications. If a wired society could be created in Britain, so the argument ran, then UK manufacturers of fibre optic cable would be able to export from a strong home base. The enthusiasm for a cabled future is clear in official pronouncements of the time:

> Cable technology poses a particular and exciting challenge because it has the potential both for removing many of the previous limitations on the number of programme services, television and sound, which can simultaneously be transmitted to the home, and for increasing the range of interactive telecommunications services available both domestically and at the office.[52]

The difficulty with this approach however was that it flew in the face of reality. Much was made of experience in the US, where cable had developed initially as a solution to the problem of poor off-air television reception. Once cable operators had signed up their clients, they were able, with the help of national providers, to offer other commercially funded channels and also subscription services, such as Home Box Office. What this meant for the viewer was a significant extension of choice. But in the UK there already were four off-air channels, offering a wider range of programming than was available on the US networks, and, in addition, there were more video recorders per head of the population in the UK than anywhere else in the world.[53] So, where was the incentive to buy cable as a way of extending viewing choice? This problem might not have mattered so much if the Thatcher government had been prepared to put public money towards creating the wired society which it believed was coming, but its deep hostility to public expenditure meant that development had to be commercially led, via entertainment. Private companies were understandably nervous about whether there really would be a move to the homeworking, home shopping socially atomised existence which was being conjured up by wired society enthusiasts, and were therefore reluctant to invest. The result was that cable staggered on for fifteen years, rarely managing to persuade residents in more than twenty per cent of the homes which it passed to buy the services which it offered. As an entertainment provider it was outpaced by satellite television, for which it quickly became a relay system, and even the telephony services which it was allowed to develop in the nineties did little to change the perception that a cable franchise was a licence to pour money down a hole in the ground.

The British dalliance with cable has been far less damaging to broadcasting than the Canadian one, though both show the dangers of believing that if something is technically possible then it is desirable, desired – or inevitable.

The debate about the development of digital broadcasting in the UK in the mid nineties needs to be considered in that light. Digital radio and television signals are produced by a process which is radically different from the one by which the traditional analogue signals are generated, in the same way that digital compact discs are different from gramophone records.[54] Because the resulting radio wave takes up far less space on the electromagnetic spectrum, it is possible to put many more signals – and hence channels – into the area of the spectrum which is allocated to broadcasting; it is also possible for satellite operators to find space for digital services on the part of the spectrum which has been allotted to them. Digital delivery is generally regarded as superior in quality to analogue, as well as being less demanding in its use of space, so it might seem obvious that if all television and radio transmission were to become digital, then there would be a substantial improvement in leisure and other associated activities in the home. Certainly a number of governments seem to think so:

> Digital broadcasting has enormous potential . . . It will provide many people with their first experience of the full potential of the information superhighway. Using a telephone return link, it will allow home shopping and other interactive news, education and information services. And viewers will be able to browse through the channels available to plan their evening's entertainment.[55]

So, it would appear, do some broadcasters:

> Digital technology will revolutionise broadcasting and enable the BBC to improve its services to audiences in two key ways. More channel space will allow us to serve an even greater range of needs and interests. Interactivity will give our audiences more control over their viewing and listening.[56]

It is undoubtedly true that a switch to digital broadcasting is technologically possible, as was the switch to compact discs from records, and to a lesser extent tapes. But is it likely and is it desirable? To answer these questions it is necessary to make some guesses about people's behaviour as consumers and as citizens. We need to know what the cost to the individual of the conversion to digital reception will be, and whether people will be happy to pay that price. Compulsion, through switching off the terrestrial analogue system, so that in order to continue to receive the services currently available consumers would be forced to buy digital conversion equipment, seems a politically hazardous course for any government to institute, although several administrations have taken tentative steps in that direction.

Willingness to pay would clearly be related to what is being offered in return, and the question then becomes one about the perceived gain in the quality of pictures and sound, and the perceived value of the new services which organizations like the BBC, British Digital Broadcasting, and several European operators say they are eager to offer. But there is a very serious difficulty about new television services. If they are not simply to be a repackaging of existing programmes – a wild life channel, a soap opera channel and so on – they are going to cost a great deal of money. Television is not like publishing: it is perfectly feasible to produce a few thousand copies of a book and sell it at a modest profit, for an initial outlay of fifty thousand pounds; on television where drama, audiences' favourite kind of programming, costs on average over £500,000 per hour, regardless of whether it is watched by several thousand people or several million, the situation is very different.[57] The economics of new television drama are not those of publishing, nor for that matter those of satellite services which act simply as transmitters, rather than originators, of programmes.

If the movement to digital does take place but some analogue transmissions continue, is there a danger of two classes of television service emerging, a danger which has already been highlighted in Britain by the way in which sporting events once available free now have to be purchased from BSkyB? Is there in any case a limit to the amount of talent in any one nation which can produce quality television? What proportion of able people is it wise for a country to encourage to work in broadcasting rather than in some other activity, such as pharmaceuticals or bio-engineering? These are important questions and they are not easy to answer, least of all in a climate where there is political and commercial pressure building up on the decision makers. Because of the nature of broadcast regulation, all cannot be left to the market, and government has to make choices. In doing so it has to balance what is good for business, even for 'Great Britain Ltd', against what is in the interests of a properly functioning democracy in which active citizenship and the cultural enrichment of the population are encouraged.

The problems of policy makers

Technology presents the policy maker with several problems. (S)he has not only to balance often conflicting considerations, but has to engage with difficult technical matters which by training (s)he may not be as well equipped to deal with as (s)he might be. We may well live in a technological age, but in the UK many of the people who become senior civil servants, government ministers – and for that matter media studies academics – do not have a strong scientific background. The public culture of Britain is much less oriented to science and technology than it is to the arts, and while that is due to an extent to the complexities of modern science, it may also derive from what some observers regard as an anti-science bias in our education system.[58] What this means is that only a few of the civil servants and politicians, whose work takes them into spheres where science and technology are central, are likely to have the kind of relevant expertise which so many of them can effortlessly display in the law or education. In practice there must be a serious risk of misunderstanding or half-understanding of what is possible or likely. It then becomes much easier for proponents of the view that we must keep up with the inevitable march of technology, and tailor our policies accordingly, to persuade policy makers of the wisdom of what they are advocating.

A further problem confronts the media policy-maker as the twentieth century ends: as globalization imposes substantial constraints on the economic power of governments, so advances in technology affect regulatory authority. Governments can regulate their domestic media and they may even be able, in cooperation with other governments, to regulate organizations which operate outside their immediate jurisdiction. The British government, for example, was able in 1993 to stop 'Red Hot Dutch', a pornographic satellite service, from being beamed into the country by action at the European Union level, and by making it an offence for the decoder smart cards to be sold in the United Kingdom. But that was a more difficult process than it would have been if 'Red Hot Dutch' had been uplinked from Manchester, where it only had an office, rather than from Denmark. Satellite broadcasting can be regulated if there is a common willingness to do so, but if that willingness does not exist it is not so easy.

Many of the world's authoritarian regimes are less than happy that news services can now be picked up in their countries without prior censorship of the sort which is imposed domestically. For decades the Communist countries of Eastern Europe did their best to jam radio stations like the Voice of America and the BBC World Service; it has been calculated that at one point Russia was spending as much money on jamming as would have paid for a new pan-Soviet radio service.[59] Jamming terrestrial radio is possible, if expensive, but satellite television signals present more intractable problems to the would-be censor. Most good democrats are therefore only too pleased when they learn that the subjects of some tyrannical regime are able to gain access to truthful accounts of what is going on in their own countries from foreign broadcasters.

But supposing a flood of satellite material were to undermine a small country's attempts to build up its own indigenous programming, would they be quite so happy? That country's policy makers may have very limited options open to them, no matter what their preferences might be.

What to do about the Internet

A similar difficulty appears to confront even the most powerful of countries when dealing with the Internet. The Internet is basically a worldwide network of computers, estimated in 1996 to total over 9 million, excluding the personal machines used by individuals to gain access to it via modems or in other ways.[60] It originated in 1969 in the United States, as a way of linking military establishments and universities conducting defence related research, in order that information might be shared among them; later it enabled users to access strategically located high-powered super computers. From that closed system has evolved the current open-access system on which any individual with the necessary equipment can send and receive messages, on a one-to-one or a group basis, and can, furthermore, have access to a staggering array of information from sources across the globe, via the World Wide Web. The Web had its origins in the European Particle Physics Laboratory (CERN) in Switzerland, and was designed to allow internationally dispersed teams of engineers to share text and images. Now it can be used by private indivduals to gain entry to libraries, government departments, citizens' groups and commercial concerns. The costs are borne by the participating computer networks and by the individual when (s)he subscribes to one of the companies which offer gateways to the Web. Some of the providers also charge additional fees, and these are usually collected via credit card.

It might well be thought that the advent of the Internet marks the beginning of electronic democracy, as everybody in the world talks to anyone else who is prepared to listen, accesses a cornucopia of information, on the click of a mouse, and participates fully in political decision making. And to the fortunate user it does indeed sometimes feel a little bit like that. The difficulty is that entry, although in itself relatively cheap, depends on the availability of personal computers, and most of these tend to be in the developed world, and in the hands of the prosperous. So, despite efforts to provide terminals in libraries and schools, electronic democracy is a long way off. However, although not everyone is travelling along it, the information superhighway, of which the Internet is an important part, is most definitely with us. Why should regulatory issues arise? Obviously authoritarian governments will be as keen to prevent 'subversive' traffic reaching their citizens via the Internet as they are to keep out foreign broadcasts and publications of which they do not approve, but the problems of such regimes need not detain us. The difficulties for democratic administrations arise from the fact that there is material on the Internet which falls into categories which would normally attract the attention of the law, such as racially offensive propaganda, incitements to violence, and pornography.

We shall return to the issue of what the criteria for acceptable publication in these areas should be in a later chapter, but for the moment let us acknowledge that there is on the Internet sexually explicit material which can be obtained by inserting in the search box of one of the finder services an anglo-saxon word or two, or even politer terms, and that, although full access is conditional on the provision of credit card details, it is perfectly possible for the non-paying user to download sample images, which certainly in Britain would not be available on any newsagent's top shelf. Let us also concede that paedophiles can use the Net to share their fantasies, and even to circulate photographs of children being forced to participate in sexual acts. Finally, let us accept that groups, such as those American militias which believe that they have a duty to wage war on the federal government, are able to talk to each other and generate a sense of solidarity by so doing.

If a government decides that it wishes to stop any or all of these activities, it faces formidable obstacles. The easiest targets are the commercial pornographers, for they tell the viewer who they are and where they are to be found. So, leaving aside for the moment the question of personal freedom, it ought to be possible to prevent XXX images appearing on the screen by taking legal action against the providers; however a difficulty may arise if the provider is in another country, and that country's government is unwilling to cooperate. Furthermore, given the way in which information moves around the Internet, there is not always a host computer which can easily be tracked down and held responsible at any one time for this traffic. The problems get worse when dealing with those non-commercial providers who take care to hide their locations, and even use the services of 'remailers' who will disguise their identities for them. It is not impossible to pursue the groups concerned but it is a very difficult task, which requires the systematic cooperation of governments and police forces. Not for the first time we are confronted with a medium of communication which offers, on the one hand, the opportunity for education, enlightenment and entertainment, but on the other, a breeding ground for hatred, cruelty and degeneracy. How can the one be maximized and the other minimized, or is the Internet the first medium of communication which, because of the technology it utilises, is beyond effective regulation?

Summary

Technology is basic to the media, as it is to many other aspects of modern life. What is not clear is whether technology has a dynamic of its own or whether it interacts with political, economic and other forces to produce a variety of possible outcomes. The history of the media is a story of continual technological innovation; this has led some policy makers to believe that unless they embrace the latest development, the prosperity of their country will suffer. Recent technological advances present new problems of regulation, for in practice they are very difficult to control.

Questions for discussion

1. Why are governments so enthusiastic about new communications technologies?
2. What will be the cultural and social consequences of a switch from analogue to digital television?
3. What are the appropriate responses to the regulatory problems posed by the Internet?

Part II
Principles

Freedom, Democracy and Enlightenment | 5

Media policy to a significant degree is citizenship policy. The approach which a government takes to regulating the media tells us a great deal about the view which that government has of its citizens and their role in society. In an authoritarian state, for example, the government, however it achieved office, will not have gained it at elections which were open to a range of political parties offering a variety of approaches to the management of the country's affairs, and in which all adult citizens were able to exercise free choice in a secret ballot. In such a state the objective of those in power is to retain and sustain their own position and to manage dissent and opposition. The methods they use to do so range from the subtle to the crude: even a casual glance at the newsletters published by Amnesty International shows that the systematic employment of brutality and torture as a way of intimidating opponents is a characteristic of a depressingly large number of regimes.[61]

Controlling dissent

As these governments seek to destroy or curtail dissent, they will inevitably give a great deal of attention to the media, for if dissent is to be contained then it is important that it is not allowed access to channels of communication. Broadcasting is the easiest medium to control internally (although signals from outside of the country present trickier problems, as we have seen). All that is required is a compliant national broadcasting organization and, if there are also private operators, a regime of censorship which ensures that they do what they are told. Where such a system exists, as in several

African and Asian countries, not only will news and current affairs programmes avoid mentioning alternative policies to those of the government, but they will often also spend much of their time detailing the activities of the 'great leader' who presides over the nation's destiny, as was the case for example in Zaire, where President Mobutu's deeds were hymned unendingly on state television during his dictatorship.

Although cinema can be censored centrally through the kind of boards which operate in democracies and non-democracies alike, when it comes to the press, control can be much more difficult, for instead of one or two organizations, there may be dozens or even hundreds. So, complicated and expensive arrangements have to be in place and working efficiently. The government can also produce its own newspapers, and do its best to eliminate or prevent alternatives appearing. The approach in the now defunct Soviet Union was rather like this: papers were owned by the state, and in effect written by the Communist Party, which meant that decisions as to what did and did not appear were essentially Party decisions. By contrast, newspapers operating in South American countries like Brazil, Argentina or Chile under military dictatorships in the 1970s and 1980s had to reckon with external censors and physical intimidation. Journalism in such a country was, and is, a very hazardous profession. Each year the International Freedom House organization reports on the number of reporters who have been killed in the course of their work: some have died in war, but many others have been murdered because they were pursuing, or had written, stories which the authorities in their country did not like and for which they had decided to exact their revenge.[62]

The media and citizenship

Governments which behave in such a fashion are alarmingly common, which might make those of us fortunate enough to live in democracies a little complacent and self-satisfied. That would be a mistake, for even in the most open of societies, the struggle over freedom of expression and publication is a constant one, and the most impeccably democratic of administrations can be tempted down the path of suppression and distortion. If media policy is part of citizenship policy, it is clear that many democratic governments are reluctant to trust their citizens with a wide range of information. The argument about the limits of knowledge is far from complete.

Although governments do have the legal right to confer and withdraw citizenship, it should be emphasized at this point that in a liberal democracy citizenship is a concept which is firmly located in the assumptions and practices of the citizens themselves. Governments may well accept the general definitions of citizenship which have evolved, and some may even have contributed to radical reformulations of the concept, but they are not the final arbiters, for that would be to contradict the fundamental characteristic of citizenship that it encompasses not only the relationship between individuals and the institutions of the state, but also the sphere of activity known as civil society. Civil society involves everything from family life and religious bodies to the host of voluntary organisations – from philately clubs to charities and pressure groups – which individuals freely join, and which are not in the control of the state or government. It is in civil society that much of what goes to make up our individual and social identities is constructed, and also where we freely engage in discourse on issues of public policy, be they local, national or international. It was the need to create such a public space in Russia which lay at the heart of Mikhail Gorbachev's reform project, for he believed that without such a development, which had been anathema to both Communist and Tsarist governments, his country could never be truly civilized.[63]

The Enlightenment, liberalism and freedom

In chapter 2 there was a brief discussion of the Enlightenment, and it is to that great movement in the history of thought that we must now return, for it is there that we shall find the basis of what is generally known as the libertarian theory of the press, on which media practice in democracies is grounded. Enlightenment thinkers were distrustful of traditional authority, whether secular or ecclesiastical, and believed that human reason offered the best guide to understanding the world, and to changing it for the better. Their approach owed much to the achievements of science from the sixteenth century on: the Polish monk Copernicus (1473–1543), for example, had argued that rather than the sun going round the earth, the planets revolved around the sun, and the German, Kepler (1571–1630), had developed laws which sought to explain planetary motion, while the Italian Galileo (1564–1642) had used his telescope to explore the solar system. All of this work depended on observation and reasoning, and as such, it represented a challenge to the traditional view of the Catholic church, which insisted that the earth, the creation of the Almighty, was at the centre of the Universe. The collision between rational science and apparently anti-rational religion was dramatised in 1633 when Galileo was forced to recant his views by the Inquisition, convicted of heresy, and compelled to spend the remaining eight years of his life under house arrest.

It was a Pyrrhic victory for the Vatican, because from that point on the Catholic church was clearly associated with ignorance and superstition, while science became a byword for education and truth. The achievments of science continued unabated with, for example, the work of Isaac Newton (1642–1727) on the laws of motion, which formed the basis of modern physics. The Protestant Reformation also contributed to the process, for although Protestant churches could be as intolerant as the Catholic one, the very nature of Protestantism, which puts the relationship between the individual and the deity, unmediated by an ecclesiastical hierarchy, at the heart of its reformulation of Christianity, strengthened the idea that each one of us could find his or her own way to truth. It is not difficult to see how that concept leads on naturally to the libertarian theory of the press, fundamental to which is the belief that freedom to publish information and opinion, unencumbered by interference from the authorities, is desirable in itself as a right of citizenship, and also contributes to the health and development of society.

The Enlightenment in general and the libertarian theory in particular are closely related not only to the rise of science and rationalism, but also to the political philosophy known as liberalism. It will therefore be useful to spend a little time exploring that philosophy. The word 'liberal' has become something of a term of abuse in contemporary American politics, where in the 1996 Presidential election campaign, for example, the Democratic candidate, Bill Clinton, expended considerable effort denying the claims of his Republican opponent, Bob Dole, that he was a 'tax and spend liberal'. In the USA the term has come to imply not only a willingness to raise taxes and utilize the revenue for community endeavours, including welfare provision, but also an enthusiasm for permissive personal behaviour in such areas as sexuality and drugs. Two hundred years ago, however, a liberal was someone who believed not only in the exercise of reason in the pursuit of human perfectibility, but also in the maximum individual freedom, untrammelled by the power of the state. In practice this meant that liberals were committed to private enterprise and to liberty of religious and political conviction, and regarded governments with considerable suspicion. In nineteenth-century Britain the economic aspect was emphasized by the so-called Manchester liberals who resisted strongly any state intervention in the business sphere, which, they averred, left largely to itself would create wealth and prosperity. The fact that laissez-faire capitalism produced not only wealth but also poverty, degradation and disease led to what might be called social liberalism, in which a commitment to private enterprise remained, but was allied to a belief in social provision and state intervention in order to modify the worst side effects of the market system. It is that kind of liberalism which is at the root of what has sometimes been called welfare capitalism, which, in varying degrees, is the economic system prevalent today in all Western democracies. In the 1980s the Thatcher – Reagan project sought, with some success, to redefine the relationship between government and economic activity, so that the former's role became rather like what it was before the advent of welfare capitalism. This has been described as neo-liberalism. But the liberalism being alluded to is not that of the social reformers who predominated in the British Liberal governments in the years before the First World War, but that of the Manchester free-traders who believed in minimal state intervention. By a further twist already mentioned, the term, in the USA at least, has come to be associated with high taxation and permissiveness, so much so that while many Americans of a progressive disposition are happy to be described as 'moderate' they now shrink from the term 'liberal'.

The point of this digression is not simply to illustrate that words change their meanings constantly, particularly abstract terms in the political arena, but also to demonstrate that there is a common thread running through the use of the term 'liberal' for the last two hundred years. That is the emphasis on the freedom of the individual, whether considered socially or economically, to pursue his or her own ends, without outside interference, except where that is necessary in order to protect the rights of others to behave in the same fashion. The collective exercise of such freedom by millions of individuals is expected by liberals to produce the just society. The very real difficulty of balancing individual good and the good of the community as a whole is a problem to which we shall return.

The disciples of the Enlightenment believed passionately that it was possible for rational human beings to distinguish clearly between truth and falsehood, and, as we have seen, in this they were much affected by the success of science in explaining the laws of nature. However, as was noted in chapter 2, belief in any kind of absolute truth is now much less common, and some contemporary philosophers go so far as to argue that there can never be an appeal to unchanging values, whether those of revealed religion or rationality; all systems of belief, they maintain, are contingent, that is to say dependent on time and circumstance. One such philosopher is Richard Rorty who describes himself as a 'liberal ironist':

> I use 'ironist' to name the sort of person who faces up to the contingency of his or her most central beliefs and desires – someone . . . [who has] . . . abandoned the idea that those central beliefs and desires refer back to something beyond the reach of time and chance. Liberal ironists are people who include among these ungroundable desires their own hope that suffering will be diminished, that the humiliation of human beings by other human beings may cease.[64]

What is rather odd about Rorty's position is that it is not at all clear why the 'ungroundable desire' that human beings should not inflict humiliation on other human beings can be concurred with, in the absence of the assertion that this is an absolute unchanging value, however contingent in origin it might appear. Be that as it may, even if we wish to argue that there are no universal truths – which is something of a contradiction, since the statement just made purports to be a universal descriptive, if not moral, truth – we would probably all be willing to accept that even in a world of contingent and conflicting value systems, it is desirable that there should be the opportunity for such pluralism to be fully expressed, if only in the hope of avoiding social breakdown. It is here that the media have a crucial role to play in encouraging the widest possible range of opinions into the public arena.

Freedom of debate

Many of the Enlightenment thinkers were Deists, that is they believed in a Creator, but were not attracted to complicated theological systems such as Christianity. However, one of the first people to contribute to the development of the libertarian theory of the press was a devout Christian. John Milton, author of *Paradise Lost*, one of the great long poems in the English language, was a civil servant during the period of the English Civil War and the Commonwealth, when, after a divisive conflict, the country was ruled not by a monarch – Charles I was finally executed in 1649 – but by a Lord Protector, Oliver Cromwell. In 1640 the licensing of printing had been abolished by the reforming Long Parliament, but in 1643 controls were reintroduced. Milton, who had been enthusiastic about the abolition, expressed his dismay at this turn of events in *Areopagitica*, a closely argued text which clearly articulates the case against censorship:

> Truth and understanding are not such wares to be monopolised and traded in by tickets and statutes, and standards. We must not think to make a staple commodity of all the knowledge in the land, to mark and license it like our broadcloth and our wool packs.[65]

For Milton the religious context is crucial, but his sentiments transcend that context:

> Well knows he who uses to consider, that our faith and knowledge thrives by exercise, as well as our limbs and complexion. Truth is compared in Scripture to a streaming fountain; if her waters flow not in a perpetual progression, they sicken into a muddy pool of conformity and tradition.[66]

Milton is firmly on the side of those who argue that dispute and debate are basic to a civilized society, indeed society profits greatly from them. And he is opposed to censorship. The third point to note – sadly – is that he failed to persuade his readers in Parliament, who went on to reimpose censorship, which survived in various forms until 1694. Even with the abolition of formal controls then, British governments continued to exercise considerable sway over the press through special taxes and straightforward bribery and coercion. The eighteenth century saw Stamp Duty being imposed on newspapers as a way of increasing their price, and thus excluding, it was hoped, the less well off from exposure to 'dangerous' information. The law of criminal libel was also used to attack radical publications, and those who produced and circulated them, many of whom were jailed. In addition, taxes were levied on advertising as a way of tightening the financial pressure on the press. As to bribery, it is estimated that Sir Robert Walpole, Prime Minister from

1721 till 1742, in one ten year period spent £50,000 on cash payments to newspapers in order to secure favourable treatment.[67] The so-called 'taxes on knowledge' continued until the middle of the nineteenth century, when they were finally abandoned as a crude and ineffective method of seeking to influence political debate.

Despite these taxes and other constraints, there developed in Britain and elsewhere a public realm, where a growing, if socially limited, number of people regularly met and discussed the behaviour of the authorities, and subjected that behaviour to critical interrogation. Informed opinion was coming into being. Jurgen Habermas has commented on the importance of coffee houses in this development – London alone apparently had 3,000 of these by the beginning of the eighteenth century. Such establishments functioned as 'centres of criticism – literary at first, then also political – in which began to emerge, between aristocratic society and bourgeois intellectuals, a certain parity of the educated'.[68] In a coffee house customers did not simply drink the beverage in question, but engaged in discussion with like-inclined men of property and business on the literary and political affairs of the day. A crucial feature of these gathering places was the availability there of newspapers and magazines, which for their part had begun to move on from elementary reporting into political debate, often in opposition to the policies of the government. And beyond the coffee house, working-class and radical organizations had been developing, and were starting to articulate a fundamental critique of social structures. So, although by no stretch of the imagination could eighteenth-century Britain be regarded as a modern democracy, it was evolving two essential features of that kind of society, namely a public willing and able to engage with issues of power and authority, and a press dedicated to the same end.

The American experience

The Enlightenment had a particularly strong impact in the American colonies, and indeed it can be argued that there was a clear symmetry between a movement which sought to overturn old ways of looking at the world, and a group of people who were actually creating a 'new world' in North America; the archetypal Enlightenment figure in the colonies was the remarkable Benjamin Franklin, scientist, inventor and politician, and one of the leaders in the independence struggle. Another such individual was Thomas

Jefferson (1743–1826), who drafted the Declaration of Independence of 1776. That document is almost a manifesto for the Enlightenment:

> We hold these truths to be self-evident, that all men are created equal, that they are endowed by their Creator with certain unalienable Rights, that among these are Life, Liberty, and the pursuit of Happiness.

Given their background in Enlightenment thought, it is not surprising that several – though not all – of the progenitors of the American Revolution set great store by the freedom of the press; indeed the First Amendment to the Constitution, which was finally ratified in 1791, states that 'Congress shall make no law . . . abridging the freedom of speech, or of the press'. The most committed proponent of press freedom in the early days of independence was Jefferson, who was President of the United States from 1801 till 1809. Jefferson had many detractors in the newspapers, and at times he was clearly weary of what he described as 'their abandoned spirit of falsehood'.[69] But his basic position was very clear:

> I am persuaded that the good sense of the people will always be found to be the best army. They may be led astray for a moment, but will soon correct themselves. The people are the only censor of their governors; and even their errors will tend to keep these to the true principles of their instititution. To punish these errors too severely would be to suppress the only safeguard of public liberty. The way to prevent these irregular interpositions of the people is to give them full information of their affairs through the channel of the public papers, and to contrive that those papers should penetrate to the whole mass of the people . . . were it left to me to decide whether we should have a government without newspapers, or newspapers without a government, I should not hesitate a moment to prefer the latter.[70]

Edwin Emery in his study of the history of the press in the United States, comments that the last few lines of this statement are frequently quoted, but what is not so often said is that in a later passage Jefferson makes the point that the people who receive the papers should 'be capable of reading them'.[71] What Jefferson is identifying here is the fundamental difficulty of the committed libertarian: he or she desires the widest possible dissemination of information about public affairs, but if, for whatever reason – ignorance, laziness, gullibility or plain stupidity – some of the readers are in no position to understand what is being said, or to take account of any partisan bias which is being displayed, then the self-righting process by which truth will drive out error, in which men like Jefferson believed, might simply not take place. This is a dilemma which lies at the heart of democratic politics, and although Jefferson retained his faith in the propositions he articulated – sometimes in the face of scurrilous newspaper attacks – he was not operating in a society where everyone had the vote or was ever expected to have it (indeed he was President of a country which tolerated institutionalized slavery). How much more acute is the problem in the age of mass democracy, when the right to vote is assumed to be inalienable, but it is far from clear that there is a concomitant responsibility to inform oneself or indeed, if some of the channels of communication are filled with propaganda, that it is always possible to do so.

The belief in liberty of thought and debate is given one of its most eloquent expressions by John Stuart Mill, whose reservations about the functioning of democracy were referred to in chapter 2. His essay, *On Liberty*, published in 1859, is a seminal statement of the position that in any society individuals should be free to do whatever they please, regardless of whom is offended, provided no harm is done to others.[72] In the chapter concerned with 'Thought and Discussion' Mill notes that it is still possible in mid-nineteenth-century England to be jailed for expressing unpopular opinions, or ones of which the authorities disapprove. He goes on to lay out several grounds for freedom of expression: if we suppress an opinion, it may be true, or it may be part of the truth; truths need to be argued over, in order that they can be seen to be valid; unless they are contested they will turn into dogma. For Mill:

> only through diversity of opinion is there, in the existing state of human intellect, a chance of fair play to all sides of the truth. When there are persons to be found who form an exception to the apparent unanimity of the world on any subject, even if the world is in the right, it is always probable that dissentients have something worth hearing to say for themselves, and that truth would lose something by their silence.[73]

What is crucial – and ironic – to note here is the contrast between Milton arguing for freedom of speech against tyrannical state authority, and Mill two hundred years later arguing for it in the face of sanctions imposed not only by the state but also by the majority of citizens who may be very hostile indeed to the expression of opinions of which they heartily disapprove.

Liberal values and current practices

In societies in which liberalism is the dominant philosophy the press is expected to reflect the diversity of opinion and outlook. Historically, liberals have also argued that it must be in private hands, in order that it be distanced from the power of the state. Those who campaigned most forcibly in the eighteenth and nineteenth centuries for freedom of the press were absolutely clear that the best guarantee of variety, and ultimately truth, was private ownership of a multiplicity of titles.

The difficulty that faces any liberal observer of the press today is that concentration of ownership and the desire for monopoly, a natural tendency in capitalists, which was foreseen clearly and warned against by the doyen of free market enthusiasts, Adam Smith, has led to a marked diminution in the range of opinion offered to the public.[74] The example of the English daily and Sunday press makes this very clear: a few firms dominate the industry, so while there is not a monopolistic situation, there is arguably an oligopolistic one. Furthermore, as many studies have demonstrated, there is a mismatch between the disposition of votes cast at elections and the disposition of the London based press: the electorate spreads its support around much more widely than do newspapers, which tend to be pro-Conservative, although in the run-up to the 1997 general election, in a remarkable volte-face, which is unlikely to be permanent, the press, led by the Murdoch titles, inclined to the Labour party.[75] The traditional pro-Conservative bias is not entirely surprising, given that Conservative parties have tended to be more supportive of business than non-Conservative ones. This situation would not matter quite so much if newspapers rigorously separated reporting and comment, but the tabloids, which account for 75 per cent of morning sales, long since gave up the effort to do so, with the result that political reporting in the *Daily Mail*, for example, will often be close to Conservative propaganda, and reporting in the *Daily Mirror* close to Labour propaganda. The approach of neither title does much to encourage the kind of informed public debate in which classical liberals believe. Overall bias towards any one particular political position accentuates the problem. The English situation is not unique, and indeed in

Scotland since the 1980s, there has been a distinct anti-Conservative tone in the press. By contrast, in both the United States and Canada there is much less overt propaganda, and a greater willingness to separate fact and comment. However, several observers of the North American scene have argued that political neutrality in reporting is often more apparent than real, and that so-called objectivity can mask the hegemony of the world-view of the powerful.[76]

The social responsibility remedy

To the committed believer in the libertarian theory the deficiencies of current practice are troubling. The problem is to find a remedy which does not violate the principle of freedom from government interference. In America the solution has been the development of the so-called social responsibility theory, which modifies the libertarian one in several important regards.[77] It even strikes at the very basis of that theory, for trust in the inherent rationality of the citizen has been replaced by deep unease about the susceptibility of the masses to propaganda of the sort generated, not only by regimes like the Nazi and Communist ones, but also by the more sensational newspapers in democracies. The new theory acknowledges that economic logic leads to concentration and, in a country where papers are local, and not national, produces regional monopolies. The solution is to ask that newspapers strive ever harder to report fairly, and open their columns to a variety of opinions, whether the papers agree with all of these or not. Substantial store is also set by professional codes of practice, to which journalists and proprietors are expected to adhere.

It is the case that a number of papers in the USA do appear in their editorial approach to acknowledge the need to represent a wide range of viewpoints and to allow different voices to be heard, although it is not at all clear how such behaviour can actually be required of them. As far as the British tabloids are concerned however, the social responsibility theory might as well not exist. If the natural tendencies within the capitalist system are therefore making it impossible for the free press to operate as it should, then it would appear that outside intervention may be necessary in order to ensure that this happens. As was noted in chapter 3, that is why governments have developed special anti-monopoly provisions. Some governments have gone much further and have intervened directly in order to protect pluralism. This is an ironic development, for the libertarian theorists saw newspapers as a countervailing force to government, yet for the press to do the job the libertarians wish it to do, governments may well need to act against the innate tendencies of the market. Of course some governments may be very happy with the 'natural' situation, if it is favourable to their own political position, but even where governments of the right have enjoyed a long hegemony, as in the UK, there has been growing unease among senior politicians about the willingness of new-spaper proprietors to use their titles to attack policies with which they disagree and to vilify particular individuals, in the way that John Major, for example, was abused during much of his tenure of office as Prime Minister of the United Kingdom in the 1990s. The dilemma is clear enough: if a government believes that it is desir-able not only to have a nominally free press but also a genuinely pluralistic one, how does it secure that end without opening itself to charges of authoritarianism and unjustifiable interference with the market?

The case of broadcasting

It has always been easier with broadcasting. As was explained earlier in the book, governments were involved in its regulation from the beginning, ostensibly for technical reasons, but also because of the perceived power of the medium. However, it would be wrong to be totally cynical about this, for it is clear from an examination of the early development of public broadcasting orga-nizations that there was a genuine commitment in many of them and in the administrations which sponsored them to 'information, education and entertainment'.[78] If we look, for example, at the history of the BBC, we can see this very much in practice, in such matters as the diffusion of culture, in the provision of information on current events and in education, whether in the shape of schools broadcasting, which began in 1924, or informal adult education. The Corporation is not directly controlled by the government, but it is the government through Parliament which establishes the frame-work within which it operates. And it is the Foreign Office that pays directly for the World Service, which transmits radio programmes in a variety of languages across the globe. The World Service enjoys a remarkable reputation for honesty and integrity. That reputation has not been gained by parroting official lines, but through a genuine attempt to offer as a central part of its schedules a reasonably accurate account of current events. If one is British, it is easy to be self-satisfied about this achievement, but it does stand as testimony to the willingness of some governments – with active encouragement from important social groups – to maintain a genuine public sphere, where ideas are contested, and the activities of those in authority are subjected to scrutiny. Habermas has commented on what he sees as the way in which mass communication has destroyed the culture of the coffee house:

> Professional dialogues from the podium, panel discussions, and round table shows – the rational debate of private people becomes one of the production numbers of the stars in radio and television, a salable package ready for the box office.[79]

But that is a generalization which simply does not apply to all government-financed and regulated broadcasting. Indeed, Habermas leaves himself open to the accusation that, like the cultural pessimists before him, he idealizes the past, and is blind to the very real achievments of broadcasting, which in many countries has produced a much more socially inclusive public sphere than was ever available in any eighteenth-century coffee house.[80]

Citizens and consumers

It does remain the case however that the idea that it is the function of the media to offer opportunities for enlightenment as well as entertainment, has taken something of a battering in recent times. In America both cinema and much of broadcasting have historically been regarded as being firmly in the sphere of entertainment, with the role of enlightening the public being left to news programming and to the press. In democratic Europe the approach, outside of the period of Nazi domination, has been that all of the media should provide both entertainment and enlightenment, although in cinema it was accepted that the emphasis was going to be on the former. The opposition between the two categories is somewhat artificial, and some post-modernists would argue that it no longer has validity. However it does remain useful, for it helps us to distinguish between the idea that the media exist to benefit the citizen, and the idea that they are there to benefit the consumer. If we are all regarded primarily as consumers, then we are deemed to be seeking various kinds of pleasures and satisfactions largely as private individuals. But, if we are regarded primarily as citizens, then we are judged to be looking for pleasure, information and enlightenment as individuals and as members of a community of active participants in the democratic process. In practice we are both consumers and citizens in much of our daily lives, but with the media it is important to consider where the balance is being struck in any particular discussion.

During the eighties and nineties public discourse about broadcasting in the European Union in general, and Britain in particular, has reflected a move from one way of talking to another. Here is the Annan Committee in 1977:

> Traditionally the State has set broadcasters their objectives. At present their role is to provide entertainment, information and education for large audiences. It is hard to conceive of a programme which would not be held in some way to inform, educate or entertain at least some section of the population. We would add to the list a further objective, unfortunately incapable of being put in statutory form, namely enrichment, to enlarge people's interests, to convey to them new choices and possibilities in life, this is what broadcasting ought to try to achieve.[81]

A decade later the Peacock Committee talked in rather different terms:

> The fundamental aim of broadcasting policy should in our view be to enlarge both the freedom of choice of the consumer and the opportunities available to programme makers to offer alternative wares to the public.[82]

Taking its cue from Peacock, the British government, in setting out its approach to the development of broadcasting in the nineties and beyond, declared:

> The Government places the viewer and listener at the centre of broadcasting policy . . . The Government's aim is to open the doors so that individuals can choose for themselves from a much wider range of programmes and types of broadcasting.[83]

Although both Peacock and the government are at pains to emphasize that what they are proposing does not represent a threat to public service broadcasting, it is quite clear that there has been a major philosophical shift. Some will argue that an old and indefensible paternalism, where broadcasters decided what was good for the public and pushed it down their unwilling throats, has been replaced by an acknowledgement that people should be free to make cultural and informational choices for themselves. It is difficult to object to this argument without being accused of elitism. But perhaps some kinds of elitism do operate in the general interest rather than simply in the interests of the elite itself. Clearly, if a financial elite wishes to assert that it is entitled to accumulate large sums of money and pay relatively little tax, then that is a self-serving argument. The question is whether a cultural elite, insisting that there should be a broad diet of programming, some of which is difficult and demanding, is simply trying to keep itself in work in television and radio studios and is thus replicating the behaviour of the financial elite.

We are back to the relationship between media policy and citizenship policy which was highlighted at the beginning of the chapter. If media policy is part of citizenship policy, what are the criteria for determining the full nature of citizenship in a democratic society? Does citizenship consist purely in the enjoyment of certain rights – freedom to express opinions, to assemble, to participate in elections, and to be subject to due process of law, for example – or does that enjoyment bring with it concomitant responsibilities, such as informing oneself about domestic and non-domestic politics? Some might argue that it is a democratic right to opt out of the democratic process entirely, indeed almost half of the citizens of the United States apparently do so during Presidential elections, and about a quarter of British citizens during general elections. Is a democracy truly functioning when this happens? And do the media have a role in trying to persuade people that it is their responsibility to vote, or is their job simply to reflect the actual political process 'out there'? Is that even remotely possible, given that 'out there' for many citizens is now brought to them via media representations?

The questions become even more difficult when we move on to consider enrichment, for we have returned to the issue of levels of culture, which was discussed earlier. Should we argue that the media have a duty to make high culture available to all or not? The European public service broadcasters have seen their role traditionally as one of offering the opportunities for a wide variety of cultural experiences, and have to some extent left it to viewers and listeners to select their own choices from a wide-ranging menu. Furthermore the most successful broadcasting systems have made their own contributions to the development of mass culture, and in British television, for example, situation comedies such as *Only Fools and Horses*, dramas like *Inspector Morse* and *Casualty*, and even shows such as *Bruce Forsyth's Generation Game* have been able to command audiences across the social classes, and to secure critical approbation. Nonetheless in the days of monopoly and semi-monopoly considerable efforts were also expended to educate audiences in classical music and drama, and these efforts continue, even although success is rather more difficult to attain in a multi-channel universe.

If we are now living in an era of cultural democracy, is it still possible to insist that the life led without serious engagement with what has traditionally been regarded as high culture is an impoverished life, or one of missed opportunity? At a time when both moral judgements and aesthetic ones have been characterized as a matter of personal preference or 'lifestyle', it is very difficult to argue that enrichment of the citizenry's imaginative lives is not just desirable but necessary. But if there is no longer a belief among policy makers that enabling people to participate in the democratic process in a more than superficial fashion, and to open themselves to a wide range of cultural experiences, is important, are they not depriving others of opportunities which they would be most unwilling to surrender in their own lives? If media policy is indeed part of citizenship policy, can value judgements possibly be avoided?

Summary

The policies which governments pursue in the media field are indicative of the view which they take of the relationship between governed and governors. In the West the belief in the primary importance of freedom of speech can be traced back to the Enlightenment, a movement which was grounded in the view that rational discussion among different individuals holding a variety of opinions is the best way to solve problems and to advance human happiness. Questions arise about how far current practice measures up to the ideal posited by Enlightenment thinkers, and whether there is now confusion over the extent to which audiences are citizens, and the extent to which they are consumers.

Questions for discussion

1. If media policy is part of citizenship policy, which principles should guide media regulators?
2. What criticisms might be offered of the Enlightenment belief that reason is the best guide to human understanding and action?
3. How easy is it for citizens to distinguish truth from falsehood in the contemporary 'marketplace of ideas'?

Protecting the State | 6

Freedom is not licence, and, as US Supreme Court Justice Oliver Wendell Holmes famously pointed out, it does not include the right to shout 'fire!' in a crowded theatre, if there is no conflagration. Liberalism has always had to grapple with the problem of what limits it is legitimate for society to impose on individuals. The view that we should all be free to act as we wish, provided we do not interfere with the liberty of others to do likewise presents serious difficulties, for it is clear that my pursuit of what I desire must sooner or later constrain the ability of others to follow a similar course. To take a simple example: in a world of relatively finite resources if I maximize my income, then it must to some extent be at the expense of those who do not manage to find a way of maximizing theirs. It might be argued however that such a situation is perfectly acceptable, provided that I make no attempt to restrict the opportunities for other people to pursue the same objective. Whether they actually attained that end would be up to them. This argument may be valid in theory, but in a world where life chances and abilities are unevenly dispersed, there are practical obstacles.

One way out of the dilemma was suggested by the nineteenth-century British social theorists known as Utilitarians, who argued that we need to construct some kind of 'felicific calculus' (the term is Jeremy Bentham's). Utilitarians believed that actions which produce the greatest happiness of the greatest number of people are superior to actions which produce less happiness overall, happiness being taken as the seeking of pleasure and the avoidance of pain.[84] This might seem an attractive way forward, but quite apart from the difficulties involved in making the necessary calculations, where it runs into complications is in dealing with situations such as one where happiness in a particular society might well be max-imized by refusing to pay the costs of relieving the suffering of a minority, whose total unhappiness is far less than the total happi-ness enjoyed by the majority. Here the classical liberal will priori-tize certain fundamental rights of the individual over and against the rights – or pleasures – of the majority. And indeed the history of liberalism is the history of a continuing struggle to insist on the inalienable entitlements and integrity of each one of us. As Tom Paine, the political propagandist, put it in *The Rights of Man* in 1791:

> all men are born equal, and with equal natural rights, in the same manner as if posterity had been continued by *creation* instead of *gen-eration*, the latter being only the mode by which the former is carried forward; and consequently every child born into the world must be considered as deriving its existence from God. The world is as new to him as it was to the first man that existed, and his natural right in it is of the same kind.[85]

The problem with rights

Such a starting point does seem preferable to any attempt to apply Bentham's felicific calculus. But there remains the crucial issue which classical liberalism, with its insistence on individual rights is obliged to address, and that is the entitlements of the wider com-munity, whether society as a whole, or that part of society con-cerned with governance and order, the state.

Rights-based cultures, it can be argued, at best put too much emphasis on the entitlements of the individual, and at worst encourage a kind of self-indulgent hedonism. Not only that, they betray a misunderstanding of the human being, who cannot exist in isolation but, for biological and psychological reasons, needs to interact with other people. The individual can only be truly him or herself, this argument runs, if part of his/her identity derives from his/her roles as member of a whole range of social groups – family, circle of friends, social class, voluntary organizations and indeed nation.[86] If this view is correct, then it follows that there will always be difficult compromises to be made, for example in the personal sphere between the rights of sexually active adults to seek new part-ners, if they feel the relationships in which they have been involved have broken down, and their duty to provide any children who have been born out of these relationships with stable emotional environments until they grow into adulthood. In an era when there has been an increased emphasis on the individual's rights in the personal arena, this kind of predicament confronts more and more people. It is emblematic of a range of similar dilemmas.

In the late 1990s public discourse in Britain and elsewhere began to couple rights and duties much more forcibly than had been the case for some time, and this seemed to be an acknowledgement of the major deficiency of an individualistic culture, that it does not emphasize clearly enough the conditional nature of rights. To take an example: if I am convicted of murdering another person in a particularly brutal and calculating fashion, does the fact that I am unlikely to be executed in a Western European state stem from my inalienable right to life, or does the very act of murder, because it involves violating the concomitant obligation not to kill one's fellow citizens, cancel that right, so that survival depends, not on an entitlement, but on the unwillingness of society to engage in judicial killing? (In many parts of the USA no such reluctance exists, and execution may well follow conviction.) Likewise, if a citizen acts as a spy for another country, perhaps because (s)he sincerely believes in the superiority of that country's political system, how is his/her right to pursue that course of action to be balanced against the right of the society of which (s)he is a part to be protected against the consequences of treason? What is being suggested here then is that the individual most certainly does have rights but other individuals and the wider community have them too, and we are all obliged to respect that fact. The problem therefore is to find a way of balancing conflicting rights and duties. This is relatively easy to do if one is possessed of complete moral certainty, but in an era when there is a painful awareness of the variety of human moral codes it is much more difficult, though not neccessarily impossible.

The dilemma which has just been outlined is central to any consideration of the right of the state to act in order to protect itself, or of the right of individual citizens or groups of citizens to protect themselves, and to seek redress for damage done by others.

For the purposes of our discussion of the former we need to make distinctions between, on the one hand, the state as a whole, that is to say the constitutional apparatus for the orderly governance of a geographically defined area, and the structures which support and ensure this, and, on the other hand, the government of the day, which utilizes the apparatus of the state, and is part of, but not identical with it. Where a particular administration is in power for a long time the difference can sometimes be hard to notice, for in practice government and apparatus of state can move very close to each other, and the particular political party which forms the administration can become almost synonymous with the exercise of power by both government and state. But it is important to remember that political parties which are not in government, but are represented in the legislature, are also part of the state, although their access to the levers of power is rather more limited.

State institutions extend beyond central government to include not only local administration but also the legal and judicial systems, the military and education. In some societies the church too can be part of the state, as is most obviously the case in a number of Islamic countries today. This does not mean that all states are monolithic, for in Western democracies, particularly where there is clear separation of powers, as in the USA, that is certainly not the situation. Indeed it is a fundamental characteristic of all liberal democracies that the judicial system operates independently, and is not under the control of the government apparatus. Whatever form the state takes, however, it has to be distinguished from civil society, which was discussed earlier; ultimately the state has coercive powers, including the use of force, but the institutions of civil society do not possess that capacity.[87]

Defending the state in war

What then are the circumstances in which a state is entitled to act in order to defend itself, not as an entity in its own right, but as the collective embodiment of a system of governance which has the endorsement of its citizens? The first and most obvious one would be if that state is facing destruction at the hands of a foreign aggressor: the UK entered the Second World War before it was attacked directly by Germany, but did so because it considered the German invasion of Poland in 1939 incompatible with the peace of Europe on which British security depended; America, however, commenced hostilities after the Japanese raid on Pearl Harbour in 1941. A state would also feel entitled to act where geographically separate territory which was linked to that state was invaded. This was why Britain felt obliged to use force in response to the Argentinian landings on the Falkland Islands in 1982. States have also been known to take military action when they consider that their vital interests are threatened. This was the justification for the American involvement in Vietnam, and for covert operations by agencies of the US government in South and Central America. It was also one of the reasons for the Allied attack in 1991 on Iraq, after the invasion of Kuwait in 1990. A state will assume, furthermore, that it is entitled to respond to subversion from within, particularly if it takes a violent form. On that basis the British army has sought to defeat the IRA and loyalist para-militaries in Northern Ireland, and the Spanish authorities the Basque separatist organization, ETA.

The reader will almost certainly by now be raising questions about the legitimacy of some of the examples cited, for clearly they are all rather different, and it could well be objected that they are being mis-described, or that a threat to the interests of a state is not the same thing at all as a threat to its very existence, and therefore cannot be used to justify a military or even semi-military response. But the examples have been chosen deliberately, for they have all involved conflict with the media, and therefore they raise acutely the question of the rights of states to restrict the freedom of these media, and the concomitant responsibilities of the media in such circumstances.

Let us return to the situation in which the state is most obviously facing destruction, total war. It would have been astonishing if during the years 1939–45, for example, the British media had been free to make their own decisions about what could and could not be published or broadcast.[88] In such a period it is inevitable that the state seeks to ensure that nothing is disseminated which might inadvertently provide the enemy with information, the possession of which would put its armed forces in danger. That seems uncontentious. What might be more controversial however is the extent to which the government of the time sought to raise morale and sustain it by a process of news management. Is such a course of action justified? Does the need to prosecute a war successfully override the citizens' right to know exactly how that war is progressing? How much information, even in a democracy, can the state allow into the public realm when the very existence of the state is in peril? But how, in such a situation, can the growth of a climate of obsessiveness be avoided, the kind of atmosphere in which the most trivial and inconsequential matters are classified as secret because they might remotely be of value to the enemy? Some observers would take the view that even pettifogging obsessiveness is part of the price which has to be paid in such extremes. However few could justify the behaviour during the First World War of

British print journalists, whose willingness to circulate fabricated German atrocity stories, and to collude in the creation of a fog of ignorance at home about the nature of the suffering at the front, is tellingly catalogued by Philip Knightley in his classic study of war reporting.[89]

When we move away from total war matters become more complicated. The Falklands War is often cited in such discussions, because it is the most recent example of a conflict – other than the Northern Ireland one – in which substantial numbers of British service personnel have lost their lives. Throughout its course the military authorities and the British government worked very hard not only to prevent the enemy gaining access to sensitive data but also to present what happened in the South Atlantic in the way most calculated to ensure continuing public support for the operation to retake the islands. It is clear that both military and government were obsessed with the belief that America was forced to pull out of Vietnam in 1973 because of the kind of reporting which had been common in the US media for several years previous to the withdrawal. If it had been possible, the argument runs, to prevent much of what appeared in the media from seeing the light of day, then that war could have been prosecuted to a successful conclusion. As Morrison and Tumber comment in their study of the interaction between military and journalists during the Falklands conflict:

> The general view among the military was that it was the nightly showing of television pictures from South East Asia which undermined popular support in America for the Vietnam War. That was the firm and unanimous opinion of . . . Task Force commanders . . . Ministers and civil servants were seriously concerned about the influence of any television pictures on morale.[90]

This perspective has not gone unchallenged, and it has been asserted on the contrary, that it was not the pictures and reports of the actual conflict which persuaded the American public that Vietnam was not worth fighting for, but the pictures and reports of dead Americans returning in body bags, and the prospect of ever more young men meeting the same fate. Morrison and Tumber argue, furthermore, that audiences respond to depictions of the sufferings of war in ways which reflect their basic attitude to the conflict: death is the price which has to be paid if a war is just, but if the war comes to be perceived to be unjust, then conversely the price is no longer regarded as acceptable.[91] If Morrison and Tumber are correct, unless it is going to be suggested that people whose relatives die in battle should not be told until the conflict is over, and the bodies should be hidden until then, then it is hard to see what could have been done to prevent the change in opinion which took place in America.

There is another point: Vietnam was not total war in the sense that the Second World War was, for, despite the so-called domino theory's assertion that if Vietnam fell to Communism, then the rest of Asia would go the same way, and thus America's vital interests would be seriously threatened, no possible analogy with the Second World War could be sustained. Military involvement in Vietnam was never overwhelmingly endorsed by the people, and as the conflict wore on interminably, then support drained away. This was a war waged on behalf of one country, South Vietnam, against its own insurgents and its neighbour, North Vietnam. No-one had declared hostilities against America. Therefore it is hardly surprising that there was fierce internal debate in the political sphere and throughout the country about the wisdom and morality of what was being done. In such a situation does the state have the right to suppress and censor, or is it obliged to continually argue its case in a way that is neither necessary nor desirable in total war?

However, as a number of commentators have observed, there is a real problem for any democratic country which orders its troops into battle in the electronic age: is it feasible for such a society to sustain a conflict, no matter how just the motives for embarking upon it, in the face of mounting casualities and television pictures of weeping relatives? Despite what Morrison and Tumber argue, might it be the case that the emotional impact of such pictures makes it impossible for democratically elected politicians to go on with a war if heavy losses are endured over a relatively short period of time? Might technological warfare be the only option open to these politicians? The Gulf conflict certainly was presented on television initially, as one in which, although missiles were landing on targets with apparently astounding precision and causing substantial damage, few Allied service personnel were being either injured or killed, although Iraqis certainly were.[92]

With the supposed Vietnam effect clearly in mind, the British military sought in 1982 to ensure, through its rationing of information, its treatment of correspondents in the field, and straightforward censorship that there was no repetition of what it perceived to be the South East Asian experience, and it can be argued that in this it was successful. But the Falklands conflict did not last very long once hostilities began. Significant casualties did occur and were reported, although for technical, and possibly other reasons, there were delays before film relating to these casualties appeared on television.[93] It is worth considering whether public support for the war in Britain would have continued at the high level which was present initially if there had been several more incidents like the destruction of the troop carriers, *Sir Galahad* and *Sir Tristram*, when fifty British soldiers were killed. In such a situation where did the responsibility of the media lie, given that the country was at war – even although no official declaration against Argentina was ever made? Should reporters in these circumstances seek to tell as much of the truth as they can, or as much as they are officially allowed to? Do they also have a duty to support the armed forces of their own country in time of conflict?

As was noted, the Gulf War was initially presented by the military as one in which technology was doing all of the fighting. Later the conflict changed when the Allies moved into Kuwait in order to eject the Iraqi army. Given the extraordinarily low level of casualties on the Allied side and the lack of 'bad news', there was little need for media management in order to minimize the impact of deaths and injuries. But the military and their governments were preparing for just such a contingency, and there was considerable tension between correspondents and army over the pooling system which was employed, and over access to the battle zones.[94] However the most important policy issue which was thrown up was about the way in which press and television appeared to accept and augment a version of the conflict which owed not a little to Hollywood – at one point, for example, BBC One's morning news bulletin began with slow-motion shots of military hardware. The relevant BBC executive stopped this style of presentation quickly, but it was symptomatic not of the sort of issue which had arisen regularly in previous conflicts, disputes between journalists and military over disclosure, but of a rather different one, namely the apparent willingness of some parts of the media to turn war – which, however just it might be, is fundamentally about killing and maiming people – into a kind of pain-free spectacle.

War, but not total war

Such a comment could not be made about the presentation of the long-running Northern Ireland conflict. The current – and possibly

final – phase of that has gone on since the late 1960s, and has provided many examples of state curtailment of the rights of the UK
media to report what is happening, including the withdrawal before
transmission of some television programmes, and ultimately the
banning from the airwaves of the actual voices of certain individuals
connected with organizations deemed to be involved in violence.[95]
Northern Ireland is not just another region of Britain, since the legitimacy of its very existence as part of the United Kingdom is questioned by a significant number of the population, and a small but
determined minority has been willing to use violent methods in
order to try to change the present constitutional arrangements, while
another determined minority has used equally violent methods to
counter the activities of the first group. Therefore journalism, and for
that matter other kinds of media output, in and about Northern
Ireland, have to take account of a clear tension between the citizens'
right to know what is being done in their name and the right of the
state to protect its agents, military and civilian, whose lives are at
risk as they seek to thwart the combatants on both sides.

News and current affairs broadcasting have had a much more
difficult time than for example, radio and television drama: several
plays have been transmitted over the years which have endeavoured to see the situation from a nationalist point of view and/or
to enable the listener or viewer to understand what motivates those
who resort to violence on both sides. Arguably a few such dra-
matizations are worth as much, if not more, than hours of the
most carefully constructed reportage. Drama in Britain has always
enjoyed high status because of the strength of the English theatrical tradition, and in a carry-over to the airwaves, the artist's right
to freedom of expression can on occasion supercede the broadcaster's obligation to ensure that nothing is said or shown which
might be considered by the authorities to be sympathetic to
terrorism.[96]

Pressure to prevent material appearing has often come from
within broadcasting organizations themselves. For example, the
governors of the BBC in 1985, on the eve of transmission, cancelled
a documentary entitled *Real Lives: at the Edge of the Union* in which
one representative of each side in the conflict outlined his view of
the situation. The governors then insisted that the film be prefaced
by a statement about the impact of terrorism, before it was broadcast at a later date. Pressure has come too from regulatory bodies:
the Independent Television Authority refused to allow a programme made by Granada Television in 1971 to be screened, as it

contained an interview with the then IRA Chief of Staff and was therefore deemed to be 'aiding and abetting the enemy'. However, in 1988 the ITA's successor, the Independent Broadcasting Authority (IBA), stood four square behind Thames Television's decision to broadcast *Death on the Rock*, an investigation which cast serious doubts on the official account of the deaths of three members of the IRA who were shot by SAS soldiers in Gibraltar. The government in effect asked the IBA to stop the programme, which it declined to do. Subsequently a campaign was waged against Thames Television by Conservative politicians, supported by the *Sun*, the *Sunday Times* and other newspapers. That ultimately led to an independent review of the journalistic procedures adopted in *Death on the Rock*, which found generally in favour of the programme, and to successful libel suits against the press by one of the people who had witnessed the shooting and had been interviewed on-screen.

The whole episode clearly demonstrated that the definition of what was in the interests of the British state was not univerally agreed by the agencies of that state, and that the state's power in a liberal democracy is not all-pervasive: the then Conservative government wished the programme not to be shown, the government-appointed regulator took the opposite position, and this was the view which prevailed. Both government and regulator no doubt agreed that what the IRA members were engaged in – planning to set off a bomb in Gibraltar – was completely unacceptable and had to be stopped; what they disagreed about were the limits of discussion about the actions of agents of the state in pursuit of that objective, particularly when evidence had been uncovered to suggest that the account given by government spokesmen was apparently at variance with some of the facts. The pivotal issue was whether in effect a 'shoot to kill' policy was in operation, and whether the IRA members were given a chance to surrender before being shot. The government version was that they were given that opportunity, but made as if to draw weapons, whereupon they were killed, although they turned out to be unarmed; the Thames Television account suggested that they were offered no real chance to surrender. What is at stake here is not public attitudes towards a 'shoot to kill' policy, whatever they might be, but the right of citizens to be informed about what is being done in their name.[97]

Because broadcasting is regulated by the British state, journalists who work in that medium have been more directly subject to pressure than their print colleagues over Northern Ireland coverage. However, although a number of newspaper reporters have attempted to raise questions which might not be so easily introduced on the airwaves, they too have been on the receiving end of sustained propaganda and PR offensives from the state and indeed from the parties to the conflict, all of whom have been seeking to have their view of events presented to the world.[98]

Hot and cold war

So far discussion has focused on unusual situations – war and incipient civil war/armed insurrection. But although these are not the norm, during the so-called Cold War, which finally came to an end with the Russian decision in the late 1980s to let Eastern Europe go its own way, extraordinary amounts of time and energy were employed by states in each of the two major power blocs in continuous clandestine activity. Spies, security apparatuses and secrecy became accepted as inevitable parts of the ways of life of even the most liberal of democracies. Time after time states sought to protect information on the grounds of threats to national security. Undoubtedly there were such threats; moreover, a climate in which there is a fundamental fear that the other side might one day seek to destroy our society, and perhaps half the world, is a climate in which it is difficult to argue that as much information as possible should be in the public realm, and all too easy to accept that the state must have the right to keep secret anything, the divulgence of which might be of assistance to the potential enemy.

There is no question that men and women in the security services of East and West lost their lives, often in very unpleasant fashions, during the forty-odd years of the Cold War. But sometimes there were episodes which, while they raised serious and troubling issues, also had their comical side. In 1987, for example, BBC Scotland developed a series of documentaries for UK network transmission, called *Secret Society*, in which the journalist Duncan Campbell explored the limits imposed on the flow of information in the UK; one of the half-hour programmes examined the case of Zircon, a satellite which had been launched by the British in order to spy on the Russians and their allies, and thus to end British dependence on American surveillance. In the course of the programme Campbell claimed that the relevant House of Commons committee, which was entitled to know in confidence about the project, had not been told, and that the information was nonetheless readily available in technical journals, although the enterprise was supposedly top secret.

One of Campbell's interviewees was the former chief scientific adviser to the Ministry of Defence, whom the journalist had clearly not told in advance the full scope of the questions which he wished to raise on camera. After a discussion of British dependence on US information, Campbell asked about Zircon. The interviewee's mouth literally dropped wide open. When he recovered his aplomb he insisted in a whisper that he could not talk about this matter. Subsequently no doubt there were many hurried telephone conversations. The BBC then abandoned transmission of this particular programme, on the grounds that the Corporation might be in danger of violating the Official Secrets Act. Shortly thereafter the Special Branch, that section of the police concerned with subversion, apppeared at BBC Scotland's premises and carried off boxes of files and video tapes. No charges were ever brought, the material was returned, and the Zircon film was subsequently transmitted within a longer programme which discussed the issues it raised. So far as is known, the security of the United Kingdom was not damaged. This was a farcical affair, but it did demonstrate acutely the conflict between the right of the state to keep secret and the right of the citizen to know, a tension which has always existed, but was central to Cold War life.[99]

Freedom of information

And yet it has to be said that despite the corrosive effect of the Cold War, in several countries progress was made towards greater openness. Even if we allow for the American emphasis on the individual's rights, it is remarkable that in 1966, four years after the Cuban missile crisis, which brought the world to the edge of nuclear disaster, a Freedom of Information Act was passed in the USA. That Act, which has been amended on a number of occasions subsequently, allows both Americans and foreign nationals to require federal government departments to produce timeously information they possess, unless there are overwhelming demonstrable reasons – the security of the state, invasion of personal privacy, for example – why that cannot be done. As a consequence of the operation of this statute – notwithstanding some official obstruction – material about the illegal US bombings of Cambodia in the 1970s, which precipitated the coming to power of the murderous Khmer Rouge regime in that country, about the Kennedy and Luther King assassinations, and estimates of Iraqi casualties in the Gulf War have come into the public realm, and appeared in the media. Most tellingly of all, from a British point of view, it was access to American intelligence files which enabled the British journalist Andrew Boyle to reveal in 1979 that the then Surveyor of the Queen's Pictures, Sir Anthony Blunt, was a former double agent and Russian spy, whom the British authorities had allowed to pursue his career after they had unmasked him in 1964![100]

Similar legislation was introduced in Canada in 1982, in Australia in the same year and New Zealand in the following year, while Sweden boasts that its statutory provision in this area dates back to 1766. Norway and Denmark caught up in 1970, and France in 1978. Freedom of information can be very useful for the individual citizen who might well wish to know what data, if any, has been stored about his or her activities, but it is also of crucial importance to the media, since the more they know about what government is doing, the more intelligently they can report, and the more informed the citizenry will be. The basic policy question is clear enough: what information should be available and what should remain confidential? There is some variation from country to country, but it is common for all such laws to exempt from disclosure matters relating to defence, national security, criminal intelligence and trade secrets. Usually freedom of information legislation has been accompanied by laws on data protection, which are designed to ensure that information held by agencies of the state about personal aspects of the lives of individual citizens is not generally available.[101] In several of the countries mentioned debate continues about whether there is enough, or too much, disclosure.

There may well have been moves towards greater openness in several countries. In the United Kingdom however the media and the citizen have confronted successive administrations which have been very reluctant to go down such a road, and, on the contrary, have ensured that scrutiny of the contemporary activities of government and government agencies is more difficult than it is in many other parts of the world. This has been achieved through a variety of laws, one of which has occupied a central position. The Official Secrets Act of 1911 had been planned by politicians for some time, but was passed amid a fortuitous panic about German spies a few years before the First World War. It allowed virtually anything the government decreed secret to be just that. In the seventies and eighties the Act came to appear more and more ridiculous and oppressive as a result of a number of court cases. In 1983, for example, Sarah Tisdall, a civil servant, leaked to the *Guardian* newspaper details of the Defence Ministry's plans for dealing with public reactions to the deployment of American Cruise missiles at Greenham Common. She was charged under the Act, found guilty and jailed for six months. Tisdall had argued that she was revealing wrongdoing, in that she believed that there was an intention on the part of the government to mislead parliament. In 1984 a civil servant at the Ministry of Defence, Clive Ponting, informed an MP that the answers which had been provided by the Defence Secretary about the events leading up the sinking of the Argentine naval vessel, the *General Belgrano*, during the Falklands War were misleading. The facts of the case were not in contention, but when it came to court in 1985 the jury, despite considerable pressure from the judge to convict, declared that Ponting was innocent.

Further embarrassment followed with the 'Spycatcher' affair. Peter Wright, a disgruntled former member of MI5, had retired to Australia and had sought several opportunities to air his view that the former head of the service had been a Russian spy. Wright wrote a book, *Spycatcher*, in 1985, and in it he repeated his allegations and made others about the supposed involvement of the British secret services during the 1970s in attempted subversion of the then Labour government. The reaction of the authorities was not to insist on a full discussion of these rather serious charges, but to try – unsuccessfully – to prevent publication of the book both in Britain and elsewhere. The affair degenerated into farce with the leading British civil servant, Sir Robert Armstrong, having an extremely difficult time in an Australian courtroom.[102]

In response to all of this, in 1989 a new Official Secrets Act was introduced, which is somewhat less wide-ranging in scope than its predecessor, but the crucial point is that no freedom of information legislation accompanied it. The position being taken by the British government, despite a few concessions to openness, was that the state still had the right to keep as much secret as it deemed fit, and, that has remained the situation. Indeed under the new Act where civil servants suspect wrongdoing they are required to use internal procedures, which contain an independent element, if they wish to rectify the situation; it is not open to them to turn to the media, for no 'public interest' defence is available, should they be charged, nor to journalists who handle the relevant information. Furthermore, post-Spycatcher, civil servants now have a lifelong duty of confidentiality in regard to a number of categories of supposedly sensitive data.[103]

As is so often the case, we see a sharp contrast between the approaches being taken on either side of the Atlantic, and indeed between Britain and other parts of Europe. However, the Labour government elected in 1997 has committed itself to introducing freedom of information legislation, and if that does happen, then the focus will be not only on this fundamental change in itself, but also on the detail – what rules of access will be stipulated, what period of time will elapse between request and disclosure, on what grounds can a request be refused, and which categories of information will be included and excluded from the provisions of the Act? Several features of the proposed legislation are encouraging: for example, disclosure can only be denied if there is a risk of 'substantial harm', rather than 'harm', there is to be an independent procedure to deal with refusals by public bodies to make data available, and enforcement as a possible remedy will be open to the new Information Commissioner.[104] However the work of the security services is not to be covered – even retrospectively – and there will be no right of appeal to the courts beyond the Commissioner. It would appear that the contrast with the American approach may continue.

There also remains one intriguing and worrisome question: how much effort will newspapers and broadcasting organizations make to utilize the new legislation, in order to increase general knowledge of the processes of government and policy making? Although freedom of information theoretically makes it possible to encourage a much better understanding of these matters, for the media there will be a significant cost in journalistic time and effort. How widespread will the necessary committment of resources be? Given the close connections which exist between newspapers and business in general, and the continuing expansion of cross-media links, will organizations, which are not always comfortable when their own activities are being scrutinized, actually be keen to support and exploit the new climate of disclosure in the interests of the citizens of Britain? Will the tabloids, which have excelled in exposing the sexual exploits of public figures, now turn their attention to the much more important political activities of these individuals?

Summary

The balance between rights and obligations is always difficult to strike, and where the state decides to curtail the rights of the individual to free speech and information, then there have to be unusual circumstances. The most obvious situation where such curtailment takes place is one of total war. Then, for reasons of military security and public morale, states feel entitled to restrict substantially the flow of information. Other situations, such as internal civil insurrection or disorder, and ideological hostility between different power blocs, are much less straightforward and have given rise to many contested cases. There has been a general movement towards freedom of information in Western democracies, but total access to all information is not on the agenda of any government.

Questions for discussion

1. In what circumstances should individual liberty be restricted in the interests of the wider community?
2. What legitimate arguments can be produced for censorship during war and warlike situations ?
3. What limits should be imposed on freedom of information?

Protecting the Citizen, Protecting Society | 7

The previous chapter was concerned to explore the question of the rights which the state has in certain specific circumstances to restrict the freedom of the individual in general, and the freedom of the media in particular. In this chapter the focus will be on the protection by the state of the citizen and of society as a whole against the media, and also on the protection of the media as they exercise their legitimate functions. The argument of the last chapter was that rights in practice have to be balanced one against the other. This will never be a simple matter. Even if we are prepared to assert, as for example the American legal theorist, Ronald Dworkin, does, that there is a 'natural right of all men and women to equality of concern and respect',[105] of which legal and political systems are therefore obliged to take account, hard cases will still need to be adjudicated. Although Dworkin himself argues that such adjudications are possible, and correct answers can be found, it is always going to be a fraught process, as the dilemmas which are about to be discussed will illustrate.

The American Bill of Rights, which contains the various amendments to the Constitution, states that 'Congress shall make no law ... abridging the freedom of speech, or of the press', and other more recent conventions contain similar provisions. The Universal Declaration of Human Rights of 1948 and the European Convention on Human Rights both assert that individuals are entitled to hold what opinions they wish, and to communicate them to others, but both also quickly add that there may be good reasons – 'respect of the rights or reputation of others or for the protection of national security or of public order or of public health or morals' – why these rights may have to be restricted in some circumstances.[106] In adjudicating between competing claims now, instead of the interests of the state being weighed in the balance against the interests of citizens, the rights of individuals will need to be considered vis-à-vis those of other individuals, organizations such as the media, and also perhaps the state. This may well mean that the state is required to protect citizens against itself, which is no easy task. And that is why a properly democratic society has to ensure that the institutions of the state are not simply branches of one overarching monolith, but component parts which have discrete, and on occasion, conflicting functions. As was noted in the previous chapter, this separation of powers is to be seen most vividly in the USA: not only is the Presidency distinct from the Congress, but the courts also, including the Supreme Court, have a role in upholding the constitution and in enforcing the rights of the citizen against the other agencies of the state, if that becomes necessary, as it did, for example, during the civil rights struggles of the 1950s and 1960s, when decisions of the Supreme Court rendered discriminatory social and educational practices illegal.[107]

Individual rights and the law

All citizens are entitled to redress for defamatory attacks, to a fair trial and to privacy. Such a statement might seem axiomatic, but in practice these entitlements are far from straightforward, nor are they universally accessible.

Defamation occurs when false statements are made about individuals, which damage them in the eyes of their fellow citizens: oral defamation is known as slander, written, libel. Different legal systems have slightly varying definitions but this is the gist of what is involved.[108] And few would wish to argue that erroneous statements about individuals should be circulated without some kind of penalty being imposed on the perpetrators. In Britain the remedy lies in suing those responsible and hoping for substantial damages if the case is won. The difficulty is that legal aid is not available, and the lawyers' fees accumulated during an unsuccessful defamation suit can be ruinous. Arguably that prevents frivolous actions, although it must also discourage people who feel they have a good case, but are unhappy about risking financial nemesis. For the media, libel is a central and ongoing concern, since newspapers and broadcasting organizations, if they are doing their jobs properly, must frequently put into the public realm material which is damaging to the individuals involved. It cannot easily be argued that if such material is a pack of lies there should be no punishment. However if the penalty for libel is very high, there must be a serious risk that the media will hesitate to publish, not simply because there might be a lingering doubt over the veracity of the allegations being made, but because, in the event of a libel suit which is successfully resisted, there might still be substantial legal bills. The situation just described is the one which has pertained in England for a very long time – not in Britain as a whole, it must be stressed, for in Scotland the procedures are different, and the rewards for the successful litigant in practice much lower than is the case south of the border.[109]

Indeed London has become known as the libel capital of the world because of the large damages awards, sometimes of half-a-million pounds or more which have been made against newspapers and on occasion broadcasting organizations.[110] Even although in the mid nineties it became possible for the English Appeal Court to reduce awards, there is still a remarkable contrast in the approaches taken in Britain and in the United States. In 1964 the American Supreme Court ruled that for a libel case against the press instituted by a public official to be successful then the official had to demonstrate 'actual malice', which was defined as 'with knowledge that . . . [the statement] . . . was false or with reckless disregard of whether it was false or not'.[111] While discussion continues as to who exactly can be regarded as a public official, what this decision means in practice is that if a newspaper or broadcasting organization makes allegations of improper conduct against a politician, which turn out to be false, but can argue convincingly that it genuinely believed the accusations to be true, and had not acted recklessly, then it will not find itself paying substantial damages. In the UK that option has not been available (however, an appeal court judgment in mid-1998 has suggested that a limited form of it might become available in the future).

The consequences of this contrast are clear enough. It is often pointed out that 'Watergate' could never have happened in Britain. This does not mean that a scandal similar to the one which enveloped President Nixon in the early 1970s could never occur in the United Kingdom. But the way it was exposed by two *Washington Post* journalists, Bob Woodward and Carl Bernstein, who made allegations about the behaviour of the President and his entourage, which in the initial stages could not have been justified in court, would have been impossible to replicate in Britain: the immediate response of the relevant public officials would have been to send for their lawyers and to sue, with every expectation of success.[112] Any British editor presented with Watergate-type allegations would be bound to hesitate before printing them, and indeed to require far more proof than Woodward and Bernstein were able to offer their editor in the early stages of their investigation. Watergate, and the resulting resignation of the President of the United States, are rightly cited as examples of how the American legal system prevents the rich and powerful from hiding their wrong doing through abuse of the law. It can also be argued however that one of the unfortunate consequences of Watergate has been the spawning of scandal-oriented journalism which in itself abuses the 1964 Supreme Court judgement. The result can be that all kinds of allegations about public figures are made with inadequate – if not reckless – attention to their veracity, and as a consequence the whole political process is brought into disrepute.[113]

In the UK, and in other countries, there is legislation which prohibits the dissemination of material designed to stir up racial hatred. In practice the British law has hardly been used against the media, and when it has, it is fringe publications produced by fanatics which have been prosecuted. What the existence of such legislation does, however, is to send a clear signal that freedom of speech does not encompass racial abuse. Again there is a marked contrast with America, where only if it can be shown, for example, that a racially offensive broadcast is likely to produce violence, will the Federal Communications Commission (FCC) take action. In recent years American talk radio 'shock jocks' have hurled abuse at minorities, women, the federal government and the President of the United States with impunity, under the protective umbrella of the First Amendment. When a show featuring one of these individuals was retransmitted by two Canadian stations in 1997, the broadcasters concerned immediately found themselves in difficulties with the regulatory authority, since in that country anyone seeking to stir up hatred against identifiable groups of individuals can be in breach of the law and/or broadcasting rules, which is not the case south of the forty-ninth parallel, where 'hate speech' appears to enjoy constitutional protection.

If citizens are entitled to redress for defamation and protection against racially motivated abuse, then they are also entitled to a fair trial, and it would therefore seem to follow that from the moment of arrest until the judicial process is completed there should be no publicity which might interfere with that objective. The approaches taken on either side of the Atlantic differ considerably.

In Britain prejudicial reporting before or during a trial consititutes contempt of court, for which the penalties include both fines and imprisonment. The law has been rather slackly interpreted on occasions in England in recent times – for example, after the arrest of the serial murderers, Frederick and Rosemary West, in 1994 the English tabloids ran stories which were openly prejudicial – although it still supposedly holds good. In Scotland however the judiciary take a very dim view indeed of any possible contempt: for example, during the trial in Glasgow of an alleged murderer in 1992, BBC Scotland, in an afternoon news bulletin, inadvertently showed a picture of the accused man being led into court. Since identification was an issue in the trial, this constituted contempt, and the relevant senior broadcasting executive was brought before the court with the very real prospect that he might be jailed, although he escaped that fate. In America, on the other hand, after O.J. Simpson was charged with murdering his wife in 1994, there was a barrage of reporting, some of it of the evidence which the prosecution was intending to present during the trial, which meant that the task of finding a jury which had not been affected by this exposure was extremely difficult. The American media would argue that their right to comment and report should not be curtailed in such a situation, and in so doing they draw on a 1941 Supreme Court ruling that only if there is 'a clear and present danger' to the administration of justice should that right be restricted; others might say that the media's freedom in this instance results in the undermining of the citizen's right to a fair trial. In cases involving prominent individuals, such as Simpson or Senator Edward Kennedy's nephew, who was charged and acquitted of rape in 1991, such reporting, as it continues through the actual trial, can turn the judicial process into a melodramatic spectacle, which is then offered as diversion to readers and viewers.[114]

Canadian journalists, who operate under contempt of court laws rather like the British ones, find themselves in the paradoxical position of reporting prominent American cases, such as the O.J. Simpson one, in ways which would constitute contempt in Canada, but having to exercise far more care in chronicling similar cases in their own country. The contrast between the two legal systems was emphasized in 1993 when, during the Karla Homolka trial, a very unpleasant case arising from the murder of two teenage girls, the judge in the St Catharine's, Ontario courtroom imposed a total ban on the reporting of the proceedings, lest such reporting prejudice the forthcoming trial of Homolka's husband, Paul Bernardo. Journalists based some ten miles from the court on the other side of the border were free to ignore the Canadian law in general and the specific ban imposed by the judge. The difference in approach of the two adjacent countries was highlighted when Canadian border officials confiscated copies of American publications which had printed accounts of the trial. But the authorities could do very little about other sources of information available to Canadian citizens, such as American satellite broadcasts or the Internet.[115]

One disadvantage of the generally strict approach to contempt of court in Britain takes us back to libel. The publisher and media mogul, Robert Maxwell, drowned in 1991, and it was soon apparent after his death that the man had been a swindler on a massive scale, who had not only broken company law on numerous occasions but had also plundered his employees' pension fund. Maxwell frequently resorted to the courts alleging libel, and won some cases, so it became very clear that his immediate response to accusations of impropriety would be to sue. If a damaging report was printed and Maxwell had then instigated proceedings, any further report which was published before the libel action was completed, would have constituted contempt. Maxwell's trick, on a number of occasions when he utilized this approach, was to delay bringing the full libel case to court, and thus to prevent further discussion of what it is now abundantly clear was thoroughly criminal behaviour which there was a very strong public interest in exposing.[116] A similar tack was taken by the Distillers Company in the 1970s to prevent the *Sunday Times* pursuing its allegations that the company had marketed the drug Distaval – which was responsible for the thalidomide deformities – without adequate pretesting, and had then ignored evidence which emerged about its possible effects. Distillers argued that, since it was negotiating compensation claims, any dissemination of additional material by the newspaper would constitute an interference with the judicial process and therefore contempt. Eventually the *Sunday Times* took its case to the European Court of Human Rights and won the right to publish, but that took several years, during which no proper discussion of the company's behaviour could take place in Britain.[117]

It appears then that laws designed to protect individuals against erroneous accusations and to ensure the fairness of the judicial process can be abused by the rich, the powerful and the criminal, and that the media can thus be prevented from carrying out their responsibilities. However, the freedom of the media to publish can lead to harassment of public officials and serious interference with the judicial process. It is arguable that neither the USA nor the UK has found the correct balance in these matters.

Privacy

In Britain during the nineties there was much discussion as to whether legislation needed to be introduced in order to protect individuals from unwarranted intrusion into their private lives by the media. Such legislation would be related to the kind of data protection law referred to in the last chapter, but it would in practice be more concerned to safeguard aspects of people's personal behaviour, for example, their sexual and family relationships, rather than say medical or financial information, although there would inevitably be some overlap. Privacy legislation does exist in some countries. For example, in France an individual's personal life is considered sacrosanct and criminal penalties can be imposed on media employees who take or publish unauthorised photographs and information; it is also open to the courts to act to prevent an infringement which is pending. That President Mitterrand had a daughter by a mistress only became general public knowledge in the last year of his life. In Britain – or in America – it is very doubtful if such information would have stayed long in the private realm, for the most intimate details of the personal lives of the famous are published regularly in the tabloid press. In the nineties it has been possible, for example, to read a transcript of a conversation which supposedly took place between the Prince of Wales and his alleged mistress, and the claims from one of the Prince's servants about where and how the heir to the throne and the lady made love. Pictures of a makeshift bed on which a cabinet minister and his mistress had intercourse, together with transcripts of the conversations which allegedly took place between them, have also been printed. Nor do relatively unknown citizens escape: for example, in 1995 one newspaper published an account of sex parties at a caravan park in south-west Scotland complete with photographic illustrations.

All of these stories appeared, the papers concerned averred, in order to meet a clear public interest: after all, the royals are financed by the taxpayers, who are entitled to know what they are up to, and whether their conduct is becoming, cabinet ministers who exhaust themselves in extramarital liaisons are clearly not able to do the job which the electorate pays them to do, and the swingers of Girvan were engaging in unprotected sex, which, in the era of Aids, constitutes a horrifying threat to public health. Despite such protestations of solicitude *pro bono publico*, cases of this sort have given rise to considerable unease, and in the mid nineties the British government toyed with the idea of introducing legislation on privacy. This would have offered a civil remedy, and individuals who felt they had a case would have been able to sue – though they would have been obliged to pay their own legal expenses in the first instance, for no legal aid was to be offered. The government was reluctant to act for a variety of reasons, not least the fact that the British newspaper industry had in 1991 reconstituted the generally discredited Press Council as the Press Complaints Commission (PCC). That body produced a code of practice, which included provisions on privacy, and sought to enforce its application by issuing adjudications against offending publications, which are obliged to print them. The work of the PCC will be examined in detail in a later chapter, but the point of significance here is that in Britain the choice was made not to legislate: if the citizen has a right to privacy then that right was to be enforced by self-restraint and self-policing by the press and the broadcasters. However the decision taken by the newly elected Labour government in 1997 to incorporate the European Convention on Human Rights into the UK's legal framework might mean that *de facto* case law develops, as individuals seek enforcement of the general right to privacy contained in that document in the courts. Such an outcome could well force parliament to legislate directly on the matter.

Similar points can be made about the so-called right of reply, that is the opportunity to correct inaccurate statements in the media about individuals or organizations. This right has statutory backing in some countries, for example France and Germany, but in Britain and North America voluntary systems apply, and where there are bodies concerned to deal with complaints from aggrieved citizens, much of their time is taken up adjudicating on whether opportunities have or have not been afforded to correct factual misrepresentations; no legal remedy is available.

One legal right which is likely to be of direct relevance to only a limited number of citizens, is that of copyright, the entitlement to payment for the publication and reproduction of a creative work, such as a play, song or game show format. A distinction is usually made between financial rights and moral rights, the latter encompassing the claim of the creator to control how what (s)he has produced is used. Not all countries have been keen to recognize both rights, and the United States, which is now determined to enforce intellectual copyright on behalf of its citizens across the globe, was once notorious for ignoring the responsibility to pay authors for their work, if they lived outside of America.[118] The purpose of copyright is to ensure that creators are rewarded for their endeavours: arguments tend to focus on how long a work should stay in copyright after the death of its progenitor – should both children and grandchildren be entitled to benefit? – and enforcement issues. When it comes to moral rights, the issues have more to do with artistic integrity and honest representation than financial returns.[119]

Although only a few of us are likely to benefit directly from copyright, we are all affected by it, for part of the price of any work in copyright is the royalty due to the author(s). If copyright in effect extends two generations beyond the death of the original holder, that arguably is a tax on the dissemination of knowledge and information, which is difficult to justify. Even if copyright were to be restricted in timespan, countries in the developing world would still have problems, for example in acquiring educational texts which they may desperately need, but can ill afford, even under the modified royalty regimes which have been introduced. In the media area there have been arguments about where exactly in collaborative works copyright should rest and how to strike a balance among the respective claims of the different participants involved in producing a film or a television programme.

The media effects quandary

In the earlier part of the twentieth century much research focused on possible behavioural changes which the media might generate. There was concern that anti-social activity might be learned from the cinema screen or comics, that crime might increase as a consequence of exposure to representations of criminality, that sexual licence might be encouraged through erotically charged imagery. There is still much anxiety about those issues, indeed such anxiety is absolutely central to public discourse about the roles of the media in society, with government officials and groups of citizens frequently arguing that restrictions need to be imposed, particularly on the depiction of violence and sexuality. Researchers, however, are much less certain than their predecessors were about what exactly the media do to behaviour, and on occasion can give the impression that, despite millions of hours and a great deal of money devoted to the task of discovery, they really have little to say which connects with public concerns.[120]

There is not space here to offer an extensive resumé of the debate about media effects but it is impossible to have an intelligent discussion about protection policies in the absence of some engagement with it. The fundamental problem which needs to be addressed is how exactly these supposed effects can be measured. It is one thing to count, for example, the number of viewers attained by a particular television programme, through the use of electronic meters distributed on the basis of well-established sampling techniques, but quite another to assess more intangible aspects of the impact of the media. All of us are subject to a variety of influences as children and adults, from our immediate family, our communities, school, society as a whole and no doubt the media. Nobody would claim that any of these has no impact whatsoever on our attitudes and/or behaviour, but how do we decide how each influence impacts on us at any one time and what its relationship is to the other influences which affect us; the difficulty comes with quantification and measurement.

For example, supposing we wished to ascertain what effect formal education had on young people, one way to find out might be to select at an early age two groups of youngsters roughly similar in terms of intelligence and social background, and to rigorously control their lives for the next five years so that one cohort went through the normal education processes and the other received no formal education whatsoever, and then to consider how they differed at the end of the experiment. Just to suggest such a project is to invite derision, for no civilized society would permit it, although perhaps there might be researchers who would be willing to organize it. A similar point can be made about the impact of television on young people. It might be feasible to devise a scheme whereby one group of children was brought up in exactly the same way as another group, with the single distinction that the first group was never allowed to see a television set, far less any programmes. Another possible experiment might involve controlling the diet of television so that one cohort of, let us say five- to ten-year-olds, was exposed to television programmes high in violence, and the other shown programmes completely free of it. At the end of a given period aggression scores would be measured and compared with those found at the outset. No such research would ever be allowed, but even if some foolish government did authorize it, implementation would involve horrendous practical problems. In the real world we have to rely on laboratory experiments and fieldwork studies, many of which are carried out with the utmost rigour, but which by their very nature can offer only tentative conclusions, and these can be undermined immediately by raising the fairly obvious objections about the artificiality of laboratory settings and the difficulties of isolating one of the many factors which influence behaviour, not to mention the effect on participants of the researchers and interviewers themselves.

Since effects research is inevitably inconclusive, it might be tempting to say that almost nothing of significance can be deduced about the impact of the media on attitudes and behaviour. And some observers have suggested that this is the only rational basis for public policy.

A more common academic response is to argue that we should be less concerned with supposedly measurable effects and more interested in the various ways in which different individuals and groups of individuals 'read' or interpret media messages. There are however very serious difficulties for policy makers if they take this apparently reasonable approach. Even if effects research does not offer definite conclusions, and may never be able to do so, it does not follow that because something cannot be isolated and observed it does not exist. Secondly, there is what might be called the 'common sense perspective'. Many people, who have never opened a book on media effects in their lives, and are unlikely to do so, genuinely believe that, for example, newspapers can have some impact on people's voting behaviour – a perspective which appears to be shared not only by the papers themselves but also by many cabinet ministers – and that exposure to violent videos and films can encourage real violence, particularly if the implication on-screen appears to be that violence is inherently attractive and helps one get what one wants in life.

It is easy for academics to dismiss such perceptions as unscientific. But in a democracy it is not so easy for policy makers in general, and practising politicians in particular. Many of them undoubtedly share with their follow citizens a series of related, and even contradictory, hunches about these matters. They know, for example, that advertisers spend millions in the belief that it is possible to persuade people to buy particular commodities; while they realize that the effectiveness of advertising derives from our propensity to consume, they are not entirely sure as to what the success of advertising means when it comes to a consideration of more general media effects. They may indeed believe that, on the one hand, the depiction of violence in fictional material could precipitate some of those viewing towards violent acts in life, that it might encourage a very small number of disturbed individuals to do something they might not otherwise have contemplated; it might, on the other hand, have a cathartic effect and thus reduce actual violence, it might have no behavioural effect whatsoever. Again, such depictions might affect our attitudes to real violence by making us believe there is more 'out there' than there actually is, they might in some insidious fashion corrupt us by offering as entertainment spectacles which should horrify and revolt us. They might so disgust us that we come to loathe violence in real life. Perhaps it is the case that repetitive viewing of the sadistic and the brutal – factual and fictional – in some subtle way corrodes our sensibilities, with the result that we lose the capacity to believe in the possibility of creating a civilized and ordered world in which cruelty and horror are, if not eliminated, at least minimized.

The trouble is that politicians, policy makers, – and all of us for that matter – will never be sure about the impact of violent imagery either on behaviour or on attitudes. If that is the case, might there not then be an argument for the exercise of discretion and care? But, it may well be countered, it is important that people are not cocooned from the true nature of the world in which they live, and from a knowledge of the kind of behaviour in which human beings engage. That is a much easier argument to put when factual material, rather than fictional, is being considered, but with fiction the argument may well still be valid. Removing violence from Shakespeare's plays or from religious paintings, for example, would render many of them incomprehensible. Even when we are dealing with extreme violence, actual and invented, the argument for inclusion can be overwhelming. Documentaries about the Nazi concentration camps, and films such as Spielberg's *Schindler's List* (1993), which is a work of fiction based on the life of particular individuals, and other films such as the Polish *Passenger* (1961), which does not use the lives of actual people as the basis for its horrifying narrative, all, it can be argued, have artistic and indeed educational value.

Discussion of what should and should not be shown must inevitably grapple with these issues, and must engage too with the generally perceived need to protect children from experiences which they have difficulty in handling before they reach adulthood.

Sex and violence are often linked in debates about what should be presented in the media, and although there is a crucial distinction to be made between violence, which involves the harming or the destruction of another human being, and sexual activity between – or even among – consenting adults, which is pleasurable and non-destructive, there is an area of overlap which has become a matter of great concern to some observers.[121] Erotic material is designed to stimulate sexual desire, and many people seem perfectly happy that this should be so, although in the Western world the sheer volume of suggestive imagery, aimed at men and women, has reached remarkable levels in the last twenty years.

Pornography is a more difficult area. The distinction between the erotic and the pornographic is not always easy to make, and the multimillion pound sexual publications industry offers examples of both, often side by side. Nonetheless it might be argued that pornography tends to focus on the mechanics of sexual acts in such a way as to exclude any kind of consensual relationship between the participants: much pornography aimed at men is dominated by representations of women displaying their genitals in ways that might seem more appropriate in an anatomy class than in any sexual encounter, and the message appears to be one of eager availability. Some material depicts women being abused, humiliated or even tortured. If we put aside the issue of whether such photographed acts actually took place, rather than being simulated – if the former were the case, it could well be a matter for the criminal law – and assume that the depictions are fictitious, might it be the case that such imagery encourages an aggressive attitude towards women? Might it even encourage acts of indecent assault and rape? We are back with the difficulties, perhaps impossibilities, of measuring specific effects. And even supposing we were absolutely convinced that exposure to such material had no impact whatsoever on actual male behaviour, could we be comfortable with the circulation of representations which suggest that women are easily available, or eager to be violated or humiliated? This is in many ways a much more intractable issue than that of non-sexual violence, for if by some chance we had a more draconian system of censorship of violent imagery than currently obtains in the Western media, it is hard to believe that human happiness would be greatly diminished. However if serious restrictions on allegedly dangerous pornographic imagery were instituted, it is highly likely that erotic material would be caught up by such measures, and there would be a significant diminution of harmless pleasure.

Policy makers who engage with these questions also have to take account of the rather nebulous concept of public taste. People may well have no wish to watch the depiction of sexual acts in their living rooms, or perhaps even in the cinema, not because the representations are pornographic or because they feel that as viewers they are being harmed, but because they believe sex is a private activity and should be presented with restraint and discretion, particularly on a public medium open to all ages and kinds of viewers, often in mixed family situations. Many parents still find explicit sexuality on television embarrassing if their children are in the room, and so too do many children.

As many viewers are unhappy about explicit sexual depictions, so many resent the use of swearing and profanity on the airwaves, indeed the major British broadcasters frequently assert that they receive far more complaints in this area than about sex or violence. People of religious convictions do not like having their sensibilities frequently assaulted by what they consider to be casual blasphemy, and many of no religious convictions whatsoever are also uneasy about the use of obscenities.

Codes of practice

The responses of policy makers to the general discussion about media effects have been varied, and they shift with perceived alterations in public mood, and pressure from lobby groups and politicians. In an attempt to deal with the difficulties they confront, bodies, such as film censorship boards or broadcasters, draw up codes of practice in order to set out the parameters within which sensitive matters are to be handled. For example, the BBC's guidelines on the depiction of violence in drama state that:

> Programme makers should ask whether the violent incident and the detail shown are essential to the story or whether it has been included simply for its own sake. The use of violence should never be gratuitous.[122]

The Broadcasting Standards Council, which was absorbed into the Broadcasting Standards Commission in 1997, has a similar clause in its code of practice, to which all British broadcasters are expected to adhere:

Violence is a legitimate ingredient of drama. It should, however, seldom be an end in itself for the purposes of entertainment, although, in the right hands, it can sometimes be so and not simply a sequence of gratuitous images.[123]

The Canadian Broadcast Standards Council, which represents the private sector in that country, returns to the same theme when it declares that 'programming containing gratuitous violence (should) not be telecast'.[124]

When it comes to sex, we find comparable provisos:

For each of us sexual activity happens after moral decisions have been made; its portrayal, therefore, should not be separated from recognition of the moral process. Drama has a part to play in illuminating the darker side of human nature. Sometimes themes and images are explored which may shock. However, we must draw the line well short of anything that might be labelled obscene or pornographic. The test to apply is one of intention and judgement: are we illuminating or demeaning?[125]

Thus the BBC Producers' Guidelines, and related sentiments are to be found in the Broadcasting Standards Council's Code:

producers should consider whether the degree of explicitness they plan is justified by the context in which it occurs. Nor should youth and physical attractiveness be used to justify a degree of explicitness which may reduce the audience to the level of voyeurs, and the participants themselves to objects.[126]

In America in the late 1980s the Federal Communications Commission introduced a ban on indecency on the airwaves between the hours of 6 am and midnight, which meant that indecency, though not obscenity, could be transmitted in a six hour 'safe harbor'.[127] In 1996 Congress passed a Telecommunications Act, which made provision for the so-called V chip – V for violence – which enables parents to shut out programming they do not wish their childen to see; the American legislators felt able to be extremely confident about the impact of violent imagery:

Studies have shown that children exposed to violent video programming at a young age have a higher tendency for violent and aggressive behavior later in life than children not so exposed, and that children exposed to violent video programming are prone to assume that acts of violence are acceptable behavior.[128]

They were also confident about the impact of the depiction of sexual activity:

> Studies indicate that children are affected by the pervasiveness and casual treatment of sexual material on television, eroding the ability of parents to develop responsible attitudes and behavior in their children.[129]

While there might be serious doubts about the unambivalent certainty of the American legislators, as far as the various codes of practice quoted from above are concerned, they are all liberal, well intentioned and commonsensical. If they were not, and a huge gap were to open up between, on the one hand, general public opinion as it manifests itself through such surveys as are conducted, the expressed views of politicians, and pressure group activity – three rather different things – and, on the other, the codes themselves, then the legitimacy of the organizations responsible for them would be seriously undermined.

Terrestrial broadcasting is not cinema, or video, nor is it quite the same thing as satellite broadcasting, and the evidence we have suggests that although there has been a marked increase in the last twenty years in explicit sexual representations on British terrestrial television and in swearing and blasphemy, there has been no corresponding increase in the depiction of violence. In the United States mainstream television has tended to be less sexually explicit and more violent than in the UK, which is why the clamour for the introduction of the V chip has been much louder there than in Britain, or for that matter Europe. On both sides of the Atlantic however there has been concern about the increasingly graphic presentation of violence in entertainment movies and videos, and to a lesser extent about explicit sexuality.

In cinema and video there are pre-release control mechanisms available. Censorship/classification boards, which exist throughout the world on either a voluntary or mandatory basis, often have the power to ban a film. Likewise, cuts can be imposed if particular scenes are considered unacceptable. Finally, films and videos are usually categorized according to the minimum age at which patrons can be admitted to cinemas showing the film in question, or are entitled to purchase or hire the video concerned. There may even be guidance to parents attached to particular classifications. What this kind of approach should mean is that heavily explicit sexual material, for example, would not be seen by minors. While that might be true of cinema exhibition, it is hard to believe that any system could ever be watertight in video rental and retail stores. Even if it were, what is to prevent an adult, if so minded, obtaining such material for minors? Or – a more likely scenario – what is to prevent children covertly viewing material which their parents have obtained for their own use? We are now in a situation where technological change has not made classification itself any more difficult, but the actual enforcement has become problematic. As a consequence, the grading of video tapes tends to be tougher than that of films.

Are there final boundaries?

Where in all of this protective activity are the rights of the citizen to express himself and to 'seek, receive and impart information and ideas of all kinds, regardless of frontiers, either orally in writing or in print, in the form of art, or through any other media of his choice'? But that right, as was noted at the beginning of this chapter, is circumscribed in the succeeding clause of the Declaration from which it comes, where it is accepted that there may be good grounds for such restriction – public order, public health or morals – and film censors in the past have been far from reluctant to act zealously in pursuit of these objectives. Indeed the history of censorship can very easily be presented as an attempt by those in power to prevent the circulation of ideas which are considered dangerous, and to impose ludicrously puritan values on the populace.[130] But the ridiculousness of past decisions need not lead us inevitably to conclude that the entire activity is wrong. What we require to be clear about is what is acceptable in the kinds of societies in which we live, and what is not. There is unlikely to be much disagreement about restrictions on the material which children can see, but real difficulty arises over what adults should be exposed to. Should we assume, for example, that all adults should be allowed to make up their own minds what they think of any film which any producer wishes to put before the public? It has to be said that in practice many film makers prefer a centralized pre-exhibition classification system, whose decisions are generally acceptable, rather than the hazard of not knowing when a criminal or civil action might be raised against them. But that is not an argument of principle so much as of convenience. To return to principle, are there any justifiable limits on the kinds of representation which adults should be free to view? Paedophilia is illegal, and depiction of it for prurient purposes must surely lead to criminal sanctions, but if, for example, there is a market for images of the sexual humiliation of adults, which there clearly appears to be, should it be catered for? If it is to be, in what conditions, and what view should we take of the fact that such depictions may involve the degradation of the participants?

In practice at the moment the final limits are drawn legally, and they vary from society to society. Britain, for example, continues to have fairly strict laws on material which is considered liable to 'deprave and corrupt' those who see it, while many European countries – Holland and Sweden, for example – are tolerant of imagery which would lead to seizure and criminal prosecution in the United Kingdom. Indeed, even although the average American book store sells magazines which depict sexual acts far more graphically than corresponding publications available in similar shops in Britain, European explicitness is generally considered to be greater than what is found in the USA.[131] Fierce controversies on the issue have ensued in America, where as a result of a Supreme Court ruling in 1973, obscenity depends on three criteria being met: that the work is deemed by the average person applying contemporary community standards, to be appealing to prurience, that sexual conduct is presented in a patently offensive fashion and that taken as a whole the work has no artistic or intellectual merit.[132] In 1983 two campaigners, Andrea Dworkin and Catherine MacKinnon, unhappy with the results of this ruling, succeeded in having a more restrictive anti-pornography ordinance passed by the Minneapolis City Council, only to have it vetoed by the mayor as unworkable.[133]

One of the most interesting attempts to balance the rights of viewer, participant and wider community has been made in Canada, where since the mid eighties, as a result of a particular court case, obscenity has been interpreted to mean what citizens in general, beyond participants and patrons, would tolerate, not simply for themselves but being available to those who might wish to peruse it (a rather different emphasis from the first of the three American criteria); that tolerance is assumed not to extend to violent pornography nor to non-violent dehumanizing material.[134]

However, the degree of explicitness is not a major issue in itself, although the context clearly is. What is striking about this approach, despite its apparent liberalism, is that it does seem to be predicated on the assumption that certain kinds of pornography are harmful, and ought therefore to be suppressed. Of crucial importance here is the right of women to equal treatment, which in the Canadian case is enshrined in the 1982 Charter of Rights and Freedoms. It is also clear that even where there has been no breach of the criminal law in the production of the material concerned, from this perspective there may still be a case for prohibition, though whether the prosecutions which are mounted to serve that end are likely to succeed is another matter altogether.[135]

Locating the ultimate jurisdiction in community standards may appear eminently rational, but there does remain the question of how judges, who are not always the most socially representative of people, ascertain exactly what these are, and keep track of their changing nature over time. Nonetheless it is clear that the law can be of value in providing a forum for discussion of the boundaries beyond which the media should not go as far as the depiction of sexual activity is concerned. However it is of rather less help when it comes to violence and matters of taste, and in these areas regulators have little option but to continue the struggle in their codes of practice and actual decisions to strike a balance between 'freedom' and 'responsibility' on behalf of the citizens with whose protection they are charged.

Summary

As the state may sometimes require to protect itself, so too there are occasions when the individual requires protection against other individuals and against the media. Sometimes this involves the law, and different countries strike different balances in the areas of defamation and contempt of court; some countries legislate in the area of privacy. The debate about the behavioural and attitudinal impact of the media continues, and various codes of practice and regulatory procedures have developed, which deal, among other topics, with sex, violence and taste. The conflict among the rights of individuals, groups, the media and society as a whole has been resolved in contrasting fashion in different societies.

Questions for discussion

1. Should the media be given exemption from some laws which constrain the freedoms of individual citizens?
2. If there were to be effective laws on privacy, which areas of the lives of public and non-public figures should be covered?
3. Given the difficulties of ascertaining exactly what impact media representations have on people, what should be the basis of regulation in regard to the depiction of violence and sexual activity?

Part III
Practice

Actors in Performance | 8

The first section of this book was concerned to explore the contexts within which media policy is formulated and implemented, while the second focused on the principles which govern that process. Throughout there have been references to the various groups and organizations which are involved, some of which, like media businesses, have been given considerable attention. In this final section the intention is to look at the ways in which policy has been made and applied in practice, through a series of case studies. Before embarking on these it will be useful to examine in more systematic fashion than has been possible hitherto the various actors involved. The term 'actor' might seem an odd one, but it has come to be used in discussions of policy making, and that convention will be adhered to here, even although it might be objected that real actors appear on the stage, or in front of cameras and microphones, and pretend to be people they are not. The assumption about actors in the policy process is that they are real people who are not dissembling as to their identities – though they might well be dissembling about aspects of their behaviour!

We need then to consider the roles of several groups, first, those who are held to be the ultimate policy makers in democratic societies, the elected politicians. Secondly, there are the civil servants who advise and interact with the politicians. Then there are the regulatory authorities, which are established by legislatures – or sometimes by other bodies – and the media organizations themselves. Beyond all of these are the citizens, in whose name and in response to whose wishes and needs media policy supposedly operates, and to whom those who develop and implement it must in the last resort be accountable.

The politicians

All politicians are interested in the media, for the obvious reason that it is through newspapers, radio and television that they make contact with most of their electorate. Members of a legislature might spend a great deal of time attending events in their constituencies but that will only give them a limited amount of exposure, so if they hold no prominent office they will rely very heavily on local newspapers and broadcasters to ensure that their activities are known to their constituents. It is not uncommon in Britain, for example, for local newspapers to invite the MPs in their areas to pen a weekly 'Westminster Commentary', and few turn down the offer. If the elected member does have a position of some note in government or opposition, (s)he will expect to appear on network radio and television and to have his/her activities and speeches reported in the national press. Again few politicians spurn such opportunities, although the more prominent and important they are, the more likely they are to seek to negotiate the terms of their appearances.[136]

At party and government level attempts are continually made to secure favourable coverage of policies and initiatives, and to gain advantage at the expense of rival parties. This is most obvious during election campaigns, when competition is at its most intense, but it is an ongoing process. Politicians have regular meetings with newspaper and broadcasting executives in order not only to exchange views but also to size each other up, and where there is clear sympathy between party and paper, the association can very easily become one of collaboration. The British Labour Party has long argued that the basic thrust of the national press is pro-Conservative, and that has certainly been the case historically, although it has not in recent years applied throughout the United Kingdom, for in Scotland, in contrast to the London situation, as was noted in chapter 5, it has been difficult to find a title which offered support to the Tories. That fact, however, did not stop the Labour Party complaining about the supposedly excessively critical stance taken by Scottish leader writers and columnists towards the New Labour project in the run up to the 1997 election which brought it to power.

Too close an association between one party and any paper or papers might seem to run contrary to the libertarian theory's view of the press as a disinterested pursuer of truth, regardless of who is damaged by disclosure, and any in-built bias towards one particular position might seem threatening to the very basis of liberal democracy. That is a theme to which we shall return in one of the case studies.

The relationship with broadcasting is markedly different, for broadcasters, certainly in most Western countries, are expected to be neutral, so any acrimonious discussion between politicians and those who work in the electronic media cannot focus on questions of support or hostility, so much as fairness and impartiality. The interaction between the politician and broadcasting is bound to be a permanently difficult one, for, on the one hand, broadcasting has to some extent undermined the power of legislatures as the supreme chambers of public debate, and has even subjugated television coverage of parliamentary deliberation in mainstream channels to the time-obsessed disciplines of the medium, but, on the other hand, without access to broadcasting the politician who seeks a national role is cut off from the people whose support (s)he needs to secure, or continue in, that role. As Anthony Smith has commented in his classic study of the relationship between electronic communication and the state:

> the prominent politician increasingly depends on radio and television for his very existence. Politics within mass society is inextricable from the technology which provides contact between the few and the many. The periodic outbursts of fury and vengeance between the broadcasting organizations of the world and their respective political communities follow inevitably from the very existence of broadcasting.[137]

The tension between broadcasters and politicians is more and more mediated by intermediaries – 'spin doctors' and their ilk – who seek not only to secure exposure for those whom they serve, but also to ensure that what is regarded as the 'on message' line is put across in news programming. Broadcasters, who are constitutionally obliged to enforce impartiality, must circumvent any attempt at overt manipulation. However there is also the programming imperative to consider, the desire to have legislators in front of the cameras, and the need to ensure that the supply of news and information does not dry up. Pressure from 'spin doctors' must be resisted in the interests of neutrality, but they cannot be ignored either, for a breakdown in the relationship can have an adverse effect on the broadcasters' ability to fulfill their role in presenting politics to the public.

The relationship is made even more complicated by the fact that broadcasting organizations exist by virtue of political decisions, and their constitutional and financial bases are subject to periodic review and scrutiny. Even the most self- denying legislators on the globe must have some difficulty in totally separating their role as performers seeking legitimation through appearances on the airwaves, from their function as the ultimate structural arbiters and gatekeepers. Indeed there are some countries where the involvement of practising politicians in the electronic media in the latter role is all too obvious. German public service broadcasting, for example, is organized largely on a regional basis, and it is an accepted fact of life that the board in charge of each station will reflect the political orientation of the area; in Italy for many years the three state channels were in effect shared out among the main political parties, Christian Democrats, Socialists and Communists. The relationship between broadcasting and politicians in France is now a more distant one than it once was, not least because of the privatization process. In 1968 however, when there were violent anti-government protests on the streets, television viewers were provided with very incomplete information about these, on the instructions of the government of President de Gaulle.[138] In the United Kingdom, by contrast, broadcasting managers are expected to operate on the basis of political neutrality and to suppress their own affiliations. There is a similar expectation of the members of regulatory bodies, although not every observer is persuaded that in practice it is an expectation which is always fulfilled.[139]

Leaving aside formal relationships, there is also a steady traffic between politics and broadcasting – and for that matter the press. Several current affairs reporters have become members of parliament and several former MPs have become broadcasters. There is a clear area of overlap in Britain at both performer and executive levels: to take one prominent example, London Weekend Television for many years had as its chairman, John Freeman, who had been a print and television journalist, and before that a member of parliament. The number of former – and even current – MPs on the airwaves – Brian Walden, Robert Kilroy Silk, David Mellor, Austin Mitchell, for example – is remarkable. In the United States, President Lyndon Johnson's personal wealth derived largely from his family's ownership of radio and television stations.

As has been noted, although politicians ultimately decide the structure of broadcasting, they have a rather more limited impact on the press, for it is organized on the same basis as most other industries, that is to say it exists within a macro-environment over which government policy has influence, but entry is not via some politically ordained or controlled process. However it would be a mistake to overemphasise this distinction, for although it may be applicable in the Anglo-American world, it is not an accurate description of the situations in several European countries where legislators intervene directly in order to affect the number of players in the marketplace, and employ a variety of devices to that end. Even where intervention is minimized, the application in practice of anti-cartel and anti-monopoly legislation is ultimately the responsibility of politicians, and, as cross-media ownership becomes a more pressing issue, so there may be more, and not less, involvement.

So far the discussion has concentrated on politicians who hold seats in national legislatures. But the centralized state on the traditional British model is not the universal norm. Many countries have federal or devolved structures, with the result that politicians who operate in the regional arena may find themselves involved in a very similar relationship to the media as has been described at the national level. This is certainly the case in Germany where, as has been noted, broadcasting policy is the reponsibility of the länder, and in Spain, where the government in Catalonia, for example, has actively pursued a media policy designed to emphasize and heighten the sense of regional identity.[140]

Politicians who operate in the pan-national stratum of government are also involved in media policy, most obviously in the European Union. The European Parliament, which is directly elected by voters throughout the EU, has been active in the media sphere, for example in supporting public service, as opposed to commercial, broadcasting across the Union. The parliament has also called for a much tougher stance to be taken by the EU on concentration of ownership and the promotion of pluralism than has been the case to date, and that call has illustrated an important contrast between the power of MEPs and national MPs: the European Parliament historically has not had the last say on European policy, for that function has rested with the Council of Ministers, which represents the member states, whereas in the UK, for example, the ultimate arbiter of national policy is the Westminster legislature. Even allowing for the fact that EU regulations can override those of national parliaments, such legislatures still remain much more powerful than the European one.

The civil servants

The relationship between the European Parliament and the Council of Ministers is not the only one of significance within the EU, for there is a strong civil service, the European Commission, which is responsible for drawing up and initiating proposals for the Council to discuss, and for policy implementation. The interaction between politicians and civil servants is a fascinating one, and has given rise to much academic analysis – and also to a very successful British television comedy series, *Yes Minister*.[141] The message of the series was that, although legislators may think they are in charge of the policy process, civil servants have a very large, if often scarcely visible, role. What is clear about the European Commission is that in the relationship with elected politicians in the Parliament, it has tended to be the dominant partner. But as far as the Council of Ministers is concerned, the interaction is much more complex and shifting, and differs from the traditional domestic one, since the Commission is entitled to be proactive in the pursuit of the EU's overall objectives.

The British civil service has traditionally been regarded as being impartial, whatever political party is in power. The accusation has often been made however that it pursues its own centrist agenda and frustrates radicals of left and right, by producing unending lists of objections to policies of which it disapproves; some commentators have gone further and suggested that its structures and recruitment procedures are one reason for Britain's relative economic decline.[142] A rather different charge, which was made during the eighties and nineties, is that with the dominance of one party in government for almost twenty years, the service had become politicized and was at times incapable of distinguishing between its legitimate role as public servant and its rather more questionable role as helpmate of the party in power.[143] However whatever lapses there may have been during the Thatcher/Major years – and subsequently – it is assumed here that much of the traditional public service ethos does survive.

When it comes to policy formulation therefore, civil servants are basically expected to take the plans with which the politicians present them, and to consider how they can be put into effect. Policy very often takes the form not of detailed proposals but rather a broad indication of the direction in which the politicians would like to move, and it is for the civil servants to consider how a general idea might be transformed into a detailed scheme of action for which politicians – ministers, governing party, and ultimately legislature – then have to take responsibility. Once a policy has legislative approval, it is for the civil service to implement it, and to monitor its effectiveness. The changes to the structure of Independent Television which stem from the Broadcasting Act of 1990 may be taken as an example. The basic thrust of the Act can be traced to the Peacock Report which had been commissioned by the Thatcher government in 1985 with the remit of considering the future finance of the BBC.[144] The committee chairman, Sir Alan Peacock, was a noted free-market economist, as was one other member, the financial journalist, Samuel Brittan. The civil servants whose job it would have been to come up with a short list of candidates to present to the relevant Home Secretary, Leon Brittan (brother of Samuel), were well aware of the government's economic and social philosophy, and would tailor their list accordingly, although they would also feel it their duty to offer less ideologically committed candidates, some of whom were in fact appointed.

When the committee actually got down to work, it ranged rather more widely than had originally been intended, and made recommendations on the future shape of non-BBC broadcasting, included among which was the proposal that, subject to number of safeguards, ITV franchises should be auctioned to the highest bidder, rather than awarded at a predetermined price to the companies deemed most suitable to carry out the task of providing the service. This radical suggestion was doubly attractive to the government, for it meant that market forces could be introduced into what Peacock called the 'comfortable duopoly' of broadcasting, and – in theory at least – it offered the Treasury additional revenue.[145] Once the idea had been accepted, it was the job of the civil service to draft the relevant legislation, which took the form ultimately of the 1990 Broadcasting Bill, and once that had become law, to ensure that it was implemented. In the drafting process not only would the civil servants in the 'host' department discuss what they were doing with each other, but they would talk to colleagues in other departments, such as the Treasury, which had an interest in the legislation.

When the Bill was going through parliament, its original direction was modified somewhat, and the relevant Home Office minister, David Mellor, claimed principal credit for this change, although much lobbying by the ITV companies and others, of both the minister and the senior civil servants concerned had taken place. Without more open government than we enjoy in Britain, it is difficult to be sure whether the crucial role was played by minister or civil servants in the discussion which led to alterations in the Bill. It seems however a reasonable assumption that the objections which had been raised in a number of quarters about the danger that, faced with the need to recover the costs of excessive bids offered in order to retain licences, a more ratings-conscious ITV, would plunge down-market, were explored at length in the papers presented to David Mellor.

Once the Bill became the Act, and the bidding procedure was embarked on, it became clear that the process was deeply flawed: some companies offered very high bids, and some virtually nothing, on the assumption that they did not face serious competition. The result was that the Treasury did not receive as great a windfall as anticipated. A consensus subsequently developed in parliament, and outside of it, that another method would have to be found to allocate franchises. So civil servants would then be expected to consider how that might best be done, so that the government, if it continued in power beyond the impending election, did not appear to be losing too much face, but nonetheless was able to extricate itself from an awkward situation.

Politicians and civil servants were prime actors in this affair, while supporting roles were played by media organizations, regulators and – at a distance – the public.

The regulators

Regulatory bodies are an important part of the democratic landscape. They are largely the creation of politicians, by whom they are given their basic responsibilities, but they operate with a degree of independence, indeed their legitimacy depends on their being perceived to enjoy that independence. They are useful devices of governance, because they remove the detail of policy implementation from the primary political arena, and to an extent transfer responsibility for decision making into a less partisan milieu, in which the 'public interest' is seen to be paramount, although that 'public interest' has to be addressed in the context of the overall policy framework which has been laid down by the legislators. In Britain, as a consequence of the privatization programme of the 1980s and 1990s, there has been a growth of such bodies, with new ones like, for example, Ofgas, which regulates the gas industry, and Oftel, which concerns itself with telecommunications, coming into being. Both of these have substantial powers including the right to fix the rates of return on capital of the industries concerned.[146]

In broadcasting the picture is a more complex one, with the BBC Governors being in practice a cross between non-executive board and regulator, and the Independent Television Commission and the Radio Authority being more conventional regulators, with the right to decide who broadcasts and who does not, within the parameters laid down by the relevant legislation. The British approach is less tidy than the American one, in which the Federal Communications Commission regulates all broadcasting and telecommunications, as does the Canadian Radio-Television and Telecommunications Commission. In the late nineties the suggestion was made more frequently in public debate that the UK should copy the transatlantic example, not least because of the growing links between telecommunications and the media.

The Broadcasting Complaints Commission and the Broadcasting Standards Council – amalgamated into the Broadcasting Standards Commission in 1997 – were no more full-blown regulatory bodies than their counterparts overseas, although they enjoyed statutory backing. Since they only possessed the power to require publication of their adjudications, and could not instruct broadcasters on their behaviour, let alone remove their licences, they were rather weaker than the regulatory bodies proper, and had to depend on persuasion, and the threat, which lurked behind their establishment, that the sanctions at their disposal might be strengthened if too many of their recommendations were ignored. A similar point might also be made about the Press Complaints Commission in Britain and Press Councils in, for example, Canada. They are essentially bodies which have been established by the industries which they are required to scrutinize. In Britain however the voluntary system is stronger than it might otherwise be because of the clear perception that if it does not work, laws on privacy will be put on the statute book, or more drastic penalties, such as the fines, which can be imposed by the Swedish Press Council, introduced.

The British Board of Film Classification (BBFC) is also an organization which was set up by the relevant industry; its judgements are generally accepted, but in law local authorities have the right to classify, or for that matter to decide which films will and will not be shown, a right which was ceded to the BBFC in 1912, but is still exercised on occasion by some councils. In the USA classification is carried out by an industry-based body on a non-statutory basis, but in Canada the Provincial authorities have statutory rights in the matter. In mainland Europe the picture varies, but all countries have classification systems of some description. In France, for example, it is the Ministry of Culture which is the body responsible for issuing certificates, which it does after receiving reports from an advisory commission.[147]

How do these various bodies, strong and not so strong, impact on the policy process? It might be thought that their function is simply to carry out the remit which has been laid down for them and let policy be decided elsewhere. But this is to oversimplify the nature of the regulatory process, which has been described by one commentator as 'a continuing transaction between the governors and the governed'.[148] An organization such as the Federal Communications Commission (FCC), although it is ultimately under political control, will, through its activities, establish principles of operation, to which broadcasters will be expected to adhere. A good example is the so-called Fairness Doctrine, under which radio and television were for many years required to provide reasonable access to differing points of view on public issues. However the FCC abandoned enforcement of this Doctrine in 1988, despite Congressional opposition, in favour of the freedom of speech sanctified by the First Amendment.[149] For its part, the British Independent Television Commission, and its predecessor bodies, have been responsible for a detailed code on advertising practice which must be followed; furthermore the Independent Broadcasting Authority had the power to review ITV programme schedules and to require changes, a power which was frequently used.[150]

To some extent regulators fill in the gaps which have been left by the broad brush of legislation, but to a significant degree they go beyond into areas of policy formulation. Here they have to proceed with circumspection, lest they be accused of usurping the proper role of the legislators, but the more firmly established a regulatory body is, the greater its scope for action.[151] When it comes to the processes of policy evolution and change, regulatory bodies seek to contribute to the discussion. This is often done discreetly: the Independent Broadcasting Authority in the approach to the parliamentary debate on the 1990 Broadcasting Bill did not wage a high profile public campaign on the issues about which it was concerned, but it did present evidence to the Peacock Committee, and its officers held discussions with the relevant government department in order to ensure that it had an input to the process which led to its reconstitution as the Independent Television Commission and the Radio Authority. Regulatory bodies are much more likely to have an impact where the government is in an open-minded mood; if that is not the case, and what is proposed is deemed by the regulators to be undesirable, it is very difficult for them to stop it by persuasion. What could then happen is that sympathetic politicians might be briefed informally, in the hope that they might persuade the government to think again, and sympathetic journalists encouraged to ensure that the regulatory body's views find their way into the public realm. This can be a dangerous game, for, on the one hand, if a regulator were to be seen to be openly opposing government policy, its future might be compromised; on the other hand, to take an independent line 'in the public interest' is likely to increase general standing and credibility.

The media organizations

The briefing of politicians and journalists is something which will be undertaken not only by regulators but also by media organizations. The nature of these was discussed at some length in chapter 3, where, it will be recalled, the point was made that, although some are commercial and some non-commercial, they can all to some extent be regarded as industries which, if they are to survive, are obliged to take account of the markets in which they operate, even although their position may be guaranteed by public funding. Companies wax and wane, but it is characteristic of most of them that, like all organizations, one of their principal aims is to continue to exist. They may well have a range of other objectives – such as making money, or producing good films or broadcast programmes – but fundamentally they wish to stay alive. So when it comes to the policy-making process they will be seeking to ensure that nothing is done to damage that prospect; if, in addition, it is possible to secure advantages, then the opportunity will not be disregarded.

In the discussions which followed the publication of the Peacock Report in 1986 the media organizations which were most concerned to ensure that their points of view were understood were the BBC, the existing ITV companies, independent production companies and new and aspiring broadcasters. It might have been expected that the BBC would have been to the fore in the debate, but as it became clear that the suggestion from Peacock that the licence fee should be replaced by subscription – rather than advertising, which had been commonly expected – was unlikely to be capable of implementation for some years, attention focused on the report's proposals for the non-BBC sector. Immediately the ITV companies found themselves having to defend a system which they were obliged to claim had operated in the public interest – ITV spokespersons had long since taken to describing themselves not as commercial broadcasters but as public service ones who, fortuitously, were financed by advertising.

However it was the view of Peacock and the legislators who supported what the report had said that the system operated more in ITV's interest than in the public's. The politicians who took this line, not least Margaret Thatcher, who had developed a hostility to what she regarded as a cossetted overmanned, uncompetitive industry, were determined on radical change, and they were still riding on the wave of free market enthusiasm which they had done so much to create, and from which a large number of the populace had derived benefit, in the shape of cheap shares in privatized utilities. In this situation it was difficult for ITV to appear as anything other than a special pleader seeking the continuation of a rather pleasant life. If the BBC, which had been described in the post-Peacock White Paper as 'the cornerstone of British broadcasting'[152] had chosen to throw its weight openly behind its beleaguered colleagues in ITV, then it would have been much easier for the commercial sector to utilize a public interest defence.[153]

The view in the Corporation however appeared to be that the best hope for its own future lay in causing minimum fuss. Although discreet support was offered to ITV, and to Channel Four in its efforts to ensure that the new independent status planned for it, in which it would sell advertising time directly, did not damage its capacity to be innovative, there was no substantial show of public solidarity. ITV was helped to present its case by a swiftly established Campaign for Quality Television, but as the membership was largely drawn from practitioners, it was difficult to avoid the accusation that it was simply an ITV front organization. Both the BBC and ITV had accepted the Peacock recommendation that they should transmit a significant proportion of independent productions – 25 per cent was the final agreed figure – and the companies which stood to benefit were enthusiastic about this aspect of the government's proposals, as is only natural. Indeed some of them had actually lobbied Peacock and the government for the inclusion of just such a provision. But none of them were ever likely to pose a serious threat to the major broadcasters.

The same cannot be said of News Corp. That company's Sky television service was only to appear fully fledged on the British scene in early 1989, but during the run up to the 1990 Act and thereafter, News Corp's papers regularly printed 'knocking copy' about both ITV and the BBC, the basic aim of which was clearly to persuade the public that both were bloated and inefficient organizations which desperately needed the bracing winds of competition, which could of course be supplied by Sky. How much impact this had on the populace is unclear, but some of the politicians were clearly receiving the message, for, as was noted in chapter 3, Murdoch's satellite operation was allowed to develop in the UK under a remarkably lenient regulatory regime, which has enabled it to concentrate on sport and movies, and thus build up a dominant position in these areas.

The public

The main theme of what can only be described as propaganda in the Murdoch press was that the British public was being denied real choice. What remains remarkable however about the whole post-Peacock debate is the virtual absence of that public. Politicians had plenty to say, as had some broadcasting organizations and, more discreetly, regulators and civil servants, but where were the people in whose name radical changes in the broadcasting system were being contemplated? Not for the first time it became clear that policy is for the most part the preserve of interested parties, and of an elite. There was no shortage of discussion in the broadsheet press – read by less than 20 per cent of the population – and in specialist journals. But as to engaging the broad mass of the public in a debate about the future of the mass medium to which most of them devote over twenty hours of their lives each week, the task was never undertaken. That is not to say that informed citizens could not write to their Members of Parliament, as no doubt many did, nor that specialist groups and organizations could not do likewise. Indeed governments often solicit views by issuing Green Papers, as was to happen in the much less ideologically charged atmosphere in the approach to the renewal of the BBC's Charter in 1996.[154] The result of that kind of consultation is that various organizations – consumers' groups, educationalists, churches and so on – and a handful of individuals do submit their views, and if the government is in a listening mode, then there is a traffic between respondents and politicians. But it does remain largely an elite activity. Successive British governments have recognized the difficulties they face in consultation, should they genuinely wish to engage in it, and have encouraged the establishment of such bodies as the National Consumer Council. These organizations are expected to find some method of ascertaining citizens' opinions before pronouncing on issues, and many of them do make considerable efforts to that end.

In Britain however there is no broadcasting or media consumer council, and some observers have argued that such a body needs to be established as a matter of urgency.[155] In Canada for many years there has been an organization called Friends of Canadian Broadcasting (FCB), which is a self-constituted group of citizens who campaign to ensure that public broadcasting, particularly in the shape of the Canadian Broadcasting Corporation, is sustained in their country. The limited success FCB has had in the nineties is not very encouraging, but the idea that such an organization should exist, perhaps with a wider remit than broadcasting, seems attractive. However if national Citizens' Media Councils were to be instituted in Britain, and elsewhere, the fundamental issue of membership would need to be addressed. If we look at the existing regulatory bodies, and indeed such consumers' councils as do exist, it is very striking how often the same kinds of people – educated, middle class, comfortable with committee work – turn up on them. It might be argued that these are the very individuals to get things done, the kind of people who know how to make the political system work to advantage. Furthermore, some of them are on the lists of the 'great and the good' held by government departments and drawn on whenever appointments to quangos (quasi autonomous nongovernmental organizations), and similar bodies are made. They are people who have no difficulty in dealing with the civil service and government, and are generally well regarded in political and adminstrative circles.

This is a seductive argument, and anyone who has been involved, even in a small way, in the kinds of selection processes which go on, inside or outside of government, will testify wearily how difficult it is to find a cross section of citizens, which is both representative and useful, even if there is a determination to do so. It is not easy for many people to operate in the kind of milieux and with the kind of discourses which typify the organizations in question; they are often uncomfortable and unsure. It is so much simpler to find concerned middle-class citizens who will take upon themselves the task of representing the unrepresented majority.[156] It may be much simpler, but is it acceptable? Are the actors in media policy to remain a relatively narrow group, or might there be ways of ensuring that if Citizens' Media Councils are to be established, they can be genuinely representative of the population as a whole, and that they will initiate real public participation? This question is obviously not unique to the media area, but because media consumption, particularly electronic media consumption, is engaged in much more by the working class than by the kind of people who are involved in policy making and implementation, it becomes particularly stark in that context.

It could be observed, by way of rebuttal of what has just been argued, that all members of the public have the right to watch or not to watch, to buy or not to buy, but if we believe that it is possible to have a genuinely participative democracy, then we cannot regard the use of the off/on switch and a credit card as substitutes for real involvement in debates about policy. It is foolish to imagine that the entire population would leap at the opportunity should it be presented to them, but a surprisingly large number of citizens might well take the chance to express their views if the opening were there. Wider participation in policy discussions would not absolve political and regulatory elites – even reformed ones – from their responsibility for making decisions, nor would it necessarily prevent them doing things they believe to be right, whether popular or unpopular, but it would mean that they were rather better informed than they currently are about what the people, on whose behalf they act, actually think.

Summary

Media policy is formulated as an ongoing process involving several principal actors. First, there are the politicians who are ultimately responsible for legislative decisions, and who take a close professional interest in media behaviour. Secondly, there are civil servants whose job it is to turn broad policy into detailed proposals, and to oversee its implementation. Thirdly, there are the regulators who, even when appointed by politicians, enjoy a significant degree of autonomy. Fourthly, there are media organizations themselves which are seeking opportunities to protect and advance their interests. Fifthly, and lastly, there are the citizens of the country in question, whose opportunities for involvement in policy making vary considerably. In any development or revision of policy all of these actors seek to secure particular ends, and the results usually reflect the balance of forces at differing points of time.

Questions for discussion

1. To what extent do the party affiliations of politicians affect their approaches to media regulation?
2. Should existing media organizations have the right to influence the development of media policy?
3. What mechanisms can be developed to ensure that the citizens of a country are more involved in the formulation of media policy?

Privacy, Accuracy and the Press Complaints Commission | 9

The British Press Complaints Commission was established as the result of a crisis which engulfed the existing self-regulatory mechanism in the late 1980s. The resolution of that crisis reveals much about the ways in which the actors in media policy deal with a threatening situation and seek to protect their various interests.

Press councils

Press councils are a feature of the media scene in many parts of the world. Sweden's council for example was set up by the country's national press club in 1916, with the aim of promoting high standards of conduct in journalism, and it was complemented in 1969 by the establishment of the office of Press Ombudsman, which deals with complaints against newspapers in the first instance, and decides whether to refer them to the Press Council. That body for its part has the power to issue adjudications, which must be published in the paper concerned, and to impose small fines. In 1956 a Press Council was instituted in Germany, with a similar remit to the one established in Sweden, although it has had a difficult history in recent years, and its legitimacy has been seriously called into question; in Germany there is also a statutory right of reply, which means that newspapers are obliged to print corrections of factually inaccurate statements. A similar right of reply has existed in France since 1881.

In the mid 1990s there were some twenty press councils of varying constitution in Europe, some of which also have broadcasting within their remit.[157] On the other side of the Atlantic, councils have had rather mixed fortune. In the United States a few have operated on a voluntary basis, for example in Minnesota and Oregon, but a national council which existed from 1973 till 1984 collapsed after a sustained campaign led by the *New York Times* which made much of the constitutional protection accorded to the press by the First Amendment.[158] In Canada however, there has been steady development, as councils have been established in different provinces, so that most of the country is now covered. In another former British dominion, Australia, a national council was instituted in 1976 and continues to function. The Australian and Canadian bodies have consciously modelled themselves on the UK's Press Council which came into being as the General Council of the Press in Britain in 1953, with the twin objectives of preserving the freedom of the press and encouraging high standards of journalism. They followed the British pattern too in being financed by the industry, being essentially voluntary and being composed of a mixture of press and 'lay' members. Now they find themselves in the position of representing an approach to regulation which has been drastically modified in the country to which they looked for example and guidance. How has this situation come about?

The British crisis

In the 1980s criticism of newspapers, particularly of the tabloids, mounted: they were deemed to be both careless with the truth, and ruthlessly intrusive. In 1983 on the first anniversary of the Falklands War, for example, the *Sun* sought an interview with the widow of a soldier who had died during the conflict and had been awarded the VC posthumously; the woman refused to cooperate, so the paper simply invented the interview. Regular accounts of the sexual activities of prominent individuals, particularly in the entertainment professions, were printed without regard for the privacy of the people concerned.[159] There was also a sense that, in addition to publishing intrusive material, newspapers often disseminated inaccurate information, but offered skimpy opportunity for corrections. It is difficult to be sure how widely the unease, which was articulated volubly by public figures, was shared, since the sales figures of the newspapers in question remained reasonably healthy; opinion polls may have suggested that the public disapproved of tabloid excess, but disapproval did not seem to greatly affect consumption patterns. The Press Council was still functioning at this time, but its legitimacy had been undermined by the withdrawal of the representatives of the principal journalists' union in 1980 (although they returned in 1990). The Council seemed unable to stop what was happening, and not surprisingly, was perceived to be impotent. Furthermore, it had acquired a reputation for being dilatory in the handling of complaints which came to it.

In the 1988–9 session of parliament a Labour MP introduced a Right of Reply bill and a Conservative member a Protection of Privacy one – the fact that the sponsor of the latter was later exposed by a television programme as someone who appeared to be abusing his position in the legislature for personal gain, proved calamitous for the individual concerned, but did not necessarily undermine the arguments for privacy legislation. Faced with the likely passage of these two bills into law, the government, mindful of the fact that their enactment would impose further restrictions on a press which was already subject to a range of legal constraints, and mindful too perhaps of its own closeness politically to some of the alleged chief offenders, decided to set up an inquiry into 'Privacy and Related Matters' under the chairmanship of a barrister, David Calcutt. For its part, the Press Council struggled to improve its performance, but the Calcutt Committee was not impressed. Indeed while it was sitting it was provided with another example of the lengths to which some papers would go to obtain stories: when an actor noted for his appearances in a television comedy series was seriously injured as the result of an accident in 1990, a photographer and reporter from the *Sunday Sport* used subterfuge to enter the hospital ward where he was being treated, conducted an 'interview' with him while he was under sedation and took pictures, all without permission from the hospital authorities. The Calcutt Committee recommended that the Press Council should be disbanded and replaced by a new Press Complaints Commission (PCC), the sole function of which would be to deal with complaints. The Commission was to be established on the clear understanding that the press 'should be given one final chance to prove voluntary self-regulation can be made to work'.[160]

The committee's proposals offered a breathing space to both government and press. The former did not feel obliged to introduce statutory regulation, something from which any administration in a liberal democracy would have shrunk, nor did it need to pursue the right of reply and invasion of privacy legislative routes. The press, for its part, had avoided confrontation with government, but at a price, since it now had to be seen to be improving its performance, for, as the minister directly involved had earlier put it, newspapers were 'drinking in the last chance saloon'.[161] The difficult position the industry found itself in did not prevent it lobbying very hard in order to ensure that the PCC which emerged was more to its liking than the one Calcutt's committee had proposed. The committee had favoured a body made up of lay members and members with substantial press experience, but the latter were not to be nominated by the industry. However, it did not take the press very long to successfully argue the case for an appointments procedure to which it has substantial input. No doubt the industry representatives made the point to the civil servants and politicians, with whom they discussed the matter, that, as they were being expected to finance the PCC, then they should have some responsibility for its composition. The actual make-up – half non-press, an independent chairman and the remaining members drawn from the industry – is similar to that of the Advertising Standards Authority, a body which deals with complaints about advertising, and which, like the Commission, is industry sponsored.

A new dispensation

Mindful of the impending closing time in the last chance saloon, the industry moved quickly to abolish the existing Press Council – despite the protests of its new chairman, who had tried to improve its performance and procedures – and the PCC was operational by January 1991, a mere six months after the Calcutt Committee reported. A Code of Practice was produced, the provisions of which are supposed to be adhered to by all the newspapers and magazines which were party to the establishment of the PCC, and had been collectively responsible for drafting it. A publicity campaign was embarked on to ensure that the creation of the Commission and the nature of its complaints procedures were widely known. The question for the press now was could this last attempt at self-regulation prevent the imposition of the statutory tribunal threatened by the Calcutt Committee. For the government the question was would further legislative intervention be necessary, and for those members of the public who were concerned about the matter, the question was would the behaviour of British newspapers improve.

The Code of Practice is fairly comprehensive, although its philosophical basis consists of little more than the injunction: 'All members of the press have a duty to maintain the highest professional and ethical standards . . . [the Code] both protects the rights of the individual and upholds the public's right to know'.[162] It is the responsibility of editors and publishers to ensure that the Code is 'honoured not only to the letter but in the full spirit'. There are clauses covering such matters as accuracy, the correction of inaccuracy, payment for articles, and intrusion into grief and shock. The line taken on privacy is that invasions of an individual's private life can only be justified if there is an overwhelming public interest, and the same public interest has to be invoked to justify the use of bugging devices, the removal of documents, subterfuge and harassment:

1. The public interest includes –
i) Detecting or exposing crime or a serious misdemeanour.
ii) Protecting public health and safety.
iii) Preventing the public from being misled by some statement or action of an individual or organisation.
2. In any case where the public interest is invoked, the Press Complaints Commission will require a full explanation by the editor demonstrating how the public interest was served.
3. In cases involving children editors must demonstrate an exceptional public interest to over-ride the normally paramount interests of the child.

The adjudication of many cases has turned on this clause, and it is obvious to any reader that, while it does not offer all-purpose defences, it is fairly generous in its interpretation of what the public interest might be. The section referring to children was added, with the position of the children of the Prince and Princess of Wales clearly in mind, after the Princess's death.

Before turning to some examples of cases dealt with by the PCC, it is worth noting in passing that clause one of the Code states that 'Newspapers, while free to be partisan, must distinguish clearly between comment, conjecture and fact'. As was pointed out earlier in the book, this injunction is totally disregarded by some sections of the British press, particularly during election campaigns, which must raise the question of why it is included in the Code at all.

The crisis continues

The PCC has been a success in one sense: at the time of writing there is no statutory regulation in Britain, so the newspaper industry and those politicians who did not relish going down that path have secured their objectives. However their relief is not necessarily widely shared. In 1992 the chairman of the committee, as a result of whose deliberations the PCC had emerged, was asked to conduct a review of the Commission's operations over its first eighteen months. During that time there had been several exposés of the lives of prominent individuals: The *Sunday People* had published a photograph of the baby daughter of the Duke and Duchess of York naked in her parents' garden, a picture which had clearly been obtained by subterfuge, and a year later the *Daily Mirror* had printed another photograph, this time of the Duchess herself, semi-naked with her 'financial adviser' beside a swimming pool in France. A complaint was made on behalf of the Duke of York about the first incident, and although the PCC upheld the complaint, the newspaper continued to assert that it was entitled to have published it in the first place. No complaint was made in the second case, although damages were sought and won in a French court under that country's privacy law. During the period Calcutt examined, there were also several stories about the personal life of the Prince and Princess of Wales, one of which seemed to have appeared with the connivance of the Princess herself, and this led the Commission into a highly embarrassing situation where, after it had issued a statement deploring the publication of such material, it became clear that it had done so without knowledge of the Princess's involvement. The presumed justification for all of these invasions of privacy is that, as the public pays for the lavish lifestyles enjoyed by the Royal Family, it is entitled to know via the press how members of this elite group are conducting themselves.

Politicians had also been at the receiving end of unwelcome attention. Clare Short, a Labour MP, who at one point had sought to ban the publication of Page Three Girls – pictures of semi-naked young women – complained to the Commission about harassment and invasion of her private life by one of the papers given to printing such material; her complaint was upheld. Most spectacularly of all, David Mellor, the minister who might have been charged with taking privacy legislation through the House of Commons, should that situation have arisen, found details – pictorial and verbal – of his alleged relationship with an 'actress' spread across several pages in the *Sunday People* and the *Daily Mirror*. The latter justified publication by saying in a leader column that if Mr Mellor was 'knackered' – a term he had used in a taped conversation with the lady, which had come into the paper's hands – then he was incapable of carrying out his duties as a minister of the crown. The

Commission met, and then issued a confused statement, at the end of which it indicated that it wished to review its work to date.

Unlike Clare Short, David Mellor never made a complaint to the PCC. It is not hard to see why, for if the allegations were true, complaining about an invasion of privacy – which this most certainly was – even although it resulted in a favourable adjudication, could only prolong the unwelcome publicity and accompanying derision. Mellor did not lose his government post at this juncture, but had to resign some months later, when it emerged that during his tenure of office as a junior minister at the Foreign Office he had accepted hospitality from a wealthy Palestinian at a time when the government was treading a delicate line between Israel and the PLO.

When Sir David Calcutt looked at this record, and at how individuals who were not public figures felt about the way in which complaints they had made to the PCC had been dealt with, he came to a very definite and stark conclusion:

> The Press Complaints Commission is not, in my view, an effective regulator of the press. It has not been set up in a way, and is not operating a code of practice, which enables it to command not only press but also public confidence. It does not, in my view, hold the balance fairly between the press and the individual. It is not the truly independent body which it should be.[163]

His preferred solution was the establishment of a statutory tribunal with the powers to deal with complaints, to award compensation and to impose fines on errant newspapers and magazines, and the introduction of privacy legislation.

The government faced a serious dilemma, for the progenitor of the PCC was in effect saying it was a sham, and would continue to be so in its current form. The clear implication was that if Mr Major's administration did nothing it would be acquiescing in a meaningless charade. But the government, politically weak, and reluctant to act against a press which had offered much support to the Conservative cause, dithered. It produced a green paper on privacy legislation which never progressed beyond the consultation stage. Before the end of that year – 1993 – the *Sunday Mirror* and *Daily Mirror* published photographs of Princess Diana, dressed in a leotard, exercising in a London gymnasium; the pictures had obviously been obtained without permission. The chairman of the PCC, Lord McGregor, described the *Mirror* newspapers as 'outlaws', and called for an advertising boycott. Mirror Group Newspapers then temporarily withdrew its support from the PCC, and characterized

McGregor as an 'arch buffoon'. In private however, away from this bizarre performance, frank discussions were clearly taking place among the parties concerned – that is to say all of the parties except the general public – in order to defuse a potentially terminal crisis. As a result, within twelve months the PCC had a new chairman, Lord Wakeham, a former Conservative politician, who promised to tighten up the Code of Practice and the Commission's procedures. Newspapers, grudgingly or otherwise, began to take the PCC rather more seriously than they had done before. This process reached something of a climax in mid 1995 when Rupert Murdoch publicly reprimanded one of his editors for invading the privacy of yet another member of the upper classes, of which more will be said below. However, although the governing party had clearly made a deal to stave off statutory regulation, much to the satisfaction of the press, not all politicians were willing to acquiesce in the situation, and early in 1997 the National Heritage Committee of the House of Commons declared that the PCC was still not doing its job well enough; the committee was particularly incensed that the Commission had no powers to fine papers which made payments to witnesses in criminal proceedings – a practice which had been openly engaged in prior to the trials of the serial murderers, Frederick and Rosemary West, in 1995 (Frederick West committed suicide before his trial began).[164]

The PCC rejected the Committee's criticisms of its performance, but it had been reviewing its Code yet again, in the aftermath of the West case. This has been the standard pattern of behaviour: when a serious problem arises which might lead to renewed demands for statutory regulation, the PCC quickly appoints a new 'tough' member, and/or adjusts the Code. That is exactly what happened in 1997 after the death of Diana, Princess of Wales, as she was being chased by freelance photographers. The Commission tightened its restrictions on the use of pictures which emanate from such sources. The overall aim is clearly to be seen as flexible and sensitive, and if this means there is some diminution in the freedom of editors to publish material they would dearly like to print, then that price is deemed to be worth paying. However the treatment by the press of the case of the son of the new Labour Home Secretary, Jack Straw, when he apparently sold cannabis to a *Daily Mirror* reporter in late 1997, and of the Foreign Secretary's extramarital relationship, which was initially revealed a few months earlier, suggests that the willingness to forego juicy stories may be more apparent than real.

Further evidence of the reluctance to abandon old habits followed. In the spring of 1998 the author Gitta Sereny published a book examining the case of Mary Bell. In 1968 Bell as a twelve year old had been found guilty of the manslaughter of two children younger than her. She was released from prison in 1980 and had pursued her life with a new identity. By 1998 she had a 14 year old daughter and, as a consequence of a court order, the media were forbidden from revealing their identities or whereabouts, in the interests of protecting Bell's daughter. Both the *Observer* and the *Guardian* reported that Sereny had paid Bell for her help in writing the book, and immediately several tabloid newspapers sought to discover her current whereabouts, which they succeeded in doing. The *Sun* boasted in a front page that it had been the first to achieve this objective. Consequently Bell's house was besieged, and although the court order was not technically breached, it became rather obvious where she was living. Members of the government were either unwilling or unable to insist on the terms of the court order being fully observed; indeed some ministerial comments may have lent spurious legitimacy to what was taking place. The harassment of herself and her daughter by journalists led Bell to seek police protection; inevitably she had to inform her daughter of the reasons for the attention she was being given by newspapers.

As a consequence of this episode, the parents of the children who were murdered were forced to relive their dreadful experiences, and Bell's daughter was obliged, in the midst of an orgy of tabloid sanctimoniousness verging on a witch hunt, to come to terms with her mother's true identity. It may well have been a very serious misjudgement for Sereny to offer money, and for Bell to take it, but how can what then happened possibly be justified in the public interest? As for the PCC, it simply said that it could do nothing unless Mary Bell made a complaint, thus emphasizing its impotence in the face of behaviour which many people found appalling.

The PCC in action

In 1995 – two years after Calcutt's damning verdict on its efficacy – the Commission received 2,500 complaints, of which almost 2,000 were outside its remit, or were considered not to involve cases that could be pursued under the Code of Practice. This left 483 – 19 per cent of the original total – which were taken further. Of these, 420 were resolved amicably without adjudication, or not pursued by the complainant. Of the 63 complaints on which adjudications were made, the complaints were upheld in 28 cases, and not upheld in the other 35. On the one hand, these figures could be interpreted to mean that there is an excellent conciliatory process at work; on the other hand, if 44 per cent of adjudications find fault with the publication concerned, it could equally be argued that there remain serious instances of misconduct.

In May 1995 *The Times* reported a criminal case involving children who had allegedly been victims of indecent assault, and did so in such a way that the children could be identified. This was a clear breach of the Code, and the paper apologized unreservedly. The Commission reprimanded it. This complaint involved private citizens with no public profiles whatsoever. In a second case earlier the same year three papers published stories about a cabinet minister's nephew who was dying of Aids, which were written in such a way that identification of the young man was possible. In response to complaints from members of his family, the papers concerned sought to justify what they had done by invoking the public interest clause, and one argued that 'the public was entitled to know that a relative of a senior cabinet minister was dying of Aids, an event which would have the effect of bringing the impact of this illness to the heart of Government'.[165] The PCC did not accept this defence, and censured all three papers.

Most dramatically of all, at much the same time the *News of the World* published an extensive report about the sister-in-law of Diana, Princess of Wales, who was in a clinic, allegedly seeking a cure for bulimia and alcohol-related problems. This was clearly an intrusion into the private life of the woman concerned – the paper even printed a photograph of her in the grounds of the clinic. The *News of the World's* editor, Piers Morgan, claimed that the complainant, her husband, Earl Spencer – who two-and-a-half-years later was to launch a savage denunciation of the tabloid press from the pulpit of Westminster Abbey during his sister's funeral service – was a public figure who had used the media to his advantage when it suited him, and therefore would have to put up with unwelcome publicity when it came his way. The Commission rejected this argument completely and activated a procedure it had announced at the beginning of 1994, a year after Calcutt's dismissive report, and just after the 'Diana in a gym' incident. It wrote to the proprietor of the paper concerned, Rupert Murdoch, indicating its displeasure. When the adjudication appeared in the *News of the World* it was accompanied by a brief statement from Murdoch –

'While I will always support worthwhile investigative journalism as a community responsibility it is clear that in this case the young man (Mr Morgan) went over the top' – and a rather grovelling apology from Morgan.[166] Earl Spencer subsequently sought to persuade the European Commission on Human Rights that the British government should be compelled to introduce privacy legislation, but failed in the attempt.

It can be argued that in all of these cases justice was done, and in one sense it clearly was, for the complainants had the satisfaction of seeing the newspapers reprimanded. But the difficulty is that as far as the aggrieved parties are concerned, the damage has been inflicted. There is a second point: if the individuals involved do not actually complain about their privacy being invaded, there is unlikely to be any redress, unless they are so prominent that the Commission feels duty bound to intervene on their behalf, as it has done on occasion, or unless the intrusion is potentially so grossly offensive that preventive action is taken by the PCC. This was what happened after the Dunblane shootings in 1996, when the Chairman backed a police request that the press presence in the town be scaled down drastically on the day when the funerals of the victims were to take place – a request which was acceded to.

In January 1995 the *News of the World* printed an exposé of the activities of 'Scottish wife swappers . . . [who] . . . are risking all with deadly party games that amount to nothing more than AIDS roulette. Hardened *News of the World* reporters have been appalled to witness couples happily engaging in unprotected sex with partner after partner'.[167] These sentences are clearly written with the 'public interest' defence in mind. If a complaint were to be made, then the editor could claim that he was highlighting the terrible threat to public health posed by people who were not using condoms, and that the subterfuge employed by the reporter, who was able to obtain photographs of several semi-naked men and women, was justified, in order to back up the allegations he was making. Titillation, it would be argued, was most certainly not the object of the exercise.

The individuals concerned could clearly be identified from the photographs by anyone who knew them, and while this might well have been productive of much mirth and perhaps some domestic difficulties, it is hard to see how the public interest defence can really be utilized, other than as an exercise in cynical hypocrisy. No-one complained to the PCC about the report. That is hardly surprising, for further publicity would have compounded the participants' embarrassment. What did happen was that one of the men involved appeared two years later in front of an industrial tribunal, claiming that, subsequent to the article appearing, he had been unfairly dismissed from his post with an organization which seeks work places for vulnerable young people, some of whom may have been the victims of sexual abuse. His employer contended that the individual concerned had lowered the standing of the organization he worked for, although there was no suggestion that he had ever abused any of those with whom he came into contact. Despite arguing that his private life was private, and that he had been deceived by journalists who pretended they wished to join the wife-swapping parties, the man was not reinstated. Many people might think very little of this person's behaviour, they might even regard him as a fool, but was it legitimate for his employment to be removed in such a fashion?

In 1994 the *Guardian* published allegations about the activities of Neil Hamilton MP and Tim Smith, a minister at the Northern Ireland Office, who, it was claimed, had both been paid by the proprietor of Harrods in order to advance that individual's interests in parliament, but had not declared their pecuniary gain in the relevant House of Commons register. In order to build its case the paper inevitably used investigative techniques which invaded the MPs' privacy. Smith resigned, however Hamilton and the public relations consultant with whom he was associated, initiated a libel action against the newspaper, but withdrew from it just as the case was about to come to court in 1996. Subsequent events demonstrated that the *Guardian* was substantially correct, and that both men had abused their positions as Members of Parliament. If a complaint had been made by either of them to the PCC, no doubt the editor of the paper would have invoked the public interest defence, and it is difficult to see how the Commission could have rejected it. What this case demonstrates clearly is that there are occasions when it is perfectly legitimate for a newspaper to invade the privacy of an individual – in the public interest. The depressing fact is that for much of the time such intrusion takes place for prurient and sensationalist reasons rather than for more substantial ones.

A few weeks before the 1997 general election the Scottish tabloid, the *Sunday Mail*, ran a story which alleged that the only surviving Conservative MP in Glasgow was having an affair with a woman whom he had met at a clinic where he had been receiving treatment for alcohol-related problems – the same paper had told its readers about that aspect of the man's life a few weeks previously. As a direct consequence of the revelations about his alleged infidelity, the MP resigned his seat, and his constituency party was obliged to find an alternative candidate at breakneck speed. It is difficult to understand how an extramarital affair bears directly on an MP's capacity to do his job, nor is it clear whether it is anyone's business but that of the people directly involved. No doubt if the former MP had made a complaint to the PCC, the *Sunday Mail* would have claimed that it was justified in publishing the story by referring to the third definition of 'public interest' in the Code of Practice, and drawing attention to the way in which the Member concerned had presented himself to his electors as a respectable family man. But does this case not suggest that the clause is nothing more than an open gateway for any editor who wishes to print salacious material about public figures?

The Commission, it should be stressed, does not only deal with privacy, indeed almost 70 per cent of the complaints received relate to accuracy – over four times the number concerned with privacy. Among those considered in 1995 was one from a major department store, which claimed that articles in the *Mail on Sunday*, alleging that the store had purchased clothes from an Indian factory which employed child labour, were inaccurate. Claim and counterclaim were submitted as to the age of the young people involved, and the Commission finally decided that it was unable to adjudicate between these assertions, but it took the view that the paper had reasonable grounds for believing that the material in its possesssion was factually accurate. So the complaint was rejected. In another case, the manager of a hospital in Liverpool maintained that a report in the *Sunday Mirror* about a disturbance in the hospital was sensationalist and 'that no attempt was made to contact the hospital's public relations department prior to publication'.[168] In its adjudication the PCC did uphold the complaint and criticised the paper for exaggerating the event; however it rejected totally the idea that newspapers have an obligation to contact official sources before printing a story, if they have reliable sources of their own.

Success or failure?

Who then gains from the existence of the PCC? It might be argued that complainants, high and low, obtain some kind of justice, although it is always after the fact, and the personal damage may be irremediable. Future potential complainants might also be regarded as beneficiaries, if the PCC is judged to have brought about a significant change in the behaviour of the press, and such people do not find themselves unfairly treated, or having their private lives exposed for all to see. Politicians, queasy about the dangerous path they might have to go down, if the clamour for legislation were to arise again, may also have profited from the Commission's existence. Above all, newspapers and magazines are major beneficiaries, for if the PCC staves off further legislative intervention, then it must be deemed a success from their point of view. Whether the general public good, and the need for ongoing accountability are best served by such an uneasy satisfying of divergent – and arguably incompatible – interests is another matter. The PCC is the central plank of a defensive strategy. If it were to be widely perceived as such, and such alone, then its fragile legitimacy could well be undermined.

There is a further point: it will be recalled that the original Press Council, in common with many other such bodies elsewhere in the world, had as one of its objectives the safeguarding of press freedom as a fundamental part of democracy. Some press councils have been more active in this area than others, but in Britain, as a consequence of the crisis out of which the PCC emerged, there is now no public body charged with the duty of upholding and defending freedom. There is reference in the Commission's remit to the need to protect the press against improper pressure, but the primary function is to deal with complaints. That surely is a major limitation. Claude-Jean Bertrand, who has made a study of press councils world wide, argues that, on the one hand, such bodies have had a poor record for a number of reasons, including government intimidation in authoritarian states, the absence of media industry support and a lack of general consensus about their usefulness.[169] On the other hand, councils are highly desirable as part of media accountability systems and have a crucial role to play not only in improving the performance of the media but also in defending their freedom. Sadly the British Press Complaints Commission, because of the way in which it has been constituted – and to an extent because of the compromising and contaminating effect of the behaviour of some British newspapers – is unable to contribute as much as it should to that defence.

Remoulding Public Service Broadcasting: the Challenge to the BBC | 10

In chapter 8 there was a brief discussion of the way in which the various participants involved in the process which produced the 1986 Peacock Report and the subsequent 1990 Broadcasting Act interacted with each other, as important modifications were made to the British broadcasting system. That system has been referred to several times in the course of the book as an exemplar of the public service model. In this chapter there will be an examination of the way in which that model came under continuing pressure in the 1990s, and an evaluation of its health – or the lack of it – as the end of the century approaches.

Public service broadcasting

There have been several defining moments in the evolution of broadcasting in the UK, most obviously the establishment of the British Broadcasting Company in 1922 as a non-profit-making organization financed by taxation, and charged with the duty of providing 'information, education and entertainment'. The introduction of commercial television in the mid 1950s – with exactly the same wide-ranging remit – was another, as was the establishment in the early 1980s of Channel Four, an advertising-financed, state-sponsored corporation which was required to provide an innovative programming service distinct from the existing ones. Each of these developments was based on an overall philosophy of broadcasting which, although it had changed over the years, and had moved from a position of rather superior certainty to one which acknowledged the increasing pluralism of British society, retained at its core the belief that radio and television have specific civic functions and are not simply ways of selling programming or commodities to the public.[170] The defining moments of the 1980s and 1990s – the Peacock Report, the 1990 Act, the 1994 White Paper on the future of the BBC – displayed no such homogenous certainty, indeed taken together they showed that a full scale ideological battle was underway, the final outcome of which could not easily have been predicted.

The British have, perhaps rather complacently, tended to regard public service broadcasting (PSB) as one of their most significant inventions, and indeed it can be argued that the most important cultural achievement of the United Kingdom in the twentieth century is not any particular school of composers or group of novelists, but the model of broadcasting which has evolved in the country, and the programming output which it has generated. PSB is actually as much a European invention as a British one, but the conflagrations which overwhelmed mainland Europe in the interwar period and during the Second World War itself, ensured that by 1945 the BBC was the supreme public service broadcaster, with imitators perhaps, most obviously in the Dominions of Canada and Australia, but no serious rivals in terms of output and prestige.[171] The expansion of the system thereafter, although it meant the end of the Corporation's monopoly, did nothing to dent the standing of Britain's radio and television domestically and internationally, at a time when the country itself was suffering a serious diminution of power in the political and economic spheres.

As was noted in chapter 2, the basic aim of PSB is to inform and enrich the listener and viewer. For this to happen certain conditions need to be met. In the first place, there must be a secure method of finance; secondly, there must be strong broadcasting organizations, which are free from government interference in programming and output; thirdly, there must be a commitment to universal coverage; and fourthly, regulation of the system as a whole must be designed to encourage broadcasters to take risks both culturally and politically.[172] Where any of these factors are not present, or are in some way weakened, then it becomes more difficult to sustain PSB. So, if, for example, broadcasters can no longer rely on a secure income, they are less inclined to schedule difficult material, or if they find themselves part of a system in which overall regulation has loosened, and in which there has ceased to be an overriding expectation that all of its component parts will seek to offer demanding programming, then again they may move away from a PSB orientation.

The challenge to PSB

The challenge to the British system, which at one point appeared to threaten the very idea of public service broadcasting in the country, can be attributed to a number of factors which were at work from the 1980s on. Most importantly, there was the overall political climate of the times, in which, as a reaction against the collectivist approach of the postwar era, there was renewed emphasis on the ability of markets to satisfy human needs. In the UK the assault on collectivist solutions had its most effective champion in Margaret Thatcher, whose governments succeeded in affecting a major ideological shift. Cynical observers might suggest that if an electorate is offered tax cuts and windfall profits from underpriced shares in denationalized industries, it is hardly surprising if that electorate appears more enthusiastic about free, rather than regulated, markets. But the change went deeper, as the approach of the Labour opposition to the 1997 election demonstrated very clearly: that party emphasized that it had no intention of going back to the 'old discredited' collectivist approach, but would retain what it considered to be the best features of Thatcherism, in particular the idea that individuals should be entitled to make the most of the economic opportunities which come their way and should not be faced by high rates of direct taxation.

Thatcherism at its zenith coincided with the collapse of communism. The achievements of Mikhail Gorbachev in dismantling the repressive apparatus of an authoritarian state and in surrendering the Soviet Union's European colonies to their inhabitants represent the most astounding political revolution of the last twenty years, only to be compared, if at all, with the abandonment of apartheid by the South African government. However one unintended side effect of what Gorbachev did was to add further legitimation to the neo-liberal approach to economics espoused by the American and British governments in power at the time. Once again collectivist solutions had been shown to lead to disaster; the way forward was to trust to the market.

Proponents of tight regulation of broadcasting have historically bolstered their case by utilizing the scarcity argument: there simply is not enough room in the electromagnetic spectrum for all comers. But the development of cable and satellite methods of delivering signals has undermined that position to a considerable degree. Furthermore, the willingness of commercial organizations to invest the necessary capital in order to make cable and satellite available to customers has strengthened the argument that PSB, whatever its merits, is rather backward, even inept, at exploiting new opportunities, an argument which was pointed up dramatically in the mid eighties when the BBC had to write off 11 million pounds after an ill-starred attempt to enter the satellite market.

As was explained in chapter 9, the first major challenge to PSB in Britain was the establishment of the Peacock Committee in 1985. Although the committee's report did not immediately provide a solution to the supposed problem posed by the continuation of the compulsory BBC licence fee, and the interference with the proper operation of market forces which such a tax allegedly represented, it did prepare the ground for an assault in due course. Peacock, it will be recalled, led in the short term to the auctioning of ITV franchises to the highest bidder and the separation of Channel Four from ITV, with the former selling advertising space directly for the first time. As was noted earlier, throughout the public debate about the impact of the proposed new system of allocating ITV franchises, the BBC kept its head down, apparently in the belief that this would secure the goodwill of the government: the Corporation's own turn was coming, for the Royal Charter under which it operated was due for renewal at the end of 1996.

For the Peacock Committee the licence fee was an antiquated mechanism which distorted the relationship which ought to exist in 'a sophisticated market system based on consumer sovereignty'.[173] The way round this difficulty was to fit into the back of every television set in the land a special socket which would enable viewers to be charged if they used BBC services. The committee did acknowledge that in the true broadcasting market which was the ultimate objective, certain kind of programmes of limited appeal, but of worth and quality, might not be made, and conceded that a special fund would have to be established to finance such work, but that realization did not deflect it from its general course. In the late 1980s it was commonly assumed that in the face of the Peacock approach, which had been endorsed by the government, the BBC would have an enormous fight on its hands if it wished to retain licence-fee funding.

What future for the BBC?

When the government published its consultation paper on the future of the Corporation in late 1992, the context had changed markedly. Mrs Thatcher had been deposed in 1990 by her own party, and her successor, John Major, had gone on to win the general election in April 1992, but with a substantially reduced majority. Mrs Thatcher had personally been very hostile towards the BBC, and her attitude appeared to derive from the perception that the Corporation was one of the few state organizations which her government had not succeeded in privatizing and, perhaps more importantly, despite some trimming under pressure, it remained committed to a consensual model of debate and argument with which she had little patience. That the overall mood had altered radically with her departure became very clear in January 1991 when during the Gulf War a Conservative backbencher rose in the House of Commons and invited the Prime Minister to join with him in condemning the 'unpatriotic' way in which the BBC was reporting the conflict. Mr Major declined to do so, and went on to praise the Corporation's journalism.

The Green Paper which appeared almost two years later reflected the alteration in the political climate. Those within the BBC who would wish to defend the failure to come to the aid of the ITV companies in their time of trial might well claim that the tone of the Green Paper justified the approach which the Corporation had taken then. A more realistic judgement would be that the departure of Mrs Thatcher from the scene, and the weak position in which the new government found itself, with a small majority and low credibility following Britain's ejection from the European Exchange Rate Mechanism in the autumn of 1992, were the crucial factors: John Major was temperamentally not inclined to pursue the BBC in the way that his predecessor had done, and the difficult situation of his administration throughout its entire term of office meant that confrontations with powerful groupings in society were only undertaken in exceptional circumstances.

'The Future of the BBC' – which is illustrated throughout by pictures of green cloud banks – reads like a genuine consultation document, and asks would-be respondents to consider a range of questions, including what the aims of PSB in general should be, what kind of services the BBC ought to provide, how its services should be paid for, how it could be made more efficient, whether it should seek to exploit the growing commercial opportunities available to it worldwide, and how it might be made more accountable.[174] Some of these issues are perennial, and are introduced in a tone which suggests that the traditional paternalist wing of the Conservative Party was in the ascendant in the Department of National Heritage, but others reflect the spirit of the Thatcher era, though in a form which has been mediated by John Major's style. The Corporation for its part had to some extent anticipated this approach – indeed a more Thatcherite approach – by developing its commercial activities, engaging in sustained efficiency drives, and by implementing a new system of resource allocation known as Producer Choice.

This was designed by John Birt, who had been appointed Deputy Director General in 1987, and became Director General in 1993. Birt rightly made much of the fact that many producers apparently had only a hazy idea of what their programmes actually cost, and in order to bring about transparency, and to encourage efficiency, he restructured the Corporation into business units, which would buy services as they needed them, either from within the BBC itself or from outside suppliers. Business units which failed to generate enough work faced the prospect of closure. The implementation of this system caused a great deal of confusion and excited much ridicule, but it did have the effect of apparently freeing more money for programming and, equally importantly, impressing the Corporation's political master, which praised this and other related initiatives in the Green Paper. Crucially for the BBC, the government had also become unenthusiastic about the possibility of utilizing subscription as a method of finance. As part of its defensive response to the Thatcher administration's endorsement of subscription, the Corporation had engaged in some modest experiments in the night-time hours, such as specialist programming aimed at the medical profession. The Green Paper notes the commercial failure of these ventures, and comments about subscription generally – 'if programmes or services were encrypted to ensure payment of the subscription, this would discourage people from sampling a wide range of programmes and could reduce the availability of programmes for those less able to pay.'[175]

The Corporation makes its case

The BBC was now able to exploit the much more sympathetic atmosphere in which it was having to present its case. A mere two days after the Green Paper appeared, the Corporation produced 'Extending choice – the BBC's role in the new broadcasting age',[176] in which it argued that, as the only publicly funded broadcaster in the land, its overriding purpose would be to 'extend choice for viewers and listeners by guaranteeing access for everyone in the country to programme services that are of unusually high quality and that are, or might be, at risk in a purely commercial market'.[177] This formulation of the Corporation's principal objective was accompanied however by the rather dangerous suggestions that the BBC's audience share might decline sharply in the face of competition from satellite and cable – one estimate which it gave suggested that the Corporation's television channels would be fortunate to secure a 30 per cent share after the year 2000 – and that the future might lie in providing an up-market service for discerning citizens. Sustaining such a position on a compulsory tax base would be a very hazardous endeavour, and the idea was quickly dropped; in any event the pessimism from which it stemmed has been shown to be unnecessary, since the new services have tended to erode the share, not of the BBC, but of ITV.

'Extending Choice' also discusses the need to improve accountability and to listen to what the audience has to say about what is being broadcast, again reflecting one of the government's preoccupations. Throughout the next twelve months the Corporation organized many public meetings, commissioned research into public attitudes and generally argued the case for its continued existence in its new efficient, accountable form. Various additional publications flowed from it, including one on its accountability mechanisms, and one which took the form of a report by McKinsey management consultants on the situation of public broadcasters around the world.[178] The latter document paints a rather bleak picture of struggle in inhospitable climes, and concludes that the licence fee method of finance is the least bad of the options available, although the report is much more circumspect on what the optimum regulatory approach might be. In its considered response to the Green Paper, which it published at the end of this period of public consultation, the BBC returned to the distinctiveness of what it had to offer, and argued that its own research and public meetings had shown that the citizens of the country supported the continuation of the Corporation, although 'they also believe that the BBC can and should do better in pursuing the objectives of publicly funded broadcasting'.[179] What was being referred to here was the view which came through opinion surveys and meetings that the representation of the life of the different regions of the country on the airwaves was inadequate, and that letters and complaints from individuals were not very well dealt with. However, bolstered by poll findings to the effect that almost two thirds of those asked felt that the licence fee was reasonable value for money, the Corporation was by now unequivocal on the issue:

> Only licence fee funding can preserve the BBC's ability to pursue public service objectives as the highest priorities in programme making and scheduling, the freedom from commercial pressures to maximise audience ratings and share, and independence from direct government or party political influence.[180]

The tone of the document as a whole is far more self-confident than the one adopted by the Corporation in the wake of the Peacock Report eight years previously. As has been noted, there are several reasons for this, including the change in the political climate, the weak position of the government, and the changes within the BBC itself which had met with government approval. The Corporation had also lobbied hard in influential circles, and had been able to exploit the general feeling that the Thatcher government had made a mess of its attempts at restructuring broadcasting. The highest bidder system of auctioning the ITV franchises could not be defended as rational or even very beneficial to the Treasury, for, as was explained in chapter 8, although some successful companies had bid large sums as annual payments for the right to broadcast, two, shrewdly guessing they would be the sole contenders in their areas, offered only a few thousand pounds, and in effect obtained access to the airwaves for nothing. As was noted in chapter 3, even the reconstitution of Channel Four on an independent basis had turned out badly, since the fall-back mechanism designed to protect its revenue base had, as a consequence of success in the marketplace, been transformed into a device whereby the innovative station found itself subsidising mainstream ITV.[181]

In the post-Peacock period a Thatcherite approach to the reform of the 'comfortable duopoly' of broadcasting had been enthusiastically supported by some sections of the press, in particular the titles owned by Rupert Murdoch, whose satellite service stood to gain from the weakening of the terrestrial channels. Murdoch's titles had not all suddenly been converted to the virtues of a strong BBC – though in a leading article, after the government's final proposals were published, *The Times* did accept that the Birt reforms had made the continuation of the Corporation a certainty – but they were no longer in tune with the tide that was running in Major's cautious government.[182] Furthermore, the criticism and abuse which the prime minister had endured after Britain's exit from the European Exchange Rate Mechanism had ensured that press/government relations were strained throughout his period of office, and certainly not conducive to special favours being offered to Murdoch, as had happened when Sky was allowed to establish itself in the late 1980s without any public service obligations.

The government announced its proposals for the renewal of the BBC's charter in July of 1994. Although it was clear from the first paragraph that the continued existence of the Corporation was not in doubt, the subtitle of the document – 'Serving the nation Competing world-wide' – gave a clear indication that the BBC of the future would be rather different from the one which had existed until then.[183] The role of the Corporation as the country's principal public service broadcaster, offering 'a wide range of radio and television programmes for people with different tastes and interests and of all ages' was reaffirmed, as was its task 'of reflecting the interests and cultural traditions of the United Kingdom as a whole', and its importance as 'a major patron of music, drama, and other entertainment, so encouraging the living arts to flourish for the enjoyment of present and future generations'.[184] Thus far what was being said seemed fairly traditional, although the reference to 'the United Kingdom as a whole' acknowledged by implication that the Britain of the 1990s had been moving towards a more regionally diverse and multicultural entity than had been the case in the recent past. However when the White Paper turned to the commercial aspects of the Corporation's activities, there was marked enthusiasm not only for traditional programme exports but also for the development of new cable and satellite services and joint ventures around the world, always provided that there were no hidden subsidies from the licence fee. That, it was confirmed, would remain the principal source of finance – at least until the turn of the century. The government also indicated that it favoured privatization of the BBC's transmission system, the proceeds from which could help the Corporation to launch digital services; thus what might have appeared a harking back to Thatcherite dogma was made to seem an intelligent way of finding new resources. It also welcomed the new accountability mechanisms which had been put in place. But it showed little enthusiasm for abandoning its own right to select BBC governors according to its preferences, a practice which many observers felt required some democratization.[185]

Beyond charter renewal

The outcome of the Charter Review process was much more positive from the PSB point of view than might have been anticipated a few years previously. However, it is noticeable that the prospect of a full broadcasting market, offering an extraordinary range of choice to viewers and listeners, as originally envisaged by the Peacock Committee, continued to resonate. In the early eighties cable had seemed like the answer to the problem of spectrum scarcity; then it was satellite. Now it was digital encoding and compression of signals, which would then be transmitted both terrestrially and by satellite. Throughout all discussion of the expanding broadcasting universe remarkably little attention has been given to possible limits to the size of the pool of potential broadcasting talent in the country. The White Paper was no exception in this regard.

There was a clear financial motive behind the British government's enthusiasm for digital broadcasting, which was seen as having the potential to both boost exports and supplement the licence fee. There was also the hope that as a result of these activities 'there ... (would be) ... programmes and services bringing a distinctively United Kingdom voice outlook and culture into the world market, with an emphasis on accurate and impartial news and high quality programmes'.[186] What is worth remarking on here is the coupling of the financial and the cultural, which exhibits a much more European inflection than had been obvious in the same administration's contribution to the debate during the 1993 GATT treaty negotiations over protection measures. The United States condemned these as barriers to free trade, and demanded that they be removed. At that time the United Kingdom was very unsupportive of its European partners as, with France in the lead, they fought – successfully in the short term – to secure exemption from the treaty for film and television support policies.

It will be recalled that in the Green Paper of 1992 the government had asked what exactly the aims of public service broadcasting should be, and indeed what was distinctive about it. Perhaps there was disappointment in Whitehall about the quality of the responses, for the White Paper does not deal directly with this issue, although the government's own view can be discerned behind the objectives being set for the Corporation in that document, and in the new Royal Charter which then emerged.[187] What is not at all clear however is whether the government, or indeed the BBC, had thought through the implications of combining a traditional public service role with a new role as in effect a commercial broadcaster competing with other such operators in the marketplace. It is one thing for a publicly owned body to demonstrate that it is using tax-payers' money responsibly; it is quite another to behave as if it were a private company seeking to maximize revenue by supplying consumers with goods and services they can be persuaded to purchase. It is an unusual development to have an organization restructured on a dual basis, with both government and the organization itself insisting that it is able to hermetically seal the activities of each part from the other.

Throughout subsequent discussion of its likely commercial ventures, particularly those paid-for digital services which it is developing in cooperation with private partners, the BBC has not only insisted that there will be no cross-subsidization, but also given the impression that licence fee payers will not find themselves deprived of original programming available only to those who are prepared to pay for it. When pressed on this issue, BBC executives have tended to fall back on the archive/themed channel argument, and to declare that viewers will be only too happy to pay for a documentary or comedy channel which uses old programming rather than original work. Given that the expansion of transmission hours on the existing terrestrial networks has meant that repeats are not uncommon at the moment, it is very hard to see how customers, in Britain at least, will be persuaded to pay for new channels, unless they are being offered something which is simply not available to other viewers. This after all is the attraction of BSkyB's satellite services – recently released films not yet in the video stores, and relays of sporting events, which have been signed up in exclusive contracts, are accessible only to subscribers, not to the general public.

The BBC's digital commitment, which had become much firmer in the period between the Green Paper's appearance and the publication of the White Paper, clearly appealed to the government, but it may well be a Trojan Horse which leads to other difficulties. It is hardly surprising that the major UK broadcaster would seek to be at the centre of any new development in technology and programming, if only to sustain its own position. However if cash is invested in paid-for digital services – terrestrial and/or satellite – in which viewers show little interest, then the Corporation will be accused of squandering public money, even although much of the investment has come from the proceeds of the sale of its own transmitter network to a private company in 1997, in line with the Major administration's wishes. If, however, these services enjoy even modest success, there could be renewed pressure on the continuation of the licence fee as the main source of finance. The BBC might claim that only a small percentage of its income will ever derive from profits from commercial ventures, but an unsympathetic government could easily insist that the proportion should be increased, and the licence fee curtailed.

A much more stable future would be in prospect if that fee, which has been frozen in real terms for some years, were to be significantly augmented, in order to ensure that the Corporation's income keeps up with those of its principal competitors, one of which seems able to extract from its customers three times the cost of the licence, despite the fact that these same customers still spend significantly more time watching BBC services than they do the services offered by BSkyB.[188] During the late 1980s and early 1990s the Corporation's senior executives shrank from any suggestion that they should argue for an 'inflation plus' increase in the licence fee, but in the mid-nineties, they became a little bolder and were heard to talk in public about the desirability of a £100 figure, which at that time would have represented an augmentation in real terms of about 10 per cent.

As the commitment to digital appealed to the Corporation's then political masters, so did the measures taken to increase efficiency, particularly Producer Choice. It was very clear to any observer of senior BBC managers in the early nineties that they believed passionately that if they did not demonstrate a continued enthusiasm for efficiency savings and staffing reductions, then this would be held against them in the run-up to Charter Renewal. It did seem at times as if they had not fully grasped that, with the advent of the Major government, there had been a significant change in tone, and, in addition, it was highly unlikely that the Conservatives would win a fifth term. So, while it may have been eminently sensible for the then Director General, Michael Checkland, to talk in the late 1980s of the BBC as 'a billion pound business', perhaps that moment had passed by the early nineties, and another more public service oriented discourse would have been appropriate. Furthermore, the zeal for cost cutting and reorganization did appear to have acquired a life of its own, or at the very least to have produced a 'change overload' situation.

It has to be acknowledged, nonetheless, that some of the critics of John Birt's regime have had rather mixed motives, and some have been unwilling to acknowledge that the Corporation under his management may not be the happiest of organizations, but it is still in business, and its relative market share has gone up, so that in mid 1997 its two channels attracted over 40 per cent of all viewing, in the face of competition from three other terrestrial channels as well as satellite and cable operations. It remains the dominant radio broadcaster, with five national services, five regional and forty local ones securing just under half of all listening in the country, despite the existence of around two hundred commercial stations, most of these regional and local, but three of them national.[189] The BBC won its battle to survive and it did so, principally by making it extremely difficult for the politicians with whom it was dealing to level the kind of charges against it which they would have been most likely to bring. The question that will continue to be asked is whether the price that was paid is greater than was necessary, and so high that there could be substantial damage to the long-term health of the Corporation and PSB as a whole in Britain.[190]

The role of the public

The principal actors in this drama were the BBC itself and the then Conservative government. Other politicians played a part, as did the civil servants involved in the long series of negotiations which took place between the BBC and the Department of National Heritage throughout the Charter Renewal process. The public figured significantly in the Corporation's documentation and arguments, but it remained largely a spectator, although a range of submissions was made to the government by bodies such as consumer councils, trade unions and church groups. There was also on the scene an organization known as The Voice of the Listener and Viewer (VLV), which had originally been a pressure group concerned exclusively with radio, and rather narrow in approach. However during the early nineties it had transformed itself into a body rather like the Friends of Canadian Broadcasting. VLV argued forcefully for the continuation of the BBC in its traditional form, but whether it, with its rather small self-selecting membership, or other similar bodies, could be considered to fully represent the public is debatable. Nonetheless the situation was rather different from the post-Peacock one when ITV companies found themselves alone in their dispute with the government. But a public which is used by a media organization to advance that organization's case and barely represented in its own right, is hardly a major actor, and no number of top-down consultative initiatives can disguise that fact. Several proposals were made during the post-Green Paper debate as to how accountability might be improved, but neither the government nor the BBC seemed very interested in substantial changes in the methods of appointment of governors or advisory boards, or in the procedures whereby the public are asked for their opinions, although both accepted that it was desirable that consultation should be a regular feature of the BBC's *modus operandi* in the future. The hour of the Citizens' Media Council has yet to come, but in a country in which radical constitutional change began in 1997, it is difficult to believe that it is an idea which will simply disappear. Indeed early in 1998 the new government signalled an important change of tack, when it announced that it intended to advertise vacant governorships, and to seek to recruit candidates from a much wider range of backgrounds than has traditionally been the case.

The British tradition in broadcasting has always emphasized the importance of having a well-trained profession at its heart; although there has been an increased commitment to access programming in recent years, that emphasis remains. If greater bottom-up account-ability were to be introduced, then it is likely that such a change would be accompanied not only by pressure for the transmission of more access/community material, but also by a far more deter-mined questioning of the professional/non-professional distinction than has hitherto been the case. It is therefore a matter of regret that the opportunity was lost in the Charter Renewal process to initiate a debate, which is bound to be long and complex, but could well lead to the creation of a much more pluralistic PSB system than has existed so far.

And now . . .

As to the 1996 settlement, it has to be said that although the BBC has a charter which will last until 2006, the impending discussion about the licence fee could well destabilize that settlement. The new Labour government indicated at an early stage that it was inclined to be sympathetic to the traditional view of PSB – indeed the rele-vant minister suggested that the Corporation needed to take more risks with adventurous programming than, in his opinion, it had been doing – and it is highly unlikely that it will seriously pursue the total abolition of the licence fee. Furthermore, it moved quickly to announce a timetable for the ending of Channel Four's payments to ITV, and stipulated that the cash released must be invested in original British and European programming.[191] However it will be obliged to deal with the tensions generated by the two-in-one restructuring of the BBC and the success or failure of the 'digital revolution'. Observers of a decade of turmoil can only hope that whatever politicians are in charge they will remember that in the final analysis it is the programmes, and only the programmes, which matter; unending organizational upheaval, interminable debate about funding, or the basic purposes of the Corporation, are distractions from the only real justification for the existence of the BBC – the production of what comes out of the cathode ray tube and the loudspeaker.

Intervention in the Newspaper Marketplace | 11

The problem of the market

It will be recalled from chapter 5 that in the development of the libertarian theory a strong link was established between freedom of the press from government interference and private ownership. This link was seen as crucial to the proper functioning of newspapers as sources of information and comment. The problem which has arisen in the intervening period is that increasing concentration has led to the situation where the press in most countries is controlled by relatively few large companies which often have interests in other media and non-media concerns. It has thus become very difficult for new competing titles to emerge. Furthermore, there is a marked tendency for newspapers to lean towards a right wing pro-business point of view, and in some countries to engage in straightforward political propaganda. Concentration of ownership, lack of diversity and shameless distortion of news are deemed by many commentators to be the central failures of the press. The solution to these deficiencies has frequently been deemed to be some kind of regulatory or financial intervention by government in order to promote the kind of genuine pluralism of ideas that so many of the early proponents of the libertarian theory argued was both necessary and desirable.

The North American experience

The United States is often cited as the country most committed to the operation of market forces, subject only to general public interest and anti-monopoly regulation. Over time, with the growth of the electronic media, the newspaper market in the USA has contracted, and as a consequence of that, fewer and fewer areas are served by more than one title. It should however be remembered that although this is a continuing trend, the availability across the country of papers such as the *New York Times* and the *Wall Street Journal* now means that locally based monopolists find themselves facing competition from much better resourced quasi-national titles – *USA Today* has taken that process to its logical conclusion, and offers itself as a mid-market national daily, the news in which is presented in such a way as to emphasize that the paper is not attached to any one part of the country. The *Globe and Mail* now seeks to perform a similar role north of the forty-ninth parallel, and has turned itself into Canada's national up-market title.

The growth of local and regional monopolists has caused concern in the USA, and, as was noted in chapter 5, it is one of the reasons for the development of the Social Responsibility Theory of the press, which emphasizes the need for newspapers to open their columns to a variety of opinions, rather than restricting themselves to the views deemed most congenial by editors or proprietors.[192] But while it is true to say that many American papers do behave to an extent in line with this theory, the theory itself has no legal force, and there is nothing in the normal operation of the economic system to give it any clout. Media businesses are subject to anti-trust law, which is designed to deal with anti-competitive behaviour, and that legislation has been used to prevent single companies dominating entire local media markets, but it has not been very effective in halting the growth of conglomerates, or in sustaining inter-newspaper competition.

Paradoxically, it was the initiation of a test case anti-trust suit by the Justice Department of the United States government in 1965 which led to the Newspaper Preservation Act, a law which is designed to counter forces which work against pluralism. In 1940 two newspapers in Arizona had merged their business operations, while keeping their journalistic endeavours separate, the overall objective supposedly being to sustain the weaker title, which might otherwise have disappeared. The Justice Department was not persuaded by the arguments advanced by the two companies involved, nor was the Supreme Court, where the case was finally resolved. Justice William O. Douglas was very clear in his summary of the Court's view – 'The First Amendment affords not the slightest support for the contention that a combination to restrain trade in news and views has any constitutional immunity'.[193] Shortly after this judgment was delivered, discussions began in Congress, and there then emerged the Newspaper Preservation Act (NPA), under which in certain circumstances competing titles are allowed to enter into Joint Operating Agreements, if there is a danger that otherwise one of the titles might cease to function. The papers concerned are required to keep editorial operations separate, but other departments may be merged. Such agreements have to be approved by the Justice Department, and the overall objective is stated in the Act to be the pursuit of 'the public interest of maintaining a newspaper press editorially and reportorially (sic) independent and competitive in all parts of the United States'.[194]

Several commentators on the process whereby this Act came into being, and on its operation, have been less than enthusiastic. William Borden in a study which compares Swedish and American interventionist policies, argues that the NPA, under the provisions of which there were in the mid 1990s seventeen Joint Operating Agreements (JOAs), has simply led to government financial favours being offered to companies, many of which have never made a credible case for them:

> The public benefit of the NPA was supposed to be diversity. No one has been able to show that JOAs truly provide different views on political issues, particularly local issues where the JOA has a common economic interest. There is no economic incentive for one JOA newspaper to improve its news coverage to outcompete its partner because both share a fixed percentage of the profits. Most of the JOA newspapers are part of large profitable chains. JOA newspapers have neither shown their readers nor the American public that the newspapers need the anti-trust exemption for economic survival.[195]

Busterna and Picard in an analysis of the impact of the NPA have argued, like Borden, that as far as editorial content is concerned the objective of ensuring diversity has not been achieved, and indeed, in their view, may be unattainable, since on present form the general political environment in the USA favours a centrist approach, so 'newspapers will be motivated to provide content that does not upset the current single mass of people in the middle'.[196]

There is no equivalent legislation in Canada, indeed the Canadian experience is one in which, despite much criticism of the process in both official and academic publications, concentration of ownership has proceeded to a remarkable degree, and the number of regions with competing newsapers has continued to decline.[197]

The European experience

To the European observer the Newspaper Preservation Act might well seem to have led to an imperfect system of intervention, and American criticism of it might be construed as stemming from a misguided belief that all interference with the operation of the market beyond anti-cartel measures, is fundamentally undesirable. For Europeans the fact that newspapers are for the most part privately owned is undeniable, but such ownership is not necessarily regarded as absolutely essential; however providing the citizen with the intellectual and informational capital necessary for the proper functioning of democracy is. Intervention in the market on the European mainland would appear to be as natural as it is unnatural on the other side of the Atlantic. A remarkable array of support mechanisms is in place, and all are usually justified by reference to the principle just enunciated, and additional principles related to such things as the need for minorities to be properly served by the media. Indirect support is provided through special postal and transportation charges, telecommunications concessions, and partial or complete exemption from certain taxes; direct aid can include general subsidies, specific targeted subsidies, capital investment loans and support for training schemes.[198] Most Western European countries, with the exception of the UK, which confines itself to postal concessions and exemption from Value Added Tax, employ some or all of these measures. Austria, for example, has both general and selective subsidies, the Netherlands uses some of the proceeds of a tax on television advertising to recompense newspapers for the loss of revenue such advertising represents, while France offers selective subsidies to both national and regional titles. The countries with the most highly developed systems of subsidy are Norway and Sweden.

Norwegians are the world's most avid consumers of newspapers, in a country where the press is organized on a regional and local, rather than on a national, basis.[199] The system of subsidy dates from 1969 and arose as a response to a situation in which the number of papers was declining and, equally importantly, the number of areas of the country where there was more than one newspaper in competition was decreasing even more sharply. Subsidies were originally designed in order to sustain weaker titles which found themselves being squeezed by stronger competitors for both sales and advertising revenue. Their introduction was supported by all of Norway's political parties, with the exception of the Conservatives, who have continued to argue that they represent an interference with the proper operation of the market, and are open to abuse by politicians seeking favourable coverage of their activities. The system has been modified over the years, and in the mid nineties it covered not only the 'number two' regional titles, but also local papers, papers directed at ethnic minorities and titles aimed at various political and social groups; in 1995 the total amount of cash allocated to the scheme was over 20 million pounds.[200]

If the success of the system is to be judged by the number of regions of Norway in which there are still competing titles to be found, then it has to be said that subsidy may have slowed the pace of contraction, but it has not reversed it; however it does seem to have led to an increase in small local papers and titles aimed at various minorities within society, so much so that supporters of the Norwegian approach are now inclined to use the cultural diversity argument, as much as the diversity of political opinion one. It is clear that some publications now depend on state support for their very survival, and have not been able to use it to improve their basic financial position; the question that must therefore be asked is whether subsidy can lead to the preservation of titles which have reached the end of their natural life, and can over-cushion papers from the bracing effects of competition either from other titles or from alternative media, which have expanded in Norway as elsewhere. Furthermore, as in the USA, where the Newspaper Preservation Act has done nothing to halt a trend towards greater concentration of ownership, the Norwegian system has been of little avail on this front either, indeed some conglomerate owners have done rather well out of it.

The Swedish experience is similar. Like Norway, it is a country where readership is high, and the local/regional press is strong. The number of communities with two newspapers declined from fifty-one in 1945 to twenty-three in 1965, and in order to counteract this tendency, and the presumed threat to pluralism, subsidies were introduced. Initially these took the form of payments to political parties, which were then at liberty to pass them on to titles with which they were affiliated. In 1971 a Press Subsidies Act became law, and since that time part of the proceeds of a general tax on advertising has been rcycled to papers which find themselves in a weak financial position, but are otherwise deemed to be important to the proper operation of democracy. Paradoxically, one long-term effect of the system has been to loosen the ties between newspapers and parties: since 1971 subsidy has come through an independent Press Support Board, rather than through the political parties themselves, and this has encouraged editors and journalists to assert their independence, and to develop a less partisan approach.

In 1995 the Swedish government spent over 30 million pounds in direct subsidies. Such a sum is substantial enough to lead to the system being questioned, particularly by those politicians on the right who have never been sympathetic to it, and the changes of government in Sweden in the nineties posed a threat to the continuation of public subvention.[201] Yet despite the fact that, as in Norway, the most that can be demonstrated is that decline has been arrested rather than eliminated, even sceptical observers such as Borden are forced to conclude that there remain strong arguments for subsidy:

> The great advantage of newspapers compared with the electronic media is that they provide comprehensive coverage of civic, particularly local, issues. Although broadcasters occasionally provide in depth coverage such as election debates, newspapers on a day to day basis provide far more civic information than do the electronic media ... It is important to keep in mind that the grants are paid for by an advertising tax targeted to pay for the subsidies. As newspapers continue to pay taxes on their advertising revenue, it is reasonable that the money be used for the newspapers' economic benefits. [202]

The British experience

The most cursory examination of academic literature on the British media will throw up numerous discussions of the current condition of the newspaper press in which the perceived political imbalance is deplored. The argument which is put constantly is that this imbalance damages fundamentally the democratic system, by making it more difficult for citizens to be properly informed about what is happening in their society, and to gain access to a range of political perspectives. The apparent enthusiasm for the election of a Labour government in 1997 in some rather surprising quarters is unlikely to undermine the consensual view in academic circles that there is an inbuilt bias to the right in the London-based press, a bias which has been exacerbated over the years by increasing concentration of ownership. This is not a new problem, nor are the analyses new either, for they have been offered by commentators inside and outside of universities fairly constantly since the war. Policy in

the ownership field has to some extent taken account of these concerns, since, as was noted earlier in this book, special conditions
have been imposed under Monopolies and Mergers legislation on
the acquisition of newspapers. However the vast majority of proposed mergers and takeovers have been given the go-ahead, either
after a Monopolies and Mergers Commission investigation, or by
the relevant government minister utilizing opt-out clauses in the
law to sanction takeover without reference to the Commission. The
most notorious use of the latter procedure was the approval given
by the then Trade Secretary, John Biffen, to News Corporation in
1981 to acquire *The Times* and the *Sunday Times* on the highly questionable grounds that if they were not taken over, they would both
go out of business. Legislation introduced in 1996 was designed to
limit cross-media ownership, and may be more effective in securing its objectives, since it contains a number of clear prohibitions,
which mean, for example, that companies which own over 20 per
cent of the national newspaper market by circulation are debarred
from acquiring a terrestrial broadcaster.[203] However the problem of
concentration within the newspaper industry remains, as does the
concomitant difficulty posed for would-be new entrants, which are
obliged to contend with the enormous power of the existing companies in attracting both sales and advertising, without both of
which no title can survive.

Over twenty years previously, in 1974, the newly elected Labour
government had set up a Royal Commission on the Press which was
charged, among other things, with considering 'the distribution and
concentration of ownership of the newspaper and periodical industry, and the adequacy of existing law in relation thereto.'[204] The Commission was chaired by the then Professor Oliver McGregor, who, it
will be recalled, was later to become the first chairman of the Press
Complaints Commission. It reported in 1977, and although it suggested a toughening up of the monopolies legislation, it turned its
back on more radical schemes. It did spend time and money inves-
tigating intervention mechanisms utilized in Europe, particularly
the Swedish ones, but could not see their relevance to Britain:

> We are sure that there would be no consensus among the public and
> the political parties in this country about the desirability of main-
> taining all loss-making national newspapers or about which should
> be preserved by public subsidies. Indeed, some of our nine national
> newspapers could close and still leave greater choice to readers than
> that enjoyed by any town in Sweden. Even if the Swedish scheme is

successful in terms of its own objectives, British circumstances are so dissimilar that it cannot serve as an exemplar to us.[205]

What is striking here is the leap from the perfectly reasonable point about the differences in the structures of the British and Swedish markets to the much more contentious one that even the principle of subsidy, which had been widely accepted throughout Western Europe by the mid seventies, had no relevance at all to the UK situation.

The Commission also spent some time debating various home-grown proposals, such as a launch fund, postal subsidies for periodicals and assistance with distribution costs, but it did not commend any of them:

> there may be circumstances in which market forces threaten the proper fulfilment of the social and political functions of the press. Nevertheless we have rejected all the proposals for Government assistance which have been put to us . . . the principal ground on which we have rejected a number of the most ambitious schemes is that they would not achieve the aims of their authors . . . Without making it easier to launch new national newspapers, they would imperil the existing number of national newspapers.[206]

Two members of the commission dissented from this view and argued for the establishment of a national printing corporation and a launch fund, both of which were designed to facilitate new entrants. The government however concurred with the majority position.

The Royal Commission was heavily criticised for its approach, and for its view that state involvement could easily lead to state censorship of publications. Among its most severe critics was James Curran who, in a collection of essays published a year after the Commission reported, condemned its failure to examine the truth of this proposition on the ground in countries which actually had subsidy and intervention schemes in operation. Curran went on to argue for an advertising deficit fund, administered by the state, though possibly funded in part by the newspaper industry, and designed to 'partially compensate publications which because of their character and audience, are unable to attract substantial advertising'.[207] However, seventeen years later Curran commented on the chances of Britain introducing some kind of Scandinavian system of launch funding and continuing support for new publications, in these terms:

In Britain, there seems to be not the remotest possibility of a similar subsidy system being introduced. And without this, the prospects of state-funded midwifery in the main sectors of the press industry are not good because gaps in the market are few, demand is gradually contracting, home deliveries make for consumer inertia, entry costs are high, and new initiatives are liable to be undermined by the anti-competitive strategies available to market-dominant groups with enormously superior resources at their disposal.[208]

Despite his pessimism, which is indicative of how badly the argument has been lost in Britain, notwithstanding all the perceived deficiencies of the press, Curran does continue to urge some intervention, in the shape of a media enterprise board, funded by an advertising levy, but with the modest objective of helping to 'facilitate the launch of new media in low-cost, niche markets by groups with limited resources'.[209] In common with many other commentators, Curran is still arguing that the state's approach to restraining concentration of ownership in the mainstream press should be stengthened – without, one suspects, much expectation of success.

It has often been observed that one of the United Kingdom's fundamental problems is that it is caught between the American social model and the Western European one, and that an inclination towards the former has led to mistaken policies on, for example, such things as public transport and out-of-town shopping centres. The paradox as far as the press is concerned is that, although the Americans have not actually offered subsidies, they have, through the Newspaper Preservation Act, intervened against the grain of the market to do exactly what the Norwegians and Swedes have done, preserve titles in particular areas of the country. Even allowing for the different structural characteristics of the British industry, and the high penetration of London-based newspapers in England and Wales at the expense of regional titles, it remains puzzling that there has been such reluctance in the UK to consider importing at least some of the schemes in operation elsewhere, if only on a trial basis.

The actors

The principal participants in the discussions which led to the establishment, or non-establishment, of intervention mechanisms have been politicians. It is they who made the running in Scandinavia, and in America too, where several members of Congress have been involved in pressing for the introduction of Joint Operating Agreements in their own states. Indeed William Borden enjoys himself pointing out how many free enterprise enthusiasts were only too happy, when the occasion arose, to argue against the operation of market forces![210] In the UK the politicians have set their faces against intervention, other than through anti-monopoly measures. It might be thought that such attitudes would have been replicated in the European Commission. But up till now the view there has been that since subsidies do not interfere with the operation of the single Europe-wide market – newspapers hardly circulate outside of their own countries – they are acceptable. Members of the European Parliament have, for their part, shown interest in addressing the issue of concentration in the press as in other parts of the media, but as yet, despite several declarations about the importance of pluralism, pan-European legislation on the matter has not materialized.[211]

The attitude of media businesses has varied. Few recipients of public funds have been heard to object, and in a country like Austria where there are general as well as specific subventions, some may have difficulty in believing their good fortune. In Britain it would be astonishing if existing successful newspaper companies were to call for the introduction of subsides. However if another London-based title, which enjoyed a respectable circulation and provided a distinctive view of the world, were to close, it is just possible that voices might be raised within the industry suggesting that the issue be reopened. But, given that many of the academics who have been the most vociferous proponents of intervention over the years have given up that fight, it does seem a remote possibility. Britain in this regard is likely to remain firmly non-European.

Media studies academics have been a growing band in the last twenty years, as degree courses in their area have expanded dramatically, and much stimulating and useful analysis has been published. However the relationship between academics and industry has been a fraught one: broadcasting organizations have been keen enough to use university-based researchers to conduct studies on such matters as the incidence of violent incidents on-screen, and the attitudes of different groups in society to particular kinds of radio and television programming, but broadcasting and press alike have been very resistant to the more radical critiques of their operations offered by many academic commentators. This is due to some extent to the fact that much media studies work has been influenced by European Marxism, and is therefore considered to be outside mainstream British thinking, but it also stems from a distrust among practitioners of those who have never had to write a thousand words against a deadline two hours hence, and who are therefore deemed – often unfairly – to have little awareness of the 'real' world. Academics in this field therefore have a very long way to go before they are established as centrally in the policy-making process as economists, for example, now most definitely are.

As for the citizens in whose name subsidies are paid and argued for, they have never been much involved other than through the operations of representative democracy. In Britain we do not really know whether there is a genuine suppressed demand for a wider range of publications. All the surveys which have been done suggest that there is a distrust of the press and a reluctance to believe much of what appears in newspapers as alleged fact, but these feelings have yet to translate themselves into a vociferous demand for action to remedy the situation.[212] Perhaps the answer to the puzzle posed at the end of the previous section is the existence of public service broadcasting, the news and information on which enjoy a much higher degree of trust than does what is offered by the press. By creating and sustaining the most successful and admired PSB system in the world, the British may have made it much easier for a private sector press, which prints some of the best and some of the worst journalism on the planet, to continue on its way with little hindrance.

Censorship, Classification and Censure | 12

In 1992 the British Board of Film Classification was considering how it would handle the awarding of a certificate to *Satin and Lace – an Erotic History of Lingerie*, a film that does not seem to have had a high artistic content. According to a newspaper account of the examiners' discussion, policy then was that 'invasive labial vaginal shots were unsuitable for 18 but acceptable for R18. But a view of the anus seen from the rear was acceptable for 18'.[213] In 1994 the Board refused to classify two so-called 'women's prison videos', one of which, *Sadomania*, featured 'gladiatorial combat to the death between naked prisoners, the torture of a prisoner by sticking needles into and around her nipples, the hunting down of a naked woman with guns and dogs, and the rape of a bound and screaming naked prisoner by an Alsatian dog, viewed by the governor and his wife as a sexy turn-on'.[214]

The first example is liable to cause the reader a certain amount of mirth, as a vision is conjured up of a group of highly qualified and sophisticated people struggling to reconcile anatomical detail and classification criteria. The second is almost certainly likely to induce a feeling of revulsion, and make the most liberal feel – even if only momentarily – that there are some kinds of imagery which should never be allowed into the public realm. In chapter 7 there was a discussion of the basis on which censorship of audiovisual material might be justified. In this chapter the work of a body charged with pre-circulation classification and censorship will be considered, as will that of an organization which seeks to offer redress after the event to aggrieved citizens.

The British Board of Film Classification

The British Board of Film Censors (BBFC) at it was known for seventy years, came into being in 1912, as a consequence of the 1909 Cinematograph Act, which gave local authorities the power to license cinemas. The authorities interpreted the responsibility for public safety which had been delegated to them to mean the moral as well as the physical, and began to pass judgement on what could and could not be shown. The resulting chaos and uncertainty led the film industry, with government encouragement, to establish a Board whose decisions and classifications would be generally accepted, even although local authorities retained their legal rights in the matter. The BBFC was a voluntary body set up and financed by the industry, and designed to ensure that it was not prevented from exploiting the burgeoning market in which it found itself, nor tarnished in the eyes of 'respectable' people as 'immoral' or 'subversive'.

Throughout its history the Board has provided much evidence of excessive puritanism and political timidity: in the period before the Second World War, for example, it made great efforts to discourage anti-Nazi films at the script stage. In the postwar era however, particularly under the leadership of John Trevelyan (secretary from 1958 till 1971) and Stephen Murphy (secretary from 1971 to 1975), the BBFC moved far beyond its previous restrictive attitudes.[215] Murphy, it must be added however, resigned after several certification decisions – including ones concerning Ken Russell's the Devils (1971), which is concerned with alleged diabolic possession in seventeenth-century France, and Sam Peckinpah's Straw Dogs (1971), which contains a very graphic rape scene – had blown up in the Board's face, and after an evangelical organization, the Festival of Light, almost succeeded in bringing a private prosecution for obscenity against the producers of Last Tango in Paris (1972) in 1974. The Director of the Board since then has been an American, James Ferman, a former documentary film maker. With the passage of the 1984 Video Recordings Act the BBFC was given, by parliament, the additional responsibility of classifying video cassettes, a responsibility which now extends to some video games. What all of this means is that the scope, and staff, of the Board – now renamed – have grown very substantially, and it occupies a central role in audiovisual culture in Britain. It also has much closer links with the state than once was the case. Although government in the shape of the Home Office has always been consulted on such matters as the appointment of a Director (formerly Secretary), it now has the power to designate officers of the BBFC as the individuals responsible for video classification, and to require annual reports on the organization's activities, despite the facts that finance still comes from the industry in the shape of classification fees, and the Council of the Board is appointed by that industry. What we now have is a hybrid, a body which is jointly sponsored by industry and state, but paid for by film and video producers. The Press Complaints Commission, it will be recalled, which has no statutory basis or responsibilities, is also financed by the industry concerned, unlike the Broadcasting Standards Commission, which is paid for by the state, as were its constituent predecessors, and has legally prescribed duties, as they did.

A reading of the Annual Reports of the BBFC suggests an organization which is genuinely concerned to balance freedom and harm – 'It is easy to recognise the possibility of harm; it is much more difficult to assess its degree of seriousness, that point at which intervention becomes necessary'. It does not have a simplistic view of the impact of media representations on behaviour, but it does believe that there are some films and videos which operate in an 'irresponsible or corrupting fashion' in the areas of morality, health and disorder.[216] The Board, unlike other similar bodies, has never published a Code of Practice, preferring to rely on precedent and discretion. This approach makes it difficult to engage with the underlying principles being drawn on when decisions are reached, but it does give the BBFC leeway to push out the boundaries of taste, should it wish to do so, without running the risk of being criticised for ignoring its own rules. However in 1997 it felt obliged to promise that a Code would be forthcoming in the near future.

In the mid nineties the Board had at its disposal six grades – Universal, PG (Parental Guidance), 12, 15, 18 and R18 (available only in licensed sex shops). The system is similar to the ones operated elsewhere in the world, although some countries have a lower adult threshold than Britain. In the USA the system runs from G (general), through PG, R (restricted, with those under 17 only admitted in the company of an adult) to NC-17 (films containing non-pornographic sexual material) and X (variable upper age limit with 17 as starting point), which almost inevitably signifies pornography. The ratings are awarded by an industry body, the Motion Picture Association of America, and are generally accepted.

The operational practice of the BBFC is best seen in its handling not of the likes of *Sadomania*, or of pictorial histories of underwear, but of mainstream commercial or arthouse movies which, because of their subject matter, and/or the particular social circumstances surrounding their appearance, are liable to give rise to public controversy. In 1994, before it had been released in Britain, there were widespread reports in the press to the effect that *Natural Born Killers*, Oliver Stone's film about the media's relationship with two teenagers who go on a homicidal rampage, was responsible for copycat killings in the USA and France. 'Never before had a film been charged with causing a whole series of murders, and it was unthinkable that a certificate could be granted before we had checked up on these allegations.' The Board, having established that starting point, then exhaustively examined the evidence, and consulted the relevant American police forces, before concluding that 'there had been no instance in which this film could be held to have been responsible, directly or indirectly, for homicide.'[217] The film was released. To judge from other pronouncements made in the annual report which discusses *Natural Born Killers*, the BBFC simply does not believe in copycat killing as a possibility, but, in order to protect its own position, and that of the film industry, it went through the procedure just described and thus sought to legitimate the action it took. However controversy over the film continues: the novelist John Grisham, for example, has argued that crimes carried out by two American teenagers in 1995, were directly copied from the movie, and that Stone should be held legally responsible for making a film which says that 'murder is cool and fun, murder is a high, a rush, murder is a drug to be used at will'.[218]

In 1997 the Board passed uncut David Cronenberg's *Crash* with an 18 certificate. Cronenberg is a Canadian film maker who has specialized in examining some of the more bizarre and troubling aspects of experience, and *Crash* is concerned with auto-eroticism: it explores the link between car crashes and sexual arousal. On this occasion the Board was at pains to publicize the fact that it had not only consulted a lawyer, and a forensic psychologist, but had also shown the film to a group of disabled adults in order to ascertain whether they felt it exploited people like them; the answer to that query was negative. James Ferman said 'Crash is distasteful in a lot of ways – all Cronenberg's films are. He makes horror movies that are about the horrifying aspects of life. But the European Court of Human Rights has ruled that you can't ban a work because it is disturbing or shocking or offensive. People can always walk out of the cinema if they don't like it.'[219] What this statement reveals is Ferman's political skill: he implies that he does not care for the film, but feels that he is obliged, after due consideration, to give it a certificate, but, with one eye on the then Home Secretary, Michael Howard, noted for his non-liberal views, he cites a Court under whose jurisdiction Britain comes, and at which it has lost a number of cases. Not that such sophisticated tactics saved Ferman from the wrath of newspapers like the *Daily Mail*, which editorialized that 'the sooner this irresponsible Board of Film Classification, together with its shockproof director, are consigned to the cutting room floor, the better for decency in Britain's cinemas'.[220] Neither *Crash* nor *Natural Born Killers* was well received critically, although the publicity generated by the manner in which they were certificated no doubt helped them initially at the box office.

The BBFC puts much emphasis on the facts that the circumstances in which films and tapes are viewed differ radically, and that there are real difficulties in utilizing cinema ratings in the video market. Indeed it has no option in the matter, for an amendment to the Criminal Justice and Public Order Act of 1994 requires the Board in its approach to classification of tapes to 'have special regard . . . to any harm that may be caused to potential viewers or, through their behaviour, to society by the manner in which the work deals with: criminal behaviour, illegal drugs, violent behaviour or incidents, horrific behaviour or incidents, or human sexual activity'.[221] The government made it clear that the BBFC would have to consider the possibility that videos might be seen by children who were technically barred from viewing by the age classification. The amendment does appear to be predicated on an assumption about the connection between screened images and actual behaviour which the Board itself does not fully endorse, but it is required to work within the law. Not surprisingly then it has been much more cautious with classification of videos than of films. The result is that it has not been possible to obtain some films on video in Britain for many years after their theatrical releases, and video versions are often cut more extensively than the ones shown in cinemas, indeed the operational assumption is that an 18 film should, on video, meet the criteria for a 15 classification. Furthermore, the BBFC has developed a voluntary labelling system for cassettes which provides information on content beyond the general guidance offered by the classification.

Should there be a BBFC?

A distinction needs to be made between criticism of the idea of pre-exhibition censorship/classification itself, and criticism of the way in which the BBFC does its job. It might well be argued that as pre-exhibition censorship was abandoned in the British theatre in the 1960s, there is no need for it to continue in the cinema. A theatre production may still fall foul of the law and be prosecuted under obscenity legislation and that is also the case with printed material. Should not the same approach be taken with cinema? A similar view was put forward by the Peacock Report on broadcasting in 1986, when it called for 'the abolition of prepublication censorship or vetting of any kind of broadcasting'.[222] The case for censorship is difficult to sustain in principle if it is not applied universally. It becomes necessary to fall back on such matters as distinctive aspects of the medium, or the relationship between audience and artifact in order to provide justification. This means talking about, for example, the vivid nature of screen imagery, the power of special effects and the commercial imperatives which encourage exploitation and so on. It is possible to be against censorship generally but still be willing to concede that some kinds of censorship may be necessary in some circumstances. That is not a very comfortable position to occupy intellectually, particularly if it involves claiming, for example, that theatre audiences are more sophisticated than film/video ones, and do not therefore need the same level of protection, but it is one in which quite a few people find themselves.

As to the practicalities of abolishing film and video censorship and classification, and allowing disputes to be resolved in the courts, that is most unlikely to commend itself to producers, distributors and exhibitors, since the present system offers certainty and minimum expense, unless a film/video is refused certification, and that is a very rare occurrence. Few in the industry would relish having to face regular legal challenges from say, well organized and funded pressure groups of an evangelical Christian persuasion. Indeed distributors seem happy to negotiate with the Board, in order to secure a classification category which will maximize the earning potential of their films, particularly if they are aimed at a pre-adult market, and will even submit 'rough cuts' in order to seek category advice. However, it could be argued that if the BBFC is operating a voluntary system without legal backing as far as cinema is concerned, the option of public exhibition without a certificate –

private club exhibition has always been a possibility – could be available, on the clear understanding that prosecution might result. If that route were open, only a few producers would be likely to avail themselves of it: from 1987–94 the BBFC refused only two films a certificate, although the number issued with cuts is generally far higher, and runs at 5 to 10 per cent of films classified per year; in 1993, for example, 38 out of 350 films (10.9 per cent) were cut, and in 1996, 21 out of 364 (5.8 per cent), while on the video front a similar percentage of titles is cut, 217 out of a total of 2,961 (7.3 per cent) in 1993, and 264 out of 3,726 (7.1 per cent) in 1996.[223]

If the BBFC looks as if it is unlikely to disappear for reasons of both principle and expediency, does it follow that the way it does its business is beyond reproach? Although it is a freestanding profit-making body, in practice its Director, President and Vice Presidents (the latter are not salaried employees) are now government appointees by virtue of their being collectively designated as the responsible authority under the Video Recordings Act. That fact was emphasized in 1997, when the new Labour Home Secretary, Jack Straw, indicated that he would be unwilling to see one of the existing Vice-Presidents succeed the retiring President, apparently because Straw disapproved of what he perceived to be the excessively liberal line which the Board had been taking with sexually explicit material. This led to uncharacteristically blunt criticism in public by James Ferman of the Home Secretary, an incident which suggested that the relationship between Board and government had entered a fractious and possibly dangerous phase: Ferman's retirement was announced shortly thereafter.

Beyond the presidency level the BBFC appoints its own full-time examiners and advisory committees, and there is a good case for opening up their procedures to greater public, and indeed parliamentary, scrutiny; the BBFC has been enriched by the Video Recordings Act, and, as the regulatory bodies in broadcasting are obliged to give an account of their activities, and face select committees from time to time, so too could the Board. There is also a case for asking the BBFC, not simply in high profile cases but generally, to make available its thinking on the processes of classification and censorship beyond the confines of its Annual Report, whether in the form of the promised Code of Practice or in some other way, so that a wider public debate about the legitimate limits of expression might at least become a possibility. The Board is clearly sensitive about this issue, for in 1995 it announced that it was setting up a Home Viewing Panel, which would be made up of regular film and video viewers drawn from a wide range of backgrounds, and would be charged with the responsibility of offering general advice on classification, and specific comment on particular decisions. It is also at pains to emphasize the willingness of its examiners to talk to schools, students and community groups about its work. Such activities are clearly designed to both extend public knowledge and strengthen the legitimacy of a body, the constitutional basis of which is not widely understood.

The Broadcasting Standards Council (BSC)

The BSC is an example of an organization which came into being largely as a result of the activity of the public, or rather those members of the public who were part of a particular pressure group. From the early sixties on, a campaign for the 'cleaning up' of television was waged by the National Viewers' and Listeners' Association (NVALA), led by a school teacher, Mrs Mary Whitehouse. The campaign achieved a high public profile, although the membership of NVALA was never more than a few thousand, and this was largely due to the ability of Mrs Whitehouse to capitalize on general unease about the permissiveness which apparently had enveloped British life. The founding objectives of NVALA are worth quoting from.

> To promote the moral and religious welfare of the community by seeking to maintain Christian standards in broadcasting by sound and vision in Great Britain . . . To press for the creation of a Viewers' and Listeners' Council, in order to influence the output of all the agencies of broadcasting by sound and vision in Great Britain. To provide means to ascertain and collate public opinion on radio and television items, and to bring positive and constructive criticisms, complaints and suggestions to the notice of the proposed Council, and of Parliament.[224]

Many readers might find the first objective, with its insistence on a Christian world view, very difficult to accept, and even thirty years ago, it would have been questionable whether it was a proposition which would have commanded even majority support in Britain. Although most citizens are in favour of a moral society, problems arise in deciding exactly what generally acceptable ethical standards should be, and NVALA has always given the impression that its criteria were excessively narrow, even for many Christians of a liberal persuasion. However it is not quite so easy to criticise the desire to establish a Viewers' and Listeners' Council. That objective was rethought, and NVALA pressed for two separate bodies, one a Broadcasting Council to deal with complaints independently investigated – the then Press Council was cited as an exemplar – and the other a Viewers' and Listeners' Council, which would seek 'to represent the opinions, ideas and experiences of the whole country to the broadcasting authorities'. The second of these would be represented on the BBC Board of Governors and the regulatory bodies, would 'promote research into current trends in broadcasting and suggest specific ways in which television and radio can best serve the interests of the country,' and would present Parliament with an annual report.[225]

Much of the time of Mrs Whitehouse and the organization she headed was devoted to attacking the alleged permissiveness and immorality of current output. The reactions of the broadcasters varied. Sir Hugh Greene who was Director General of the BBC from 1960–9, treated Mrs Whitehouse with disdain, but she was taken much more seriously in other quarters, and at gatherings of practitioners and academics which she attended it was possible on occasion to see her being treated with some deference by representatives of the Independent Broadcasting Authority. Nonetheless her campaign remained largely an irritant and little else, until the advent of the Thatcher government. Before that time, the Annan Committee on the Future of Broadcasting, when it reported in 1977, had recommended the setting up of an independent organization to deal with complaints about invasion of privacy and unfairness, and that body was created in the 1980 Broadcasting Act. It replaced internal complaints mechanisms which both the BBC and the IBA had introduced in the 1970s. So, although the new Broadcasting Complaints Commission was not concerned with the areas on which NVALA had focused, the principle of an independent body from which aggrieved individuals could seek redress had been established. Credit for this should not be laid solely at the door of Mrs Whitehouse's organization, for there had been pressure from other quarters too, but from the NVALA point of view it was significant progress. Annan also proposed the creation of a Public Enquiry Board for Broadcasting which would hold hearings on how broadcasters had discharged their duties, on a seven year rolling basis. To date this Board, which was modelled on the Canadian Radio-television and Telecommunications Commission, has not been set up.[226]

The basic approach to broadcasting favoured by the Thatcher government combined a commitment to deregulating the market with a desire to tighten content regulation. The Broadcasting Complaints Commission, as has just been noted, had been established at the beginning of the Thatcher period; it was given the power to require broadcasters to publish its adjudications, but no other sanctions. In 1988 a new body was created to deal specifically with the kind of matters about which Mrs Whitehouse and NVALA had been agitating for the previous twenty years, 'the portrayal in television and radio programmes and broadcast adverts of violence, sexual conduct and matters of taste and decency'.[227] The Broadcasting Standards Council (BSC) was actually brought into being before it was given statutory authority, which followed in the 1990 Broadcasting Act. It might be thought that having two separate bodies charged with handling complaints from the public was confusing, but the political aim was clearly to give the alleged permissiveness of the broadcasters a higher profile than would otherwise have been the case. It was 1997 before the two organizations were amalgamated into the one Broadcasting Standards Commission.

As with other quangos, appointments to the BSC were in the gift of the relevant government department, in this case the Home Office, and the lists of 'the great and the good' were examined to find suitable establishment figures – retired civil servants, former BBC governors, prominent clergymen and the like – to serve. Perhaps in order to avoid giving the impression that the BSC was in effect simply there to do what Mrs Whitehouse and NVALA were generally perceived as wishing, the Council was asked not only to produce a Code of Practice, of which broadcasters are legally obliged to take account, but was also required to commission a range of research work and to liaise with similar bodies overseas. It will be recalled, however, that NVALA's proposed Viewers' and Listeners' Council was also intended to do rather similar work, although that fact is not widely understood.

Complaints to the BSC from members of the public about programming rose steadily over the years, a fact which may reflect either growing unease or increased awareness of the existence of the Council. In 1992–3, 1,355 complaints which were within its remit, were received, while in the last year of the Council's independent existence that number had reached 2,769. Throughout its life most complaints were about taste and decency – 48 per cent in 1992–3 and 60 per cent in 1996–7 – while complaints about the depiction of sex – 24 per cent and 19 per cent were lower, and those about violence – 8 per cent and 12 per cent – lower still, with the remainder being concerned with more than one aspect of output. The proportion of complaints upheld rose – it was only 4 per cent in 1992–3, but had reached 29 per cent in 1996–7.[228]

Handling violence

As was explained in chapter 7, broadcasters worldwide have felt obliged to produce codes on the depiction of violence. The BSC's view on violence in fiction was referred to in that chapter. As far as news programming is concerned, its Code of Practice states:

> Where scenes of violence are necessarily included in television bul-letins, the fact that violence has bloody consequences should not be glossed over. However, it is not for the broadcaster to impose a moral judgement on the audience and care should be taken not to linger on the casualties nor on the bloody evidence of violence.[229]

In order to gain some idea of how the Council – half a dozen indi-viduals nominated by the Home Secretary and its professional full-time staff – dealt with complaints, the 1991–3 period in television will be considered. The topic of violence has been chosen for detailed analysis because it is such a sensitive and difficult area – although, as has just been noted, most complaints have been about other aspects of output – and because the way in which the BSC handled the issue is particularly illuminating about its general prac-tice. Some reference will also be made to early adjudications issued by the Broadcasting Standards Commission, in order to explore the issue of continuity of practice.

It will be recalled that during the 1991–3 period the Gulf War took place and the Bosnian conflict began. As far as the structure of British broadcasting is concerned, the new system of ITV franchise allocation came into operation, while on the programming front the major ITV company, Granada, launched *Cracker*, its series about a psychologist who specializes in helping the police to track down psychopaths and other assorted murderers, while the BBC mystified its audiences with David Lynch's *Twin Peaks*.

A clear distinction emerges between the handling of complaints about actuality and those concerned with fiction. Not surprisingly, there were a number of complaints about news relating to the Gulf War and the Bosnian conflict. In August 1992, for example, in evening bulletins both the BBC and ITN (Independent Television News), the news provider for ITV and Channel Four, screened shots of the bodies of refugee children who had been shot outside Sarajevo, lying in a mortuary. In response to the view that this particular footage should have been cut from the report, the BSC said that while 'recognising the very distressing nature of the material . . . (it) . . . nevertheless accepted that the circumstances of the killing of the children warranted the showing of the pictures complained of'.[230] This was typical of the response to complaints concerned with news broadcasts. In 1997, however, an item in the BBC's *Six o'Clock News* about sexual abuse was criticised by the Standards Commission, but on the grounds that it contained too much detail for a programme transmitted before the so-called adult watershed of nine o'clock in the evening.[231]

Not all actuality escaped censure in the earlier period. An edition of Channel Four's *The Word* in December 1992, for example, was criticised for retaining in the recorded repeat an interview with a reggae singer who advocated the crucifixion of homosexuals.[232] In January 1993 ITV screened, late at night, a programme about offender profiling of serial killers, which included an interview with Dennis Nilsen, who had been responsible for a particularly gruesome series of murders in London. Complaints were made about the distress which might be caused to relatives of Nilsen's victims, and the allegedly sensationalist presentation – at one point, before a commercial break, the next part of the documentary was trailed by showing Nilsen in a prison interview saying 'The most exciting part of the little conundrum was when I lifted the body, carried it. It was an expression of my power, to lift and carry and have control', while the caption unrolling slowly at the bottom of the screen, to the accompaniment of melodramatic music, said 'Coming next – serial killer Dennis Nilsen's own story'. The BSC accepted that the programme had serious intent and did not criticize its transmission, but it upheld the complaint about the way in which the subject was treated.[233] Four years later another ITV documentary, this one about the so-called Yorkshire Ripper, the murderer Peter Sutcliffe, which used reconstructions to allege that Sutcliffe had attacked a number of women, who had survived his assaults, was also censured. The Standards Commission adjudication decreed that the violence 'went beyond acceptable limits and could have generated fear' and that the use of pop music on the sound track, apparently to indicate the passing of time, 'was inappropriate in the context of such a disturbing case'.[234]

Complaints were made about films in regard to both content and time of transmission. Where the BSC upheld complaints, it usually focused on scheduling or the lack of adequate warnings about subject matter. On occasion, it would argue that a film should have been cut. In February 1992, for example, ITV transmitted late evening a movie called *Visiting Hours*, which was about a woman reporter being pursued by a psychopath. The film had not been preceded by a warning, but even if it had been, the BSC was of the view that 'the level of violence could not be justified'.[235] It required of Yorkshire Television that it publish a summary of the finding in a national newspaper. Five years later David Cronenberg, whose *Crash*, it will be recalled, caused the BBFC some heart searching, fell foul of the Standards Commission, after BBC2 transmitted *Videodrome* as part of a season of his work. The movie was, according to the Corporation, 'a serious, intelligent and well-made horror film about the commercial and political exploitation of cable-television pornography'. The BSC took the view however that, despite the nature of the genre, the pre-transmission warning and the hour of broadcast, 'the intensity of the violence, the graphic scenes of mutilation and the explicit nature of the sado-masochism strayed beyond the boundaries of acceptability even for a horror film broadcast late at night'. Similar treatment was meted out to *Shivers*, which was transmitted immediately after *Videodrome*, at ten past midnight.[236]

What is striking here is that the Commission, like the Council before it, is making it very clear that the standard of acceptability in television must continue to be stricter than that applied by the BBFC in cinema, and that some scenes which might well have been passed as suitable for a cinema audience will never be acceptable on television, regardless of time of transmission. In a sense what the Commission is doing is applying the 15 test that the BBFC applies when it classifies videos. However in the same year as the transmission of *Videodrome* was criticized, complaints about a screening of Tarantino's *Reservoir Dogs* by Channel Four late evening were rejected, on the grounds that the channel had provided sufficient warning as to content, and 'Difficult writing or art or music has to find a place alongside more comfortable programming'.[237]

Film apart, it is in the field of drama that most problems arise. Towards the end of the American serial, *Twin Peaks*, there is an episode which contains a pivotal scene in which a woman is brutally murdered. The serial was transmitted on BBC2 after the nine o'clock watershed, but was not preceded by a warning. When the

BSC asked the Corporation for its response to the complaints it had received, to the effect that 'the violence was gratuitous, unnecessarily protracted and explicit, and compounded by the fact that it was directed against a woman at home', the BBC argued the artistic merits of the series and the crucial importance of this scene in revealing one of the central mysteries of the drama, but conceded that a warning should have been broadcast. However the Council took the view that even with a warning 'the murder scene went beyond acceptable limits', and it drew attention to a section of its Code of Practice which declares that 'the degradation of women, as objects of male violence, should be handled with particular sensitivity, requiring the details of an attack to be given sparingly'. The BBC was required to publish the finding in its programme journal *Radio Times*.[238]

What is worth remarking on about this adjudication is the emphasis on the avoidance of on-screen violence against women; the Council made much of its concern in this area, and whether that was the intention or not, it was a politically astute move. When the BSC was established, it was almost certainly going to find itself attacked as excessively puritanical on the sexual front. Censuring violently degrading images of women not only diverted attention from the non-violent sexual arena, but also appeared to locate the Council in the 'progressive', rather than the 'reactionary' camp.

A similar point can be made about the judgement issued in response to complaints about several episodes of *Cracker*. The first episode of the first story in that series was transmitted in September 1993 at nine o'clock in the evening on the ITV network. It began with the discovery of the body of a girl who had been murdered by a psychopath in a train compartment. In one scene a pathologist – for some reason a North American – described to policemen in some detail, and with apparent relish, how exactly the girl had been killed, and asked that a photograph be taken of him pointing at some of the bloodstains – 'something for the album'. This scene, and others, led to several complaints to the BSC. Granada Television insisted that the violence was not gratuitous and was necessary, although it offered apologies for any offence caused. The Council was not impressed, and insisted that 'the scenes of the murdered young woman in the train and of the heavily bloodstained carriage ... were too protracted and unnecessarily graphic, compounded as they were by the description given by a pathologist standing at the scene, of the effects of the stabbing'. However when the episode was repeated some months later, the scenes in question were still there, a neat illustration of the limits to the power of the Council.[239]

Was the BSC worth having?

Any fair-minded observer would be likely to conclude that the Broadcasting Standards Council was not particularly authoritarian – indeed Mary Whitehouse has been less than complimentary about its activities. It tried to develop a balanced approach in its judgements and sought to locate its work in a context which extended far beyond reacting to complaints, by regularly commissioning research on audience attitudes to various aspects of broadcasting content. It was not however popular with the industry, any more than its companion body was. Latterly, it was arguing for its own demise and for the establishment of a Broadcasting Consumers' Council which, in addition to carrying out the functions of the BSC and the BCC, would have 'wide responsibilities for research, for publications, for stimulating debate and promoting media education'.[240] The Standards Commission which emerged from the 1996 Broadcasting Act does not have as wide a remit as that: it remains firmly focused on complaints, and the monitoring of the broadcasters' performance in the areas with which the constituent bodies were previously concerned. By no stretch of the imagination then could the Standards Commission be regarded as a Broadcasting Consumers' Council, although it does carry out some of the functions such an organisation might have.

As to the value of the Council, if there is a case for a Press Complaints Commission, even a reformed one, then it is difficult to argue against the existence of the BSC and its successor. Indeed the element of independence from the industry concerned that is lacking in the PCC has always been present in the statutory bodies which deal with broadcasting complaints. The most fundamental question of all however remains: in a mature democracy, with legal safeguards, is there any need for such bodies? The Peacock Committee's answer, it will be recalled, was robustly in the negative. However, even if we were persuaded by Peacock's arguments in principle, could we be sure that all of those entitled to seek legal redress would be able to do so, given the cost of going to law in Britain, and the limited scope which exists for civil action in the areas concerned? It is hard to believe that the vast majority of the people who took complaints to the BSC, if that option had not been available, would have brought actions against the broadcasters, even if a legal route had been open to them. Although it is clear from its Complaints Bulletins that the time of the BSC, particularly in its early years, was wasted by fatuous or eccentric complainants, not all of the citizens who wrote to the Council came into these categories. In whose interests would it have been to force those with legitimate and serious concerns to choose between expensive legal action and silence? Broadcasters do make mistakes, and have tended to be reluctant to apologize when apology is clearly called for. Are citizens not entitled to some form of redress when it is required, and should not that redress be cheap and easily obtainable?

A final comment

The two bodies – and for the purpose of what is said here the Standards Council will be regarded as continuing to exist in the shape of the Standards Commission – which we have been examining in this chapter share the basic assumptions that there are boundaries of taste, and that there is the possibility of harm. Both have been reluctant to insist that they are dealing in absolutes, and have made much of their continued attempts to ascertain what the public thinks at any given time as to where the limits actually lie, but behind the judgements and pronouncements of both there does seem to lurk an assumption that in a civilized society certain kinds of imagery – and in the case of radio, aural depictions – are not acceptable, and that somewhere there are lines which should not be crossed.

One organization reacts to what has already been done, while the other decides what will and will not be seen. The BSC may have had an indirect influence on what comes into that part of the public realm with which it is concerned, the BBFC can actually decide what receives an entry permit and what does not. One is in the business of offering redress, and the other protection. In membership one emphasizes the 'great and good' tradition, whereby men and women of distinction are invited to carry out a civic responsibility, albeit with a professional staff, while the other puts much more emphasis on the full-time employment of professionals in its work, although the 'great and good' are involved in its constitutional and committee structures. Both organizations purport to act on behalf of the public, and both strive constantly to demonstrate their fitness to do so. Whether the methods of appointment employed ensure that the citizens as a whole are properly represented is quite another matter. That is an issue which has been raised several times in this book and must continue to lie at the heart of any discussion about the approach to the constitution of regulatory bodies favoured in the United Kingdom; it is more than likely, however, that the British way of handling these matters will be subject to significant revision in the near future, as pressure mounts for the diminution of the centralized and centralizing power of Westminster.

Coping with Cultural Imperialism | 13

Governments are keen to protect themselves and their citizens from the harm which they fear the media might do, and they often also declare themselves to be committed to the promotion of knowledge and enlightenment. Many of them have another concern, which is that the media, like other cultural activities, should express aspects of the life of the nation. This has both internal and external importance, internal, for through such expression the nation may enlarge its self-knowledge and cohesion, and external, for such cultural products as emerge may, if they are good enough, enhance the standing of the nation abroad, and, if they are commercially successful, generate income and employment. Governments are rarely alone when they seek to promote culture, for they are usually joined by groups of citizens who share the assumption that nations are not truly themselves unless there is some concrete expression of that nationhood. Some of these groups may have motives which are not entirely disinterested, for they may be composed of people who make their livings in the media and the arts, but others are genuinely committed to the coupling of polity and culture.

A glance at the programme of any international arts festival such as the most wide-ranging one of all, which takes place each summer in Edinburgh, shows the process just described at work: orchestras, particularly if they have their countries' names in their titles, will be officially subsidized to travel abroad, exhibitions of painting will be mounted with the support of the government of the nation of origin of the painters, and theatre companies will perform under the patronage of their cultural ministries. This is generally accepted as normal practice, and excites little controversy. However, when we move from the traditional arts to the media we find that matters are not quite so straightforward, for, while film and broadcasting are clearly part of culture, they are also part of commerce, in a way that opera and ballet are not deemed to be. This means that the criteria for public support are not as self-evident as they have become in the world of the high arts, and while it is inconceivable that the American government would seek to force the French one to desist from subsidizing its symphony orchestras on the grounds that this represented an interference with the operation of a competitive market in classical music, when it comes to measures designed to support French cinema and television, US administrations have tried very hard indeed to have these mechanisms abolished or curtailed. The contrast which arises here is rather bizarre, for it is much easier for classical music to travel, since it encounters no language barriers, and there is therefore a sense in which the Orchestre de Paris is in much more direct competition with the New York Philharmonic than French television is with American television. However the high arts, no matter the salaries commanded by their super stars, and no matter the ruthless way in which some of those involved conduct their activities, continue to be regarded as noncommercial in a way that the media are not.

But in a world in which the dominant forms of expression are those which have emerged in the twentieth century, no country which is serious about promoting its own culture as a means of self-expression, and of encouraging national feeling and awareness, can afford to ignore the media. An added incentive, as has already been noted, is the economic benefit which comes from employment and exports (a benefit which, it should be remembered, is also available in the more traditional arts: campaigners in Britain have often made the point that the amount of money spent by tourists on the theatre in London greatly exceeds the public subsidy to drama[241]). General competition is fierce and so is media competition, and as major economies seek to dominate world trade in manufactured goods, likewise in the media. We have already noted the way in which large media corporations, many of them based in the USA, have extended their operations across the globe. It is not therefore surprising to find that these organizations and the countries where they are domiciled are often charged with imperialism.

Varieties of imperialism

Imperialism is the term used to describe the way in which powerful nations impose their will on the less powerful, whether through military intervention or other pressures. In the nineteenth century the dominant imperialist was Britain, and a child at school, even in the 1950s, could look at a map of the world, most of which was coloured red, by way of signifying that the countries concerned had been part of the British Empire, although by then they were members of the Commonwealth. This kind of imperialism – usually called colonialism – is no longer to be found in the world, with the last modern empire finally collapsing with the Berlin Wall in 1989. However major countries do continue to be accused of imperialism through the application of either military or economic pressure. Indeed it is very difficult for the most powerful nation in the world, the United States, to use force at all without exciting such charges, which is why in recent times it has sought to build international support for its interventions, for example in Kuwait and Iraq in 1991 and Bosnia in 1996.

It is against America too that charges of cultural and media imperialism are most often levelled, although other Western nations also find themselves in the dock. It is certainly true that in the nineties the Americans have sought to eliminate trade barriers worldwide, and it is far from clear that weaker economies necessarily benefit in the short or medium term from being exposed to the full blast of free competition, even if in the longer term there may be substantial advantages. When it comes to culture generally and the media in particular, the issues for debate are relatively clear cut: does access to the culture of the United States necessitate the weakening or destruction of the cultures of other less-economically powerful nations, and if it does, is that price worth paying?

Some snapshots: winter, 1991 in Moscow, not long after the failed coup against Mikhail Gorbachev, across the street from the uninspiring state restaurant, a huge queue has formed outside of a recently opened pizza parlour; summer 1993 in Prague, facing the beautiful art nouveau Municipal House, a colossal billboard shows the location of the city's new and forthcoming McDonald's restaurants; July 1996, outside of a little cinema on Lake Balaton, the billboards announce current and forthcoming attractions, only one of which is Hungarian. Readers can no doubt supply their own examples of the process which is at work here. And Eastern Europe is a fascinating place to observe it, for because of the relatively closed nature of most of the societies there until very recently, American culture was not nearly as prevalent as it was in the rest of the continent. In a sense a dam has burst, and what was once forbidden has been leapt upon and devoured, literally and metaphorically. However it is highly unlikely that McDonald's and assorted pizza chains will eliminate either authentic Russian or Czech restaurants, no matter how popular they are with the young. The success of these fast food companies, sometimes in the most improbable places, is due not just to the fare which they offer, nor to their marketing skills, but owes much to the kind of symbolic transaction which takes place every time a young Russian, Czech or, indeed, Briton buys a Big Mac: it is not only meat, flour and potatoes which are being consumed but also the very image of America, the land of opportunity, the land of immense wealth, and the land which has produced the most exciting and vibrant mass culture in the world. Young people dream rather more than the middle aged, who have been forced by time and circumstance to grapple with reality, and it would be surprising if their dreams were not full of images and sounds from across the Atlantic. That surely is only a problem when it becomes impossible to dream in any images other than those provided by the American media industries.

So it is not difficult to be sanguine about the impact of fast-food chains on the ways of life of the world outside of America, for they have arrived at the end of culinary histories that may be thousands of years old, and although these histories may change, they are certainly not going to vanish. When it comes to the media – and cinema and television in particular – matters are a little more complicated. Unlike the traditional arts, which in most countries – like cooking – enjoy a long lineage, the media are modern in origin. Early on in its existence cinema was organized in the United States on an industrial basis with division of labour and large production lines. Like the motor industry, it enjoyed a huge home market which enabled it to spend generously on product development with a reasonable expectation of a return on investment; and like the auto business, it used that home market as the basis for launching an export drive which has grown as the century has progressed. Indeed in 1996 it was reported that for the first time the income from theatrical exhibition of American films abroad was expected to exceed the income generated from theatrical exhibition at home.[242] The United States is by far the most successful exporter of audio-visual material, followed some distance back by Canada (though only as far as television programming is concerned). Britain also, as was noted in chapter 3, has, until recently, enjoyed a modest trade surplus in the area, and is the most successful European exporter. Australia too has found foreign markets, particularly for its soap operas, as have Brazil and other South American countries for their telenovelas.

Some observers regard all of this as part of a process, the objective of which is world domination. Herbert Schiller, a radical American commentator, has remarked of his own country's behaviour:

> the concept of cultural imperialism today best describes the sum of the processes by which a society is brought into the modern world system and how its dominating stratum is attracted, pressured, forced, and sometimes bribed into shaping social institutions to correspond to, or even promote, the value and structures of the dominating center of the system.
>
> The public media are the foremost example of operating enterprises that are used in the penetrative process. For penetration on a significant scale the media themselves must be captured by the dominating/penetrating power. This occurs largely through the commercialisation of broadcasting.[243]

Twenty years after these words were written, anyone who has watched the enthusiasm with which American agencies based in Russia have encouraged broadcasters there to go down the commercial route, rather than the public service one, would have to agree that Schiller's analysis is still very relevant, and that there is clearly a dynamic within capitalism which seeks to universalize its practices. A distinction however needs to be drawn between the attempt to globalize the capitalist system, and the endeavours of particular countrties to market their products to others. Whatever the judgement might be about whether the USA has indeed been seeking to do what Schiller believes to have been the case, there is no doubt about its behaviour as an exporter: historians of the film industry have shown how the Americans, with the support of the federal Department of Commerce, sought to restrict the entry of foreign films to the US market and to improve their own access to foreign markets. Kristin Thompson has described the approach of Will Hays – from 1922 head of the Motion Picture Producers and Distributors of America organization (MPPDA) – to countries which tried to protect their domestic film industries through quotas and other devices: by a mixture of persuasion and the threat of total withdrawal of American films from the markets in question he managed to secure very favourable terms in most of Europe. What is also clear is that movies were seen by US administrations as both a commodity and a vehicle for spreading appreciation of the American way of life.[244]

The taste of the colonized

It is tempting to view this as a sinister process in which one nation has sought to ruthlessly obliterate the audiovisual cultures of the less-economically powerful. But that is to ignore some inconvenient facts. In the first place it is clear that millions of people throughout the world like American mass culture, which is why, when Hays threatened European governments with boycotts, they had to back down, since their own populations would have been outraged if they had been prevented from seeing any more US films. And if, by way of further example, we look at what might now be regarded as the classical era of the American musical theatre, the interwar period, when writers such as the Gershwins, Irving Berlin, Rodgers and Hart and Jerome Kern were at work, we are confronted with an array of songs which are sung, played, hummed and whistled across the globe. It might be suggested that this is due to the power of the American recording companies, and behind them the American capitalist system. Equally – as the comment by Wilfrid Mellers quoted at the beginning of chapter 2 suggests – it can be argued that these writers had the ability to encapsulate in memorable words and tunes universal feelings and aspirations; indeed, if we wish to understand their success, it might be more profitable to look at their ethnic origin – many of them were the sons of Eastern European Jewish immigrants, Berlin actually being born near Minsk – and to explore the relationship between the musical traditions from which they came and the kind of material they produced.

A similar point can be made about Hollywood cinema: it would be stupid to ignore the power and determination of the industry, and its leaders like Hays and the studio bosses, but it would be equally foolish to deny that the mode of narrative developed by Hollywood is a very economical and effective way of telling stories. Ironically, as Pierre Sorlin has commented of 'classical' Hollywood approaches:

> [they] . . . are merely an extension of the style of narrative which has existed in Europe since the eighteenth century; initially they might have developed as successfully on this side of the Atlantic as on the other. Hollywood won at the beginning of our century because it was the first to settle the formula and it was financially stronger than its European competitors.[245]

And which of us would really be willing to surrender the pleasures we have had, and expect to have in the future, from American film, music and television? However, most of us would also like to have music and imagery which arise from our own culture. Nor are we uninterested in other non-American cultures: it is, for example, surely one of the advantages of living at the close of the twentieth century that it is possible to walk into a record store, and find ourselves in a sea of ethnic music of all kinds from around the globe. Furthermore, cultures continually interact with each other, for it is in the nature of artistic creativity that it will both ground itself in a tradition and seek to learn from other traditions. To take one instance, consider the way in which Scots and Irish fiddle music crossed to North America with immigrants, changed and adapted, and fed into musical genres which developed there, including Country and Western, which in its turn has re-crossed the Atlantic in the other direction to be taken up enthusiastically in Britain.[246] In such a situation is it possible to distinguish clearly the authentic from the inauthentic?

What all of this means is that there are difficult balances to strike in media policy. Cultural imperialism in the sense that one culture sets out to destroy another is obviously undesirable, but so is a closed culture policy, not simply because it is impractical, but because it denies the possibilities of enrichment which come from exposure to other traditions. For some countries, sadly, the available choices are very limited, for they do not have the resources to produce the range of material which can be purchased off the shelf at trivial prices from foreign suppliers. So, for example, in the Caribbean, although indigenous popular music has found a way of surviving alongside the international variety, many television stations will offer viewers an unending stream of images of a rich and glamorous lifestyle remote from their own experience.[247] The effect of this kind of exposure is a matter of some controversy but one or two points do seem obvious. In the first place, all of the evidence from throughout the world tells us that while American films are universally popular, if audiences have the choice between American and indigenous television drama, they almost inevitably go for the home-grown material, even although the production values are much less glossy.[248] The film/television drama distinction seems to owe something to the perception that film is to a degree a fantasy medium, whereas television, with its wider range of output, much of it factual, is more firmly rooted in reality.

Secondly, if the media are foreign dominated, then the survival of a country's culture will depend on what is done outside of the media rather more than would otherwise be the case, and in an age when the media are so dominant, that can render some cultures very fragile. It is for this reason that the Welsh campaigned for Britain's fourth television channel to devote much of its air time in the principality to programmes in the indigenous language, and the Gaels of Scotland pressurized the British government to set up a special Gaelic Television Fund, which helps finance a range of material which is screened on mainstream channels.[249] Finally, where the gap between the ordinary conditions of living of the viewers and the conditions depicted onscreen is huge, as in the Caribbean, it would be surprising if, in addition to a sense of cultural domination, a feeling of economic exclusion was not also generated.

The European dimension

The European Union came into being as the European Economic Community in 1957 as a consequence of the Treaty of Rome, which was signed by France, West Germany, Italy and the Benelux countries. From 1974, the year in which the United Kingdom joined, a process of enlargement began, so that by 1995 it was composed of fifteen Western European nations, and was pondering how it would respond to the desire of the post-Communist countries of Eastern Europe to become members, which only one of them, East Germany by virtue of reunification, had managed to do. In its early days the Community was known as the 'Common Market', and that was an appropriate title, for the basic aim of the project was the removal of internal trade barriers so that goods and services could move freely across national boundaries. It would be a gross simplification however to neglect the politics which lay behind the economics: the Common Market locked together the two major powers of mainland Europe, France and Germany, in an embrace which the founders of the Community believed would remove forever the possibility of a war between these two former adversaries and the general conflagration which would flow from such a disaster.

If the political thrust has been clear from the beginning, it has to be said that there has been no comparable cultural thrust for most of the Community's existence, that being left to the much larger Council of Europe, a body established in 1949, which has also been very active in the sphere of human rights. However as the European Community has grown larger, and the vision of its ultimate destiny – perhaps even a Federal Europe – has become grander, it has started to interest itself in matters cultural – 'The commitment of citizens to the European idea depends on positive measures being taken to enhance and promote European culture in its richness and diversity' declared the EU heads of government in 1989.[250] And in the Maastricht Treaty of 1991, which marked a quickening of the pace of integration, there was specific reference to the need to encourage 'artistic and literary creation, including the audio-visual sphere'.[251]

There have been occasions when it looked as if there was a desire for some kind of transcendent pan-European culture, and that was reflected in a number of unsuccessful television dramas. However, as the first statement quoted above makes clear, the link between polity and culture which is being sought is one in which diversity is the key characteristic. And it is in the audiovisual sphere that the EU has been most active. The reasons are obvious enough. There is no threat to the continued European domination of classical music, theatre and ballet across the continent, but in film and television it is a different matter. In 1993 the countries of the Union produced 502 feature films, compared to 450 made by the United States, yet unlike the vast majority of the American films, no more than 20 per cent of the European movies were shown beyond their country of origin, and very few of them crossed the Atlantic. American films had a 75 per cent share of the EU box office, while national films picked up 15 per cent. In 1986 the figures were 59 per cent and 24 per cent respectively; it is very clear in which direction the situation has been moving.[252] Of fiction programmes, including films, shown on eighty-eight television channels within the Union in 1993, 69 per cent were American.[253] However, although American movies tend to be the most popular at the box office in European countries, as is the case elsewhere in the world, television audiences for domestic drama when it is available are usually much larger than those for US fiction.[254] A casual glance at the weekly ratings in the UK demonstrates the point: it is rare for an American programme – unless it is a transmission of a blockbuster film – to get anywhere near the top ten programmes, and material from the other side of the Atlantic usually only appears in the bottom half of the top seventy.[255]

It is not therefore surprising that the EU has concluded that there is an unsatisfied demand for more indigenous television, particularly in those countries which because of their population size do not have a strong broadcasting industry like the British one. Nor is it at all puzzling that the Union feels that Europe is grossly under-represented on its cinema screens. There is a cultural imperative to act, and there is also an economic one, an audiovisual trade imbalance of over 6 billion dollars.[256]

The measures which have been undertaken have been embarked upon by an organization which is tugged in two rather different directions from within its own structure. On the one hand, there is an enthusiasm for economic liberalism which leads to an emphasis on the removal of barriers to trade within the Union and ultimately in logic, if not always in practice, to support for measures which eliminate obstacles to the operation of market forces worldwide. This approach is to be seen most clearly in the Bangemann report on telecommunications, which goes out of its way to play down suggestions that there should be interference with these forces, or calls for public investment.[257] On the other hand, there is a commitment to interventionism in order to secure objectives which the market by itself would be unlikely to deliver. That is obvious in a number of areas, such as the employment-related Social Chapter, and in the MEDIA programme, which has been designed with the aim of bolstering European audiovisual production.

The European Union operates to a significant degree through Directives, which are enforceable under EU law, though member states have some discretion in implementation. The major directive in the media policy field is *Television Without Frontiers*, which appeared in 1989.[258] The two approaches outlined above are clear in that document. The basic aim was to ensure that there should be no restriction on the retransmission of services which originate anywhere in the Union, a provision which was immensely helpful to the largely commercial satellite sector. However that provision was accompanied by restrictions on the amount of advertising which would be allowed, the banning of all tobacco advertising, a right of reply stipulation, and, most important of all, the introduction of a quota requirement. This stated that 'Member states shall ensure where practicable and by appropriate means, that broadcasters reserve for European works . . . a majority proportion of their transmission time, excluding the time appointed to news, sports events, games, advertising and teletext services'. This is not a new idea, with, for example, the United Kingdom having had for many years prior to the appearance of the Directive a requirement that broadcasters carry no more than 14 per cent of non-British programmes, and, on the other side of the Atlantic, Canada expecting broadcasters to transmit 60 per cent Canadian content.

The argument about the quota clause was long and hard, and the final form it took, with the insertion of the phrase 'where practicable', was much less demanding than it might have been. But even this weak formulation was too much for the Americans, who, during the 1993 Uruguay round of the GATT talks, endeavoured to have it set aside, and to force France to curtail its special support measures for the cinema. At one point it looked as if these trade negotiations, which involved over a hundred countries, might well collapse over this issue, but at the last minute it was agreed that audiovisual goods would be set to one side and a solution sought after the conclusion of the discussions. American pressure did not subside thereafter, but it took more subtle forms, with Hollywood production companies agreeing to open up their distribution networks in both the US and Europe, to share dubbing technology and to contribute to technician and scriptwriter training.[259] Jack Valenti, the chairman of the US Motion Picture Association – successor to the MPPDA – called for 'flexibility' and drew attention to the level of his members' investment in Europe.[260]

This did not greatly impress the European Parliament, and it demanded that the Commission, the EU's executive body, toughen up and enforce the television quota. However the free market approach won, and in 1996 the Commission refused to amend the existing wording – 'where practicable' stayed in the revised version of the Directive – thus paving the way for a clash with the Parliament, which continues to be much more concerned about the cultural importance of the media than the Commission.[261] Jack Valenti, with a little help from European free marketeers, had succeeded in securing the objectives set by his employers – backed by the US government at the highest level – just as Will Hays did sixty five years previously. Nonetheless the quota system has had some impact, for efforts have been made in a number of countries to increase domestic production. The Commission could claim in mid 1996 that:

> At least half the output of most mainstream terrestrial EU channels was European in origin in 1994 . . . A total of 91 channels broadcast a majority of European works, out of 148 surveyed . . . Many of those channels not reaching the 50% threshold were channels that had been launched recently and/or satellite channels with limited audience share, often providing specialist programming on a pay-TV basis.[262]

However, it should be noted that in a country like the United Kingdom the introduction of the quota allowed broadcasters to increase their imports of American material, should they wish to do so, and that is in fact what has happened.

If the quota system then is of limited value, what of the MEDIA programme? It was instituted in 1988 on a pilot basis, formally adopted in 1990 as a five year initiative, and renewed thereafter on what appears to be a permanent footing. Its aim is to encourage the development of film and television projects and the wider circulation of the finished products. Initially a dizzying array of schemes with appropriate acronyms, such as EVE, BABEL, CARTOON and SCRIPT, was embarked on, but after 1995 it was decided to concentrate the relatively limited resources – £40 million per year – on development, distribution and training.

MEDIA has been criticized for its diffuseness, the size and cost of its bureaucracy and the low level of its funding. It is not easy to measure the impact of the programme to date, although anyone who watches European films in the cinema and on video – for example, *Cyrano de Bergerac* (1990), *Land and Freedom* (1995), even *Four Weddings and a Funeral* (1994), or such BBC television productions as *Nostromo* (1997) – must be aware of the fact that MEDIA money is involved at some point in their production and distribution. Whether any or all of these films would have been made without this funding can only be a matter of speculation, but it is difficult to believe that the loans and grants available have not helped them on their way to the large and/or small screens. But even with a MEDIA fund of several times the size of the present one, the competition would remain very uneven: the average production budget for French and British mainstream films in the mid nineties was just over £3 million while the average budget for an American film was almost £23 million.[263] A similar gap exists in post-production marketing budgets. There does also remain the nagging question of how willing audiences in one European country are to watch the films and television drama of another European nation, if the American option is open to them. The answer appears to be 'not very', and changing that attitude has proved very difficult.

France and Britain – a contrast

If the EU's involvement in the audiovisual industry has been marked by a certain timidity, structural fragmentation and intellectual confusion, the approach of France to the support of its national cinema has been much more vigorous and determined, notwithstanding the financial disparities mentioned above. The Centre

National de la Cinematographie had at its disposal in 1998 £263 million, which was raised largely by taxing television companies, but also through a levy on cinema tickets and one on video cassettes. The money is used to bolster the income of French films, to encourage their distribution and to improve exhibition facilities. Support is also offered to drama, documentary and animation production for television. The basic aim is to make the French audiovisual market more attractive and rewarding than it would otherwise be, and thus to sustain French culture.

Although American films dominate French cinema screens as they do the screens of all other European countries, indigenous product has a 35 per cent market share, over twice the EU average, and by far the highest figure in the Union.[264] Paradoxically, in the 1930s, of the European nations, the Germans were most successful in boosting their share of the cinema market with the British not far behind, while the French struggled against the American presence. German films and British ones now have shares of their home makets of around 10 per cent. In the 1990s France has not only enforced the Television without Frontiers quota, but has imposed a 60 per cent one, with the additional proviso that two-thirds of that should be in the French language. However, neither France nor any other EU country any longer uses screen time quotas in the cinema, a device which was very popular in the interwar and postwar periods.

France now stands out in Europe by virtue of the determination of its policies, particularly in cinema, and the question that must be asked is whether it offers an example which other countries should follow. Several of these countries do have schemes designed to offer some assistance to indigenous film makers, but none are on the French scale.[265] The case of Britain is particularly interesting. Quotas were introduced in the 1920s and were gradually increased, until in the postwar period the figure settled at 30 per cent of screen time. In addition, in 1950 the Eady levy was established, a scheme rather like one currently employed in France, whereby a tax on all cinema tickets was recycled to top up the receipts of British films, and the National Film Finance Corporation (NFFC) was set up with £5 million in working capital – some of which helped pay for the *Third Man* (1949). All of these measures contributed to the development of a significant movie industry. The Thatcher government abolished the Eady levy, the quota system and the NFFC, on the grounds that, since cinema was an industry, it should compete in the marketplace like other industries. However a little public money was made available for investment via British Screen Finance, and when the National Lottery arrived in the 1990s, film projects were deemed eligible for funding from that source, and this has made a significant difference to the situation.[266] Television – particularly Channel Four, but the BBC too – has also been helping with the finance of feature films. But nothing has yet been done about the iron grip which American and American-oriented companies have on distribution and exhibition.

As has been noted earlier, Britain continues to have a substantial export trade in television – and in film – and a spectacular success such as *Four Weddings and a Funeral* can inflate earnings considerably. (*The Full Monty* (1997) however was largely American financed, so most of the profits were repatriated to the USA.) It is not therefore surprising that those who work in the industry often cite economic justifications when they seek government support in the form of, for example, tax concessions; after a long period when they made little headway, the Labour government elected in 1997 re-introduced just such a provision. The cultural argument however remains a secondary one, because it has not been deemed to be politically effective, whereas in France it is paramount, although in France too there is a keenness to export where that can be done, with Europe the principal market.

The Canadian experience

The one country in the world which has always been in the front line of the cultural struggle is Canada, although its experiences are not as well known as they should be on the other side of the Atlantic. An independent nation, Canada has nonetheless found itself by virtue of its small population base – 30 million compared to the 266 million of the US – experiencing acutely the problem of sustaining indigenous activity in the face of the most dynamic mass media industry in the world, a problem compounded by the fact that, at least as far as English-speaking Canada is concerned, there is no language barrier. Attempts were made to establish a Canadian film industry in the early days of cinema, but they came to very little as Hollywood gained control of distribution and exhibition and threatened retaliatory action whenever a European style quota system was suggested.[267] Crumbs were thrown to the Canadians in the shape of location shoots north of the forty-ninth parallel, and American movies which offered the world 'positive' images of

Canada. The situation was a little better in Quebec, but until the 1960s many of the films made there were full of the suffocating clericalism with which that Province was imbued, and had little general appeal.

So what Canada did as far as cinema was concerned, was to admit defeat: indigenous radio did develop with the BBC as a model, as was explained in chapter 2, but feature film production was virtually abandoned. However, in 1939 the Canadian government set up the National Film Board (NFB), which under its first director, John Grierson, and his successors, concentrated on documentary and animation, in both of which fields it achieved much; indeed the NFB became a byword internationally for quality in these areas.[268] However, its films were rarely to be found in mainstream cinemas, so until television developed many Canadians were only dimly aware of this attempt to represent Canadian life on the screen.

Latterly the NFB began to put a little money into feature film production, and in 1967 the government set up the Canadian Film Development Corporation (CFDC) in order to try to develop a feature film industry. When television was added to the CFDC's remit in 1983, and it became Telefilm Canada, the politicians were clearly acknowledging that without state intervention it would never be possible for a wide range of indigenous stories to be told on the large or small screens. The simple facts were, and are, that most Canadians most of the time watch American films and American television fiction. Public funding, and the requirement that at least 60 per cent of what broadcasters transmit is Canadian in origin – cinema distribution and exhibition quotas, which could be crucial, are not as yet in prospect – are an attempt to curtail the impact of American audiovisual culture. But nobody believes that it will ever be possible to Canadianize film and television in a way that, for example, Canadian theatre has been Canadianized as a consequence of the funding policies pursued by the Canada Council.[269] The aim is the more modest one of finding a small space for Canadian material, and there have been some successes, with film makers such as Denys Arcand, Atom Egoyan and David Cronenberg being able to access public funds in order to develop their talents and add something to the cultural prestige of their country. Because their work circulates internationally it also brings in export earnings. The same point can be made about some of CBC's socially realistic dramas, several of which have been sold abroad.

One of the most interesting examples of a Canadian attempt to take on the American competition is the television series *Due South*. That series offers an original approach to the well-worn cop show genre by having a Mountie work alongside the Chicago police department. It continually contrasts the differing approaches to solving crime and the general social attitudes of the two countries, while drawing on the standard conventions of the format; however there is far less lethal gunplay than in the average American series.

Due South was developed by an independent production company, Alliance of Toronto, in conjunction with CTV, the Canadian commercial network, and CBS, one of the American networks, which met over half the cost. It was the first Canadian series to be given a peak time placing in an American network's schedule, where in the autumn of 1994 it achieved tolerable ratings, although when it was renewed for a second series CBS preferred to wait until it was made before deciding to purchase it. The series has also been shown in a number of other countries, including Britain, where on BBC1 it secured a place at the bottom of the top seventy. *Due South* was, particularly in its first series, enjoyable popular television: it also was both perceptive and witty about the differences between Canada and America. The fact that it was able to be so and to achieve reasonable ratings on a major commercial network in the US is a tribute to the talent of the people who were responsible for it; its success also tells us something about the difficulties faced by minority cultures which exist in the shadow of much more powerful ones, and about the compromises which may have to be made.

There was no Telefilm Canada money invested in the first *Due South* series, but Alliance had secured finance from this source in several of its other projects, including its series about television news, *ENG*, and Telefilm contributed to the cost of the pilot which was used to attract CBS's interest. But to make a series of this kind for the home Canadian market alone is financially very difficult, particularly when the audience is well used to American production values. So export potential can be crucial, and/or so is public investment, which in practice may well turn out to be a subsidy. Indeed when CBS refused to offer money up-front for the second series of *Due South*, Alliance had to go back to Telefilm; it also secured some co-production finance from the BBC. Repeating the *Due South* success may not be easy, and it is clear that public funding will remain vital if Canadian fiction is to continue to appear on Canadian screens, and if Canada wishes to export audiovisual culture.

The struggle continues

Canada has a small population but it is a very rich country. Even allowing for the peculiar difficulties of its situation if it has had an unending struggle to develop its own distinctive media ouput, what hope is there for much smaller and poorer nations? The questions which policy makers there have to confront relate to what is desirable and what is feasible in both cinema and television. Even although the two media interact so much with each other, they are different, not least in production costs: even at an average of over £500,000 per hour in the UK, television drama remains cheap compared to feature films, particularly Hollywood feature films. But poorer countries, and even relatively rich nations with small population bases, do not have the range of choices open to them which large prosperous ones like Britain and France enjoy. It may simply be the case that some countries have little option but to forego a significant presence – or any presence at all – on their own cinema screens. It may be too that even a 50 per cent target in television programming as a whole is almost impossible to attain, and when it comes to fiction, utterly beyond reach. Unless of course the decision is made that a national presence in the audiovisual sphere is so crucial that it becomes a major political goal. Policy makers would then have to form a judgement about how much money the electorate are prepared to see spent to achieve such an end, rather than have the cash used for other worthy purposes. If it is possible to buy foreign programming for a tenth of the cost of original programming, how much can a country with modest resources afford to spend on its own indigenous work? But, with the growth of commercial terrestrial and satellite services, both of which are more likely to use foreign programming than public service broadcasters, can a country afford the cultural cost of not finding ways of telling its own stories on the small screen?

In the final analysis there is no avoiding the fact that for most of us our experience of cinema has been, and will continue to be, dominated by American film. There is a scene in the Italian *Cinema Paradiso* (1990) when the old Sicilian projectionist, who has been blinded in a fire in his picture house, tells the young lad who has befriended him that the boy needs to leave Sicily and then return – 'Right now,' he says 'you are blinder than I am'. 'Who said that?' he is asked. 'Gary Cooper, James Stewart, Henry Fonda?'. 'No' the lad is told, 'this time it's all me.' It is a poignant moment which epitomizes the way in which American movies have suffused not only the cinema going of Europeans but the very texture of their films as well. The contest may well have been settled on the large screen; on the small one however it has yet to be finally resolved.

Further Reading | 14

In what follows there will be an emphasis, where appropriate, on primary texts before secondary ones, since it is always desirable to read at first hand what particular commentators have said before going on to consider what other commentators have had to say about the original commentators.

Arising out of chapter 2 then, the first books to turn to should be Tocqueville's *Democracy in America*, Arnold's *Culture and Anarchy*, F.R. Leavis's *Mass Civilisation and Minority Culture*, Dwight Macdonald's *Against the American Grain*, Horkheimer and Adorno's essay on the 'Culture Industry', Raymond Williams's *Culture and Society* and Richard Hoggart's *The Uses of Literacy*. The relevant texts are listed at the end of this chapter, as are all the works cited. As far as secondary reading is concerned, Lesley Johnson offers a useful historically based survey, while John Storey and Fred Inglis both offer good introductions to cultural theory; Inglis, it should be noted, remains a firm Leavisite but an open-minded one.

The reactions of the intelligentsia to the arrival of mass culture are explored by D.L. LeMahieu and John Carey, while Scannell and Cardiff examine the evolution of cultural policy within the BBC; Erik Barnouw considers the development of broadcasting in the USA over several volumes, a task carried out for Britain by Asa Briggs, while the Canadian situation is discussed by a number of writers including Marc Raboy and W.H.N. Hull.

Hirsch and Gordon's analysis of *Newspaper Money* remains a first-rate introduction to the impact of press economics on newspaper content, while Curran and Seaton's general history of the media in Britain explores many of the relevant issues. Jeremy Tunstall has provided useful studies of the power of the American media companies and of the media moguls themselves. Herman and McChesney have examined the growth of the dominant global media companies, while the globalization thesis itself has been discussed by John Tomlinson from a more sceptical perspective than some other commentators offer. Congdon and colleagues have written on the policy challenges posed by cross-media ownership, as have Collins and Murroni, while the International Institute of Communications has brought together a series of essays which examine the situations in a wide range of countries and areas of the world. Granville Williams has provided a useful 'map' of the British media ownership landscape.

Raymond Williams's *Television, Technology and Cultural Form* is still an excellent introduction to the relationship between media and technology, while Marjorie Ferguson and Robert Babe offer useful critiques of technological determinism. The account by Akio Morita, the head of Sony, of his company's rise is illuminating.

As with chapter 2, so with chapter 5. Milton's *Areopagitica* is not easy to read, but it is worth the effort, as are Mill's *On Liberty* and Habermas's the *Structural Transformation of the Public Sphere*. John B. Thompson offers a very useful critique of Habermas, while Edwin Emery sets the American debate on freedom of the press in context. Indispensable still is Wilbur Schramm's *Four Theories of the Press*.

Jeremy Bentham should also be looked at in the original, as should Tom Paine. Andrew Vincent offers a useful analysis of the different forms of the state, while Charles Taylor explores the conflict between rights and duties in the contemporary context. As far as the media and war are concerned, Philip Knightley's study remains indispensable, while both the Glasgow University Media Group and Morrison and Tumber explore state–media relations during the Falklands conflict; Alex Thomson and R.J. Denton offer studies arising out of the Gulf War.

Roger Bolton, who as a programme maker was in the thick of controversies which stemmed from the reporting of the Northern Ireland situation, has written a lively narrative of his travails, while Bill Rolston and Martin McLoone offer more widely based studies of media–state relations in the Irish context. As far as the UK's approach to secrecy is concerned, the account offered by Clive Ponting is particularly interesting, given his own role in seeking to open up government activities to public scrutiny. The British love of secrecy is also explored in two sets of essays, one edited by Des Wilson and the other by Norman Buchan and Tricia Sumner. The legal position of the media in the UK is set out by Geoffrey

Robertson and Andrew Nicol, while the situation in the USA is described by Roy L. Moore.

Both of the works just cited also provide useful further reading arising out of chapter 7. Woodward and Bernstein have written an account of the Watergate affair, while Tom Bower has charted Robert Maxwell's career. The tussle between the *Sunday Times* and the Distillers company is related by the then editor of the paper, Harold Evans.

When it comes to media effects there is a vast literature. Joseph Klapper's very canny review of the subject is a good place to begin. Cumberbatch and Howitt provide a more recent overview, as does David Gauntlett. On violence, contrasting perspectives can be obtained from Barker and Petley, on the one hand, and Eysenck and Nias, on the other. The debate about sexual representation can usefully be explored through the essays in Catherine Itzin's collection, which includes contributions from Catherine MacKinnon and Andrea Dworkin; Brian McNair takes an even-handed approach in his study of the subject.

The interaction of the various actors in media policy can be taken further with a number of authors. Anthony Smith's book remains an excellent starting point, while Nicholas Jones offers an account of the contemporary situation. Peter Hennessy's *Whitehall* is an extremely useful guide to the British way of doing things, while Barnett and Curry discuss the aftermath of the Peacock Report. Kenneth Dyson has explored the formation of policy at the European level, as does Peter Humphreys, who also offers a comparative discussion of press and broadasting policy in a number of Western European countries. Stuart Hood deftly analyses the British approach to the recruitment of the 'great and the good' to public bodies.

The genesis of the Press Complaints Commission is dealt with by Jeremy Tunstall, Colin Seymour-Ure and Raymond Snoddy, but it is worth reading the two Calcutt reports cited in the text in order to get the flavour of the arguments involved. The situation in Europe is discussed in a number of essays in the *European Journal of Communication* (Vol 10, 4), and by Gustaf von Dewall, while Peter Desbarats offers a lucid explanation of developments in North America. The Press Complaints Commission's regular bulletins should also be consulted. Belsey and Chadwick have edited a series of essays on journalism and ethics.

The arguments over the future of the BBC have been recounted by Barnett and Curry, and Curran and Seaton, while Collins and

Purnell have suggested alternative modes of governance. The regional situation in the UK is explored in a series of essays edited by Harvey and Robins. John Keane has argued for a redefinition of public service broadcasting, while Nicholas Garnham has sought to distinguish PSB as it ought to be from the BBC as it has been. Marc Raboy has edited a useful collection of essays on the situation of PSB in different parts of the world. Sakae Ishikawa has brought together a group of writers who examine attempts which have been made in the West and elsewhere to quantify 'quality' in broadcasting. Again, the actual documents produced by government and the BBC – which are cited in the text should also be read firsthand, in order to grasp both the substance and the flavour of the arguments.

There is not an extensive list of publications on press support systems, but William Borden's study, which contrasts the situations in the USA and Sweden is very illuminating. Joint Operating Agreements have been explored and critiqued by Busterna and Picard, while Paul Murschetz has produced a detailed study of the support mechanisms in several European countries; Eli Skogerbo has written a useful analysis of the situation in Norway. James Curran's essays on the applicability of subsidy to Britain should be read, as should the Final Report of the 1977 Royal Commission on the Press. Tunstall in *Newspaper Power* – and Curran and Seaton, among others, point up the deficiencies of the current UK situation.

Tom Dewe Mathews has written a useful and entertaining history of cinema censorship in Britain, while Richard Maltby has described the evolution of the American system. The annual reports of the BBFC offer invaluable insights into the thinking of the Board, while John Trevelyan's memoir of his time as Secretary is a useful account of the working of the Board at a crucial time in its history. Martin Barker has cast a very sceptical eye over the way in which video recordings were brought under the scope of the BBFC. The genesis of the Broadcasting Standards Council can be explored through the relevant government publications, in particular *Broadcasting in the 90s: competition, choice and quality*, and in Mary Whitehouse's own book, *Cleaning Up TV*. Mitchell and Blumler have produced a useful report on broadcasting accountability mechanisms in different parts of Europe.

The cultural globalization thesis is considered – sceptically – by Mike Featherstone and John Tomlinson, who was referred to earlier, while Dallas Smythe and Herbert Schiller offer much more convinced analyses. Ian Jarvie and Kristin Thompson explore the behaviour of the American film industry abroad, while the series of essays edited by Ali Mohammidi offers a perspective beyond the Western one, and those under Michael Dorland's editorship deal with the Canadian situation. Richard Collins and Mario Hirsch with Vibeke Petersen have explored the development of media policy in Europe, while Sophia Kaitatzi-Whitlock has analysed the EU's approach to the concentration of ownership issue.

Of books which seek to cover the field of policy as a whole, Dennis McQuail's, which attempts to set out normative criteria for judging the effectiveness of the media, is particularly valuable. The series of essays edited by Kenneth Thompson focuses on a number of specific topics, including sexual moralities and multiculturalism. Lorimer and Scannell offer in outline a range of international policy comparisons.

Many websites are worth accessing: of particular interest are that of the European Union's Directorate concerned with Information, Communication Culture and Audiovisual matters, DG10, to be found at europa.eu.int/en/comm/dg10/dg10.html, the Federal Communication Commission's – www.fcc.gov – and the BBC's – bbc.co.uk. A good search tool will quickly provide access to others.

List of publications referred to:

Arnold, M. 1932: *Culture and Anarchy*. Cambridge: CUP.
Babe, R. 1989: *Telecommunications in Canada: technology, industry and government*. Toronto: University of Toronto Press.
Barnett, S. and Curry, A. 1994: *The Battle for the BBC*. London: Aurum.
Barker, M. and Petley, J. 1997: *Ill Effects: the media violence debate*. London: Routledge.
Barker, M. 1984: *The Video Nasties: freedom and censorship in the media*. London: Pluto.
Barnouw, E. 1966: *A Tower in Babel*. New York: OUP.
Barnouw, E. 1968: *The Golden Web*. New York: OUP.
Barnouw, E. 1970: *The Image Empire*. New York: OUP.
Belsey, A. and Chadwick, R. (eds) 1992: *Ethical Issues in Journalism and the Media*. London: Routledge.
Bentham, J. 1948: *Principles of Morals and Legislation*. Darien, Connecticut: Hafner.
Bolton, R. 1990: *Death on the Rock and other stories*. London: W.H. Allen.
Borden, W. 1995: *Power Plays*. Goteborg: University of Goteborg.
Bower, T. 1991: *Maxwell: the outsider*. London: Mandarin.
Briggs, A. 1961–95: *History of Broadcasting in the United Kingdom*. Oxford: OUP.

Buchan, N. and Sumner, T. (eds) 1989: *Glasnost in Britain*. London: Macmillan.

Busterna, J.C. and Picard, R.G. 1993: *Joint Operating Agreements: the Newspaper Preservation Act and its application*. Norwood: Ablex.

Carey, J. 1992: *The Intellectuals and the Masses*. London: Faber.

Collins, R. 1994: *Broadcasting and A-V Policy in the Single Market*. London: Libbey.

Collins, R. and Murroni, C. 1996: *New Media, New Policies*. Cambridge: Polity.

Collins, R. and Purnell, J. 1995: *The Future of the BBC: commerce, consumers and governance*. London: Institute for Public Policy Research.

Congdon, T. 1995: *The Cross Media Revolution*. London: Libbey.

Cumberbatch, G. and Howitt, D. 1989: *A Measure of Uncertainty – the Effects of the Mass Media*. London: Libbey.

Curran, J. 1978: Advertising and the Press. In Curran, J. (ed.): *The British Press: a manifesto*. London: Macmillan.

Curran, J. 1995: *Policy for the Press*. London: Institute for Public Policy Research.

Curran, J. and Seaton, J. 1997: *Power without Responsibility* (5th edition). London: Routledge.

Denton, R.J. (ed.) 1993: *The Media and the Persian Gulf War*. Westport, New Jersey: Praeger.

Desbarats, P. 1990: *Guide to Canadian News Media*. Toronto: Harcourt Brace Jovanovich.

von Dewall, G. 1997: *Press Ethics: regulation and editorial practice*. Dusseldorf: European Institute for the Media.

Dorland, M. (ed.) 1996: *The Cultural Industries in Canada*. Toronto: Lorimer.

Dyson, K. (ed.) 1988: *Broadcasting and New Media Policies in Western Europe*. London: Routledge.

Emery, E. 1972: *The Press and America* (3rd edition). Englewood Cliffs, New Jersey Prentice Hall.

Eysenck, H.J. and Nias, D.K.B. 1978: *Sex, Violence and the Media*. London: Temple Smith.

Evans, H. 1983: *Good Times, Bad Times*. London: Weidenfeld and Nicholson.

Featherstone, M. 1995: *Undoing Culture*. London: Sage.

Ferguson, M. (ed.) 1990: *Public Communication: the new imperatives*. London: Sage.

Gauntlett, D. 1995: *Moving Experiences*. London: Libbey.

Garnham, N. 1990: *Capitalism and Communication*. London: Sage.

Glasgow University Media Group 1985: *War and Peace News*. Milton Keynes: Open University.

Habermas, J. 1989: *The Structural Transformation of the Public Sphere*. Cambridge: Polity.

Harvey, S. and Robins, K. (eds) 1993: *The Regions, the Nations and the BBC*. London: British Film Institute.

Hennessy, P. 1990: *Whitehall*. London: Fontana.

Herman, E. and McChesney, R. 1997: *The Global Media*. London: Cassell.

Hirsch, F. and Gordon, D. 1975: *Newspaper Money*. London: Hutchinson.

Hirsch, M. and Petersen, V.G. 1992: Regulation of Media at the European Level. In Siune, K. and Truetzschler, W. (eds.) *Dynamics of Media Politics*. London: Sage.

Hoggart, Richard 1958: *The Uses of Literacy*. Harmondsworth: Penguin.

Hood, Stuart 1997: *On Television*. London: Pluto.

Horkheimer, M. and Adorno, T. 1977: The Culture Industry: Enlightenment as Mass Deception. In Curran, J., Gurevitch, M. and Woollacott, J. (eds.) *Mass Communication and Society*. London: Arnold.

Hull, W.H.N. and Stewart, A. 1994: *Canadian Television Policy and the BBG 1958–1968*. Edmonton: University of Alberta.

Humphreys, P.H. 1996: *Mass Media and Media Policy in Western Europe*. Manchester: Manchester University Press.

Inglis, F. 1990: *Media Theory: an introduction*. Oxford: Blackwell.

International Institute of Communications 1996: *Media Ownership and Control in the Age of Convergence*. London: IIC.

Ishikawa, S. (ed.) 1996: *Quality Assessment of Television*. Luton: University of Luton Press.

Itzin, C. (ed.) 1992: *Pornography: women violence and civil liberties*. Oxford: OUP.

Jarvie, I.C. 1992: *Hollywood's Overseas Campaign*. Cambridge: CUP.

Johnson, L. 1979: *The Cultural Critics*. London: Routledge.

Jones, N. 1995: *Soundbites and Spin Doctors*. London: Cassel.

Kaitatzi-Whitlock, S. 1996: Pluralism and Media Concentration in Europe. *European Journal of Communication*, 11, 4.

Keane, J. 1991: *The Media and Democracy*. Cambridge: Polity.

Klapper, J.T. 1960: *The Effects of Mass Communication*. Glencoe, Illinois: Free Press.

Knightley, P. 1982: *The First Casualty*. London: Quartet.

Leavis, F.R. 1930: *Mass Civilisation and Minority Culture*. Cambridge: Minority Press.

Lorimer, R. and Scannell, P. 1994: *Mass Communications: a comparative introduction*. Manchester: Manchester University Press.

Macdonald, D. 1965: *Against the American Grain*. New York: Vintage.

McLoone, M. (ed.) 1996: *Broadcasting in a Divided Community: seventy years of the BBC in Northern Ireland*. Belfast: Queen's University Press.

McNair, B. 1996: *Mediated Sex*. London: Hodder.

McQuail, D. 1992: *Media Performance*. London: Sage.

LeMahieu, D.L. 1988: *A Culture for Democracy*. Oxford: Clarendon.

Maltby, R. 1996: Censorship and Self Regulation. In Nowell-Smith, G. (ed.) *The Oxford History of World Cinema*. Oxford: OUP.

Mathews, T.D. 1994: *Censored*. London: Chatto and Windus.

Mill, J.S. 1910: *Utilitarianism, Liberty and Representative Government*. London: Dent.

Milton, J. 1968: *Areopagitica*. London: University Tutorial Press.

Mitchell. J. and Blumler, J.G. 1994: *Television and the Viewer Interest*. London: Libbey.

Mohammadi, A. (ed.) 1997: *International Communication and Globalisation*. London: Sage.

Moore, R.L. 1994: *Mass Communication Law and Ethics*. New Jersey: Erblaum.

Morita, A. et al. 1987: *Made in Japan*. London: Collins.

Morrison, D. and Tumber, H. 1988: *Journalists at War*. London: Sage.

Murschetz, P. 1997: *State Support for the Press: theory and practice*. Dusseldorf: European Institute for the Media.

Paine, T. 1969: *The Essential Thomas Paine*. Hook, S. (ed.) New York: Signet.

Ponting, C. 1990: *Secrecy in Britain*. Oxford: Blackwell.

Raboy, M. 1990: *Missed Opportunities*. Kingston: McGill/Queen's University Presses.

Raboy, M. (ed.) 1996 *Public Broadcasting for the 21st Century*. Luton: Libbey.

Robertson, G. and Nicol, A. 1992: *Media Law* (3rd edition). London: Penguin.

Rolston, B. (ed.) 1991: *The Media and Northern Ireland: covering the Troubles*. Basingstoke: Macmillan.

Scannell, P. and Cardiff, D. 1991: *A Social History of British Broadcasting, Volume One*. Oxford: Blackwell.

Schramm, W. et al. 1956: *Four Theories of the Press*. Urbana: University of Illinois Press.

Schiller, H. 1976: *Communication and Cultural Domination*. White Plains, New York: M.E. Sharpe.

Seymour-Ure, C. 1996: *British Press and Broadcasting since 1945* (2nd edition). Oxford: Blackwell.

Skogerbo, E. 1997: The Press Subsidy System in Norway. *European Journal of Communication*, 12, 1.

Smith, A. 1976: *The Shadow in the Cave*. London: Quartet.

Smythe, D. 1981: *Dependency Road*. Norwood, New Jersey: Ablex.

Snoddy, R. 1993: *The Good, the Bad and the Unacceptable*. London: Faber.

Storey, J. 1993: *Introductory Guide to Cultural Theory and Popular Culture*. New York: Harvester.

Taylor, C. 1992: *The Malaise of Modernity*. Boston: Harvard University Press.

Thomson, A. 1992: *Smokescreen: the media, the censors and Gulf War*. Tunbridge Wells: Laburnham and Speellmount.

Thompson, J.B. 1995: *The Media and Modernity*. Cambridge: Polity.

Thompson, Kenneth (ed.) 1997: *Media and Cultural Regulation*. London: Sage.

Thompson, Kristin 1985: *Exporting Entertainment: America in the world film market 1907–34*. London: British Film Institute.

de Tocqueville, A. 1968: *Democracy in America*. London: Fontana.

Tomlinson, J. 1991: *Cultural Imperialism*. London: Pinter.

Trevelyan, J. 1973: *What the Censor Saw*. London: Michael Joseph.

Tunstall, J. 1977: *The Media are American*. London: Constable.

Tunstall, J. 1996: *Newspaper Power*. Oxford: Oxford University Press.
Tunstall, J. and Palmer, M. 1991: *Media Moguls*. London: Routledge.
Vincent, A. 1987: *Theories of the State*. Oxford: Blackwell.
Whitehouse, M. 1967: *Cleaning Up TV*. London: Blandford.
Williams, G. 1994: *Britain's Media*. London: Campaign for Press and Broadcasting Freedom.
Williams, R. 1963: *Culture and Society 1780–1950*. Harmondsworth: Penguin.
Williams, R. 1974: *Television, Technology and Cultural Form*. London: Fontana.
Wilson, D. (ed.) 1984: *The Secrets File*. London: Heinemann.
Woodward, B. and Bernstein, C. 1974: *All the President's Men*. New York: Simon and Schuster.

References and Notes

Chapter 2

1 F.R. Leavis 1930: *Mass Civilisation and Minority Culture*. Cambridge: Minority Press, pp. 9–10.
2 Wilfred Mellers 1996: All the things they were. *TLS* 19 July 1996, pp. 18–19.
3 Karl Marx and Friedrich Engels 1967: *The Communist Manifesto*. Harmondsworth: Penguin, p. 78.
4 Raymond Williams 1963: *Culture and Society 1780–1950*. Harmondsworth: Penguin, p. 289.
5 Alexis de Tocqueville 1968: *Democracy in America, Volume One*. J.P. Mayer and M. Lerner (eds). London: Fontana, p. 302.
6 Ibid. p. 303.
7 W. Kaufman (ed.) 1976: *The Portable Nietzsche*. New York: Penguin, p. 545.
8 Jose Ortega y Gasset 1961: *Revolt of the Masses*. London: Unwin, p. 74.
9 P.J. Keating (ed.) 1970: *Matthew Arnold Selected Prose*. Harmondsworth: Penguin, p. 226.
10 Q. Hoare and G. Nowell Smith (eds) 1971: *Selections from the Prison Notebooks of Antonio Gramsci*. London: Lawrence and Wishart, p. 175. In a footnote the editors discuss Gramsci's borrowing of the phrase from Romain Rolland.
11 F.R. Leavis: *op. cit.*, pp. 3–4.
12 Dwight Macdonald 1965: *Against the American Grain*. New York: Vintage, p. 5.
13 Ibid., p. 39.
14 Theodor Adorno and Max Horkheimer 1977: The Culture Industry: enlightenment as mass deception. In J. Curran, M. Gurevitch and J. Woolacott (eds): *Mass Communication and Society*. London: Arnold, p. 351.

15 Raymond Williams: *op. cit.*, p. 296.
16 Asa Briggs (ed.) 1962: *William Morris Selected Writings and Designs.* Harmondsworth: Penguin, p. 172.
17 Richard Hoggart 1958: *The Uses of Literacy.* Harmondsworth: Penguin, p. 340.
18 Asa Briggs 1961: *The Birth of Broadcasting.* Oxford: Oxford University Press, p. 59.
19 Erik Barnouw 1966: *A Tower in Babel.* New York: Oxford University Press, p. 281.
20 John Reith 1924: *Broadcast over Britain.* London: Hodder, p. 34.
21 Roger Bird (ed.) 1988: *Documents of Canadian Broadcasting.* Ottawa: Carleton, p. 112.
22 See P. Scannell and D. Cardiff 1991: *A Social History of British Broadcasting, Volume One.* Oxford: Blackwell, pp. 277ff.
23 Dwight Macdonald: *op. cit.* p. 74.

Chapter 3

24 Government Statistical Service: *Standard Industrial Classification of Economic Activities.* London: HMSO.
25 See Variety's Global 50. *Variety* 25 August 1997.
26 US Studio Revenue to grow by 8.4 per cent. *Screen Finance* 2 May 1996, p. 17.
27 The Fortune 500. *Fortune* 4 August 1997.
28 See note 25.
29 See J.P. Stopford (ed.) 1992: *Directory of Multinationals.* London: Macmillan.
30 Statistics on satellite and cable penetration in Britain and elsewhere are published regularly by the *Financial Times's New Media Markets.*
31 Roger Cowe and Lisa Buckingham: How the Murdoch global tax maze leads to a fortune in savings. The *Guardian* 16 July 1996, p. 5.
32 The FCC ruling turned on the view that, since Murdoch dominated the company and had become an American citizen, the fact that the actual share structure broke US rules was not considered relevant.
33 Democrats flirt with the left. The *Guardian* 10 January 1997.
34 See Raymond Snoddy: The renaissance that fizzled out. *Financial Times* 25 January 1996, p. 23.
35 See Fred Hirsch and David Gordon 1975: *Newspaper Money.* London: Hutchinson.
36 See *Screen Finance* 2 May 1996, p. 16 and also Paul Krugman 1994: Competitiveness: a Dangerous Obsession. *Foreign Affairs* 73, 2, pp. 28–44.
37 Overseas Transactions of the Film and Television Industry. London: Office for National Statistics.

38 Department of National Heritage 1995: *Media Ownership: the Government's proposals* p. 3.
39 See discussion in Peter Desbarats 1990: *Guide to Canadian News Media.* Toronto: Harcourt Brace Jovanovich.
40 See E. Herman and R. McChesney 1997: *The Global Media.* London: Cassell for an account of the current ownership situation.
41 See, for example, Ian Jarvie 1992: *Hollywoood's Overseas Campaign.* Cambridge: Cambridge University Press.
42 Anthony Giddens 1990: *The Consequences of Modernity.* Cambridge: Polity, p. 64.
43 See Eric Hobsbawm 1968: *Industry and Empire.* London: Weidenfeld and Nicolson.
44 J.M. Stopford 1995: Impact of the Global Political Economy on Corporate Strategy. London: London Business School, p. 2.
45 Robin Wood 1981: Art and Ideology: notes on *Silk Stockings.* In Rick Altman (ed.) *Genre: the musical.* London: Routledge, p. 66.
46 See David Thompson 1997: *Howard Hawks.* London: British Film Institute.

Chapter 4

47 See George Boyce (ed.) 1978: *Newspaper History: from the seventeenth century to the present day.* London: Constable.
48 See Asa Briggs 1961: *The Birth of Broadcasting.* Oxford: OUP.
49 See Raymond Williams 1974: *Television, Technology and Cultural Form.* London: Fontana.
50 European Union 1994: *Europe and the Global Information Society* (Bangemann Report). Brussels: European Union.
51 See Marc Raboy 1990: *Missed Opportunities.* Montreal: McGill University.
52 Home Office and Department of Industry 1983: *The Development of Cable Systems and Services.* London: HMSO, p. 6.
53 Timothy Hollins 1984: *Beyond Broadcasting: into the cable age.* London: British Film Institute, p. 293.
54 See for example J. Watkinson 1994: *The Art of Digital Video.* Oxford: Focal.
55 Department of National Heritage 1995: *Digital Terrestrial Broadcasting.* London: HMSO, p. 3.
56 British Broadcasting Corporation 1996: *Extending Choice in the Digital Age.* London: BBC, p. 31.
57 British Broadcasting Corporation 1995: *Annual Report 1994–95.* London: BBC, p. 94.
58 See for example Correlli Barnett 1995: *The Lost Victory.* London: Macmillan.

59 See Julian Hale 1975: *Radio Power: propaganda and international broadcasting*. London: Elek.

60 The data is taken from the judgment handed down in the US District Court for the Eastern District of Pennsylvania in the case of the American Civil Liberties Union v Janet Reno, Attorney General of the United States, in 1996, which is available from the ACLU website – http: //www.aclu.org/.

Chapter 5

61 See the Annual Reports published by Amnesty International, London.

62 See Reporters sans Frontières 1995: *Freedom of the Press throughout the World*. London: Libbey.

63 See Jonathan Steele 1994: *Eternal Russia*. London: Faber.

64 Richard Rorty 1989: *Contingency, Irony and Solidarity*. Cambridge: Cambridge University Press, p. xv.

65 John Milton 1968: *Areopagitica*. London: University Tutorial Press, p. 96.

66 Ibid., p. 104.

67 Boyce *op. cit.*, p. 95.

68 Jurgen Habermas 1989: *The Structural Transformation of the Public Sphere*. Cambridge: Polity, p. 8.

69 Edwin Emery 1972: *The Press and America* (third edition). Englewood Cliffs, New Jersey: Prentice Hall, p. 9.

70 Ibid., p. 131.

71 Ibid., p. 131.

72 J.S. Mill 1910: *Utilitarianism, Liberty and Representative Government*. London: Dent.

73 Ibid., p. 107.

74 See, for example, Adam Smith 1976: *An Inquiry into the Nature and Causes of the Wealth of Nations*. Oxford: Oxford University Press, Book IV, chapter five.

75 See for example Ralph Negrine 1989: *Politics and the Mass Media in Britain* (second edition). London: Routledge.

76 See Peter Desbarats 1990: *Guide to Canadian News Media*. Toronto: Harcourt Brace Jovanovich, chapter five, for a discussion of this issue from a North American perspective.

77 See F. Siebert, T. Peterson and W. Schramm 1956: *Four Theories of the Press*. Urbana: University of Illinois Press.

78 These words are taken from the Royal Charter governing the operation of the BBC; the most recent was issued in 1996 and runs for ten years.

79 Jurgen Habermas *op. cit.*, p. 164.

80 See James Curran 1991: Rethinking the Media as a public sphere. In

P. Dahlgren and C. Sparks (eds) *Communication and Citizenship*. London: Routledge.

81 Home Office 1977: *Report of the Committee on the Future of Broadcasting*. London: HMSO, p. 27.

82 Home Office 1986: *Report of the Committee on Financing the BBC*. London: HMSO, p. 125.

83 Home Office 1988: *Broadcasting in the 90s: competition, choice and quality*. London: HMSO, p. 1.

Chapter 6

84 Jeremy Bentham 1948: *Principles of Morals and Legislation*. Darien, Connecticut: Hafner, pp. 29–32.

85 Sidney Hook (ed.) 1969: *The Essential Thomas Paine*. New York: Signet, pp. 149–50.

86 See for example Charles Taylor 1992: *The Malaise of Modernity*. Boston: Harvard.

87 See for example Ernest Gellner 1983: *Nations and Nationalism*. Oxford: Blackwell.

88 See Asa Briggs 1970: *The War of Words*. Oxford: Oxford University Press.

89 Philip Knightley 1982: *The First Casualty*. London: Quartet.

90 David Morrison and Howard Tumber 1988: *Journalists at War*. London: Sage, p. 169.

91 Ibid., pp. 348ff.

92 See for example R.J. Denton (ed.) 1993: *The Media and the Persian Gulf War*. Westport, New Jersey: Praeger, and Alex Thomson 1992: *Smokescreen: the media, the censors and Gulf War*. Tunbridge Wells: Laburnham and Speellmount.

93 See Morrison and Tumber, *op. cit.*

94 See Glasgow University Media Group 1985: *War and Peace News*. Milton Keynes: Open University.

95 See Ed Moloney 1991: Closing Down the Airwaves: the story of the Broadcasting Ban. In Bill Rolston (ed.) *The Media and Northern Ireland: covering the troubles*. Basingstoke: Macmillan.

96 However see Martin McLoone (ed.) 1996: *Broadcasting in a Divided Community: seventy years of the BBC in Northern Ireland*. Belfast: Queen's University, for a more pessimistic account.

97 See Roger Bolton 1990: *Death on the Rock and Other Stories*. London: W.H. Allen.

98 See David Miller 1994: *Don't Mention the War*. London: Pluto.

99 See Murray Ritchie and Alistair Bonnington 1989: Whom the truth would indict. In Norman Buchan and Tricia Sumner (eds) *Glasnost in Britain*. London: Macmillan.

100 Andrew Boyle 1980: *Climate of Treason*. Sevenoaks, Kent: Hodder.

101   See James Michael 1984: FOI in Other Countries. In Des Wilson (ed.) *The Secrets File.* London: Heinemann.

102   See Clive Ponting 1990: *Secrecy in Britain.* Oxford: Blackwell.

103   See Geoffrey Robertson and Andrew Nicol 1992: *Media Law* (third edition). London: Penguin.

104   See Chancellor of the Duchy of Lancaster 1997: *Your Right to Know.* London: HMSO.

Chapter 7

105   Ronald Dworkin 1977: *Taking Rights Seriously.* London: Duckworth, p. 182.

106   See Rowland Lorimer with Paddy Scannell 1994: *Mass Communication: a comparative introduction.* Manchester: Manchester University Press, chapter three.

107   See for example, R. Divine, T. Breen, G. Fredrickson and R. Williams 1991: *America Past and Present* (third edition). New York: Harper Collins, pp. 869ff.

108   See for example Geoffrey Robertson and Andrew Nicoll, 1992: *Media Law* (third edition). London: Penguin, and Roy L. Moore 1994: *Mass Communication Law and Ethics.* New Jersey: Erblaum, for a comparison of the British and American situations.

109   See B. McKain, A.J. Bonnington and G.A. Watt 1995: *Scots Law for Journalists* (sixth edition). Edinburgh: Green.

110   See Robertson and Nicoll *op. cit.*, pp. 43ff.

111   See Roy L. Moore *op. cit.* and R.L. Weaver and G. Bennett 1993: New York Times Co. v Sullivan: the 'Actual Malice' – standard and editorial decision making. *Media Law and Practice,* 14, 2–16.

112   See Bob Woodward and Carl Bernstein 1974: *All the President's Men.* New York: Simon and Schuster.

113   See Paul Starobin 1995: A Generation of Vipers. Journalists and the New Cynicism. *Columbia Journalism Review.* March/April 1995, pp. 25–32.

114   Roy L. Moore *op. cit.*, p. 97.

115   See George Bain 1995: Suspicions of a Hidden Agenda. *Maclean's,* 26 June 1995 for a discussion of the issues involved.

116   See Tom Bower 1991: *Maxwell: the outsider.* London: Mandarin.

117   See Harold Evans 1983: *Good Times, Bad Times.* London: Weidenfeld and Nicolson.

118   See H. Laddie, P. Prescott and M. Vitoria 1980: *The Modern Law of Copyright.* London: Butterworth, pp. 7ff.

119   Ibid., pp. 483ff.

120   See for example Guy Cumberbatch and Denis Howitt 1989: *A Measure of Uncertainty – the Effects of the Mass Media.* London: Libbey, and Oliver Boyd-Barrett and Chris Newbold 1995: *Approaches to Media: a reader* (section three). London: Arnold.

121   See Catherine Itzin (ed.) 1992: *Pornography: Women Violence and Civil Liberties*. Oxford: Oxford University Press.
122   BBC 1996: *Producers' Guidelines*. London: BBC, p. 65.
123   Broadcasting Standards Council 1994: *A Code of Practice* (second edition). London: BSC, p. 27.
124   Canadian Broadcast Standards Council 1988: *Voluntary Code Regarding Violence in Television Programming*. Ottawa: CBSC, p. 3.
125   BBC 1996 *op. cit.*, p. 56.
126   Broadcasting Standards Council 1994 *op. cit.*, p. 37.
127   See Roy L. Moore *op. cit.*, p. 254.
128   *US Telecommunications Act* 1996, section 551, a(4).
129   Ibid. section 551, a(6).
130   See for example Tom Dewe Mathews 1994: *Censored*. London: Chatto.
131   See Brian McNair 1996: *Mediated Sex*. London: Hodder.
132   See Roy L. Moore *op. cit.*, p. 525.
133   See Itzin *op. cit.*, and McNair *op. cit.*
134   See James V.P. Check 1992: The Effects of Violent Pornography, Nonviolent Dehumanising Pornography and Erotica: some legal implications from a Canadian perspective. In Itzin, *op. cit.*
135   See Paul Kaihla 1994: Sex and the Law. *Maclean's*, 24 October 1994.

Chapter 8

136   See for example Nicholas Jones 1995: *Soundbites and Spin Doctors*. London: Cassell.
137   Anthony Smith 1976: *The Shadow in the Cave*. London: Quartet, p. 181.
138   Ibid., pp. 82ff.
139   See Steven Barnett and Andrew Curry 1994: *The Battle for the BBC*. London: Aurum.
140   See Hugh O'Donnell 1997: Catalan TV in E. Rodgers (ed.) *Encyclopaedia of Contemporary Spanish Culture*. London: Routledge.
141   See for example Peter Hennessy 1990: *Whitehall*. London: Fontana.
142   See for example Martin Wiener 1980: *English Culture and the Decline of the Industrial Spirit*. Cambridge: Cambridge University Press.
143   Peter Hennessy *op. cit.*, part four.
144   Home Office 1986: *Report of the Committee on Financing the BBC*. London: HMSO.
145   Ibid. pp. 38ff.
146   See Michael Moran and Tony Prosser 1994: Privatisation and Regulatory Change: the case of Great Britain. In M. Moran and T. Prosser (eds) *Privatisation and Regulatory Change in Europe*. Buckingham: Open University Press.
147   See American Film Marketing Associates 1994: *International Market Fact Book*. New York: AFMA.
148   G.B. Doern (ed.) 1978: *The Regulatory Process in Canada*. Toronto: Macmillan, p. 1.

149 See Roy L. Moore 1994: *Mass Communication Law and Ethics* (third edition). New Jersey: Erblaum, pp. 258ff.

150 See Jeremy Potter 1989: *Independent Television in Britain, Volume Three.* London: Macmillan.

151 See for example the discussion of the experience of the Canadian Board of Broadcast Governors in Andrew Stewart and W.H.N. Hull 1994: *Canadian Television Policy and the BBG 1958–1968.* Edmonton: University of Alberta Press.

152 Home Office 1988: *Broadcasting in 90s: competition, choice and quality.* London: HMSO, p. 7.

153 See Steven Barnett and Andrew Curry 1994: *op. cit.,* pp. 120ff.

154 Department of National Heritage 1992: *The Future of the BBC.* London: HMSO.

155 See for example Richard Collins and Cristina Murroni 1996: *New Media, New Policies.* Cambridge: Polity.

156 The present author was a member of the Scottish Selecting Panel from 1988 until 1996, and chairman for five of these years. The Panel is charged with the task of nominating to the BBC Board of Governors suitable persons to become members of the Broadcasting Council for Scotland, a body which has general oversight of the Corporation's operations in Scotland. There are similar Councils in Wales and Northern Ireland. The remarks made draw on the experience of the selection process.

Chapter 9

157 See Tina Laitila 1995 Journalistic Codes of Ethics in Europe. *European Journal of Communication* 10, 4, pp. 527–44.

158 See Peter Desbarats 1990: *Guide to Canadian News Media.* Toronto: Harcourt Brace Jovanovich, and David Pritchard 1992: Press Councils as Mechanisms of Media Self-Regulation. In J. Zyleberg and F. Demers (eds) *L'Amérique et les Amériques/America and the Americas.* Sainte-Foy, Quebec: Les Presses de l'Université Laval, pp. 99–116.

159 See for example Colin Seymour-Ure 1996: *The British Press and Broadcasting since 1945* (second edition). Oxford: Blackwell.

160 Home Office 1990: *Report of the Committee on Privacy and Related Matters.* London: HMSO, p. x.

161 Mr Mellor appeared on Channel Four's *Hard News* and made this comment, specifically about the tabloid press. See *The Times,* 22 December 1989.

162 Press Complaints Commission 1991 (and subsequently): *Code of Practice.* London: PCC. The quotations are taken from the version published in November, 1997.

163 Department of National Heritage 1993: *Review of Press Self-Regulation.* London: HMSO, p. xi.

164   Heritage MPs attack PCC. *UK Press Gazette*, 24 January 1997.
165   Press Complaints Commission 1995: *Report Number 29*. London: PCC, p. 15.
166   Ibid., pp. 6–8. See also *News of the World*, 14 May 1995, p. 4.
167   *News of the World*, 15 January 1995, p. 23.
168   Press Complaints Commission 1995: *Report Number 28*. London; PCC, p. 1.
169   Claude-Jean Bertrand 1990: Media Accountability: the case for press councils. *Intermedia* 18, 6, pp. 10–14.

Chapter 10

170   See Paddy Scannell 1996: Public Service Broadcasting, from National Culture to Multiculturalism. In Marc Raboy (ed.) *Public Broadcasting for the 21st Century*. Luton: Libbey, for a discussion of this transition.
171   See Asa Briggs 1961: *The Birth of Broadcasting*. Oxford: Oxford University Press, and Paddy Scannell and David Cardiff 1991: *A Social History of British Broadcasting, Volume One*. Oxford: Blackwell for accounts of the early history of the BBC.
172   See British Film Institute 1986: *The Public Service Idea in British Broadcasting*. London British Film Institute, for a discussion of the principles of PSB.
173   Home Office 1986: *Report of the Committee on Financing the BBC*. London: HMSO, p. 133.
174   Department of National Heritage 1992: *The future of the BBC. A consultation document*. London: HMSO.
175   Ibid., p. 34
176   BBC 1992: *Extending Choice: the BBC's role in the new broadcasting age*. London: BBC.
177   Ibid., p. 82.
178   BBC 1993: *An Accountable BBC*. London: BBC. BBC 1993: *Public Service Broadcasters Around the World*. London: BBC.
179   BBC 1993: *Responding to the Green Paper*. London: BBC, p. 13.
180   Ibid., p. 53.
181   The distortions produced by the bidding system can be illustrated by comparing the annual charge of £43.17 million. paid by Yorkshire Television, and the £2,000 (sic) paid by Central Television, which enjoys advertising revenue almost two-thirds greater than does Yorkshire. The fall-back mechanism was designed to ensure that if Channel Four's share of total television revenue fell below 14 per cent, then the shortfall, up to 2 per cent, would be made up by ITV, and if Channel Four's share exceeded 14 per cent, then the reverse would happen to half of the surplus so generated. The assumption was that, on balance, ITV would continue to subsidise Channel Four. Because Channel Four's advertising revenue has

continued to grow there has been a constant flow of funds one way.

182 See the leading article in *The Times*, 7 July 1994.

183 Department of National Heritage 1994: *The future of the BBC. Serving the nation Competing world-wide*. London: HMSO.

184 Ibid., p. 1.

185 See for example Richard Collins and James Purnell 1995: *The Future of the BBC: commerce, consumers and governance*. London: Institute for Public Policy Research.

186 Department of National Heritage 1994: *op. cit.*, p. 24.

187 Department of National Heritage 1995: *Broadcasting: draft of Royal Charter proposed by Her Majesty's Secretary of State for National Heritage for the continuance of the British Broadcasting Corporation*. London: HMSO. Department of National Heritage 1995: *Broadcasting: A draft of an agreement between Her Majesty's Secretary of State for National Heritage and the British Broadcasting Corporation*. London: HMSO.

188 In 1997 the average share of viewing in 'cable/satellite homes' of BSkyB services was 17 per cent, while the average share of the BBC channels in these homes was 29 per cent. These figures can be obtained on a weekly basis from *Broadcast* magazine, but see in particular William Phillips: Yesterday's Dish, *Broadcast*, 6 March 1998.

189 Audience figures for radio are produced on a regular basis by RAJAR (Radio Joint Audience Research), and published intermittently in *Broadcast* magazine.

190 See for example Steven Barnett and Andrew Curry 1994: *The Battle for the BBC*. London: Aurum, for a discussion of this issue.

191 *Broadcast*, 1 August 1997.

Chapter 11

192 See for example Ben Bagdikian 1991: *The Media Monopoly*. Boston: Beacon.

193 Quoted in William Borden 1995: *Power Plays*. Goteborg: University of Goteborg, p. 148.

194 Ibid., p. 259.

195 Ibid., p. 235.

196 J.C. Busterna and R.G. Picard 1993: *Joint Operating Agreements: the Newspaper Preservation Act and its Application*. Norwood: Ablex, p. 91.

197 See for example Christopher Dornan 1996: Newspaper Publishing. In Michael Dorland (ed.): *The Cultural Industries in Canada*. Toronto: Lorimer.

198 See A. Sanchez-Tabernero 1993: *Media Concentration in Europe*. London: Libbey.

199 See World Association of Newspapers 1997: *World Press Trends*. Paris,

World Association of Newspapers, according to which 592 copies of daily newspapers are sold for every 1,000 inhabitants; the corresponding figure for Sweden is 438, for the United Kingdom 330 and for the USA 297.

200 See Eli Skogerbo 1997: The Press Subsidy System in Norway. *European Journal of Communication*, 12(1), 99–118.

201 I am indebted here and elsewhere to research on press subsidy systems on the European mainland carried out by my colleague, Paul Murschetz. See Paul Murschetz 1997: *State Support for the Press: theory and practice*. Dusseldorf: European Institute for the Media.

202 Borden *op. cit.*, p. 234–5.

203 See *Broadcasting Act, 1996*. London: HMSO.

204 *Royal Commission on the Press, Final Report*. London: HMSO, p. i.

205 Ibid., p. 115.

206 Ibid., p. 126.

207 James Curran 1978: Advertising and the Press. In James Curran, (ed.): *The British Press: a manifesto*. London: Macmillan, p. 266.

208 James Curran 1995: *Policy for the Press*. London: Institute for Public Policy Research, p. 23.

209 Ibid., p. 23.

210 Borden *op. cit.*, pp. 176ff.

211 In early 1997 in response to pressure from the European Parliament the Commission was considering a draft directive which contained specific ceilings on media shares, but it was split on the proposals.

212 See for example Richard Tait 1997: Switching Off Politics. *British Journalism Review*, 8, 3, pp. 19–24. Tait quotes a Harris opinion poll commissioned by Independent Television News (ITN), which showed that, as far as the forthcoming 1997 General Election in Britain was concerned, 62 per cent of respondents were prepared to trust television news, while only 37 per cent were prepared to trust the press.

Chapter 12

213 See report in The *Guardian*, 18 February 1994.

214 British Board of Film Classification 1995: *Annual Report. 1994–95* London: BBFC, p. 21.

215 For a history of film censorship in Britain see Tom Dewe Mathews 1994: *Censored*. London: Chatto and Windus.

216 See BBFC 1995: *op. cit.*, p. 3.

217 Ibid., p. 8.

218 John Grisham 1996: Don't Sue the Messenger. In Karl French (ed.) *Screen Violence*. London: Bloomsbury, p. 234.

219 See report in The *Scotsman*, 25 March 1997.

236 REFERENCES AND NOTES

220 *Daily Mail*, 24 March 1997.
221 H.M. Government 1984: *Video Recordings Act*. London: HMSO, section 4a, as amended 1994.
222 Home Office 1986: *Report of the Committee on Financing the BBC*. London: HMSO, p. 150.
223 See British Board of Film Classification: *Annual Reports* London: BBFC for these statistics.
224 Mary Whitehouse, 1967: *Cleaning Up TV*. London: Blandford, p. 194.
225 Ibid., p. 196.
226 Home Office 1977: *Report of the Committee on the Future of Broadcasting*. London: HMSO, pp. 57ff.
227 Home Department 1988: *Broadcasting in the 90s: competition, choice and quality*. London: HMSO, p. 35.
228 See Broadcasting Standards Council 1993 and 1997: *Annual Report 1992–93* and *Annual Report 1996–97*. London: BSC.
229 Broadcasting Standards Council 1994: *Code of Practice* (second edition). London: BSC, p. 20.
230 Broadcasting Standards Council 1992: *Complaints Bulletin 21*. London: BSC, p. 6.
231 Broadcasting Standards Commission 1997: *Bulletin 3*. London: BSC, p. 6.
232 Broadcasting Standards Council 1993: *Complaints Bulletin 26*. London: BSC, p. 6.
233 Ibid., p. 2.
234 Broadcasting Standards Commission 1997: *Bulletin 1* London: BSC, p. 1.
235 Broadcasting Standards Council 1992: *Complaints Bulletin 15*. London: BSC, p. 2.
236 Broadcasting Standards Commission 1997: *Bulletin 4*. London: BSC pp. 5 and 7.
237 Broadcasting Standards Commission 1997: *Bulletin 5*. London: BSC p. 10.
238 Broadcasting Standards Council 1992: *Complaints Bulletin 3*. London: BSC, p. 6.
239 Broadcasting Standards Council 1993: *Complaints Bulletin 35*. London: BSC, pp. 21–2.
240 Broadcasting Standards Council 1993: *Annual Report 1992–93*. London: BSC, p. 15.

Chapter 13

241 The basis of the argument relates not only to receipts from overseas visitors, which can be regarded as part of the nation's 'invisible' earnings, but also to the payment of VAT on ticket sales.

242 *Screen Finance*, 2 May 1996, p. 19.

243 Herbert Schiller 1976: *Communication and Cultural Domination*. White Plains, New York: M.E. Sharpe, pp. 9–10.

244 Kristin Thompson 1985: *Exporting Entertainment: America in the world film market 1907–34*. London: British Film Institute.

245 Pierre Sorlin 1991: *European Cinemas, European Societies 1939–90*. London: Routledge, p. 2.

246 See for example Donald Clark 1995: *The Rise and Fall of Popular Music*. London: Penguin.

247 See K. Malm and R. Wallis 1992: *Media Policy and Music Activity*. London: Routledge.

248 See for example the charts of the most popular television programmes in different countries published regularly by *TV World* magazine.

249 The pressure from Wales included a threat to fast to death by a Welsh Nationalist politician; the Gaels simply hired a lobbyist whose economic credentials appealed greatly to the then Prime Minister, Margaret Thatcher.

250 Commission of the European Communities 1990: *The European Community Policy in the Audiovisual Field*. Luxembourg: Office for the Official Publications of the European Communities.

251 See *Financial Times*, December 12 1991, p. 7.

252 Centre National de la Cinematographie 1995: *CNC Info-Results 199*. Paris: CNC.

253 European Audiovisual Laboratory 1996: *Statistical Yearbook*. Strasbourg: EAL.

254 See note 248.

255 See *Broadcast* magazine, which publishes these statistics on a weekly basis.

256 See *Screen Finance*, 14 November 1996, p. 12.

257 Commission of the European Communities 1994: *Europe and the Global Information Society*. Luxembourg: Office for the Official Publications of the European Communities.

258 Commission of the European Communities 1990: *op. cit.*

259 Europe and Hollywood close to peace deal. The *Guardian*, 2 November 1994.

260 Valenti asks EC to be flexible. *Broadcast*, 11 November 1994.

261 This difference of emphasis has also shown itself in the contrasting approaches to the question of concentration of ownership, with the Commission being more concerned to remove barriers to competition and the Parliament being exercised about the dangers to pluralism.

262 European Commission 1996: *The Week in Europe*, 18 July 1996. London: European Commission.

263 See *Screen Finance*, which publishes regular data on these matters.

264   Centre National de la Cinematographie 1995: *op. cit.*
265   See Patricia Perilli 1991: *A Level Playing Field*. London: British Film Institute, for a discussion of the approaches taken by different European countries.
266   See John Hill 1993: Government Policy and the British Film Industry 1979–90. *European Journal of Communication*, Volume Eight pp. 203–24, for a discussion of these policy changes.
267   See for example Ted Magder 1993: *Canada's Hollywood*. Toronto: University of Toronto Press.
268   See Gerald Pratley 1989: The Eyes of Canada. *Sight and Sound*, 58, 4, pp. 229–33.
269   See for example Paul Rutherford 1993: Made in America: the problem of mass culture in Canada. In D. Flaherty and F. Manning (eds) *The Beaver Bites Back*. Montreal: McGill and Queen's University Presses.

Index